Spinoza and Relational Autonomy

Spinoza and Relational Autonomy

Being with Others

Edited by Aurelia Armstrong, Keith Green
and Andrea Sangiacomo

EDINBURGH
University Press

Edinburgh University Press is one of the leading university presses in the UK. We publish academic books and journals in our selected subject areas across the humanities and social sciences, combining cutting-edge scholarship with high editorial and production values to produce academic works of lasting importance. For more information visit our website: edinburghuniversitypress.com

© editorial matter and organisation Aurelia Armstrong, Keith Green and Andrea Sangiacomo, 2019, 2021
© the chapters their several authors, 2019, 2021

First published in hardback by Edinburgh University Press 2019

Edinburgh University Press Ltd
The Tun – Holyrood Road
12(2f) Jackson's Entry
Edinburgh EH8 8PJ

Typeset in 10/12 Goudy Old Style by
Servis Filmsetting Ltd, Stockport, Cheshire

A CIP record for this book is available from the British Library

ISBN 978 1 4744 1969 7 (hardback)
ISBN 978 1 4744 8127 4 (paperback)
ISBN 978 1 4744 1970 3 (webready PDF)
ISBN 978 1 4744 1971 0 (epub)

The right of the contributors to be identified as the authors of this work has been asserted in accordance with the Copyright, Designs and Patents Act 1988, and the Copyright and Related Rights Regulations 2003 (SI No. 2498).

Contents

Acknowledgements		vii
Abbreviations		viii

    Editors' Introduction   1
    Aurelia Armstrong, Keith Green and Andrea Sangiacomo

1. Relational Autonomy: State of the Art Debate   10
   Catriona Mackenzie

2. Epistemic Autonomy in Descartes, Spinoza and Kant: The Value of Thinking for Oneself   33
   Ursula Renz

3. Spinoza on the Interaction of Ideas: Biased Beliefs   50
   Martin Lenz

4. Spinoza on Natures: Aristotelian and Mechanistic Routes to Relational Autonomy   74
   Matthew Kisner

5. Spinoza's Path from Imaginative Transindividuality to Intuitive Relational Autonomy: From Fusion, Confusion and Fragmentation to Moral Integrity   98
   Heidi M. Ravven

6. Revisiting Spinoza's Concept of *Conatus*: Degrees of Autonomy   115
   Caroline Williams

7. Bodies Politic and Civic Agreement   132
   Justin Steinberg

8. Power, Freedom and Relational Autonomy   149
   Ericka Tucker

9. Spinoza on Affirmation, *Anima* and Autonomy: 'Shattered Spirits'   164
   Keith Green

10 A Spinozistic Approach to Relational Autonomy: The Case of
    Prostitution   194
    Andrea Sangiacomo

Notes on Contributors   212
Index   213

Acknowledgements

This collection grew out of a collaboration that began in 2014 with a workshop organised by Andrea Sangiacomo at the Faculty of Philosophy at the University of Groningen. The editors are grateful to Martin Lenz (chair of the department of history of philosophy) and to Lodi Nauta (dean of the Faculty of Philosophy) for their support at various stages of this project. Participants from the original workshop included the editors and other contributors: Matthew Kisner, Martin Lenz, Beth Lord and Ericka Tucker. We are grateful for the additional editorial help provided by Ericka Tucker. We would like to acknowledge and thank Francesco Lombardo, of Marshall, North Carolina, for permission to use an image of his painting, 'Sy' for the cover of this volume. The editors found in the image, so beautifully rendered, a powerful visual evocation of themes and ideas that are central to this volume. This publication is supported by the Netherlands Organisation for Scientific Research (NWO) as one of the outputs of the project 'Occasionalism and the secularization of early modern science: Understanding the dismissal of divine action during the scientific revolution' run by Andrea Sangiacomo at the University of Groningen. Finally, we are grateful for the help and patience of our editors, Carol Macdonald and Kirsty Woods, who have done so much to see this project completed.

Abbreviations

Commonly used abbreviations

AT — *Œuvres de Descartes*, René Descartes, ed. Charles Adam and Robert Tannéry. Paris: Vrin, 1964–74, 12 vols.

C1 — *The Collected Works of Spinoza*, vol. 1, ed. and trans. E. Curley. Princeton: Princeton University Press, 1985.

C2 — *The Collected Works of Spinoza*, vol. 2, ed. and trans. E. Curley. Princeton: Princeton University Press, 2016.

CSM — *The Philosophical Writings of Descartes*, ed. and trans. John Cottingham, Robert Stoothoff, Dugald Murdoch. Cambridge: Cambridge University Press 1984–91, 3 vols.

E — *Ethica more geometrico demonstrata*, in *Spinoza Opera*, im Auftrag der Heidelberg Akademie des Wissenschaften, hrsg. von C. Gebhardt, 4 vols, Heidelberg, Carl Winter, 1925. English translation in C1.

Ep — *Epistolae*, in *Spinoza Opera*, im Auftrag der Heidelberg Akademie des Wissenschaften, hrsg. von C. Gebhardt, 4 vols, Heidelberg, Carl Winter, 1925. English translation in C1 and C2.

G — *Spinoza Opera*, im Auftrag der Heidelberg Akademie des Wissenschaften, hrsg. von C. Gebhardt, 4 vols, Heidelberg, Carl Winter, 1925.

KV — *Korte Verhandeling van God de Mensch en deszelvs welstand*, in B. Spinoza, *Oeuvres I, Premiers écrits*, texte établi par F. Mignini, Puf, Paris, 2009, pp. 157–474. English translation in C1.

NS — *Nagelate Schriften*, Xenographic version available from Proquest, Ann Arbor, MI: UMI Books on Demand.

PPC and CM — *Principia Philosophiae Cartesianae* and *Cogitata Metaphysica* in *Spinoza Opera*, im Auftrag der Heidelberg Akademie des Wissenschaften, hrsg. von C. Gebhardt, 4 vols, Heidelberg, Carl Winter, 1925. English translation in C1.

TIE — *Tractatus de intellectus emendatione*, in B. Spinoza, *Oeuvres I*,

	Premiers écrits, texte établi par F. Mignini, Paris, Puf, 2009, pp. 19–155. English translation in C1.
TP	*Tractatus Politicus/Traité Politique*, texte établi par O. Proietti, traduction, introduction, notes, glossaires, index et bibliographies par C. Ramond, notice de P. F. Moreau sur la réception du TP, notes d'A. Matheron, Paris, Puf, 2005. English translation in C2.
TTP	*Tractatus Theologico-Politicus/Traité Théologico-Politique*, texte établi par F. Akkerman, traduction et notes par J. Lagrée et P. F. Moreau, Paris, Puf, 1999. English translation in C2.

Other abbreviations

ad	Definitions of affects (E3)
app	Appendix
ax	Axiom
c	Corollary
def	Definition
dem	Demonstration
l	Lemma
p	Proposition
post	Postulate
pref	Preface
s	Scholium

Editors' Introduction

Aurelia Armstrong, Keith Green and Andrea Sangiacomo

1. From Relational Autonomy to Spinoza and Back Again

From Kant to Rawls, a consolidated tradition has conceived of 'autonomy' as an individual capacity for rational self-rule. During the last two decades, this account has been widely challenged. Feminist philosophers in particular have argued for the necessity of rethinking the notion of 'autonomy' on the basis of the social, political and moral relationships that shape and sustain individual lives and beliefs. This 'relational' approach to autonomy is gaining growing consensus in contemporary debates in political and moral philosophy as a promising way to redefine and reassess many controversial topics such as the liberal attitude toward paternalism, the problem of adaptive preferences, and the conditions of social and political oppression.

However, contemporary philosophers have largely neglected the problem of uncovering the historical roots of the relational approach to autonomy. The reference to historical figures is far from being a fee to be paid to tradition and antiquarian curiosity. As the contemporary revival of Aristotelian and Kantian accounts shows, authors of the past are crucial discussants for present-day debates and are often able to both challenge our assumptions and suggest new directions for investigation. Moreover, exposing past philosophies to present-day concerns is often a highly stimulating hermeneutical exercise, capable of generating new insights into past figures and producing new interpretations of canonical works.

Philosophical interpretations are themselves historical products. Interpretations are filtered through and determined by the interpreters' own commitments and by the context of their creation. By exposing Spinoza's texts to the contemporary concern raised by feminist debates on relational autonomy, this collection aims to deconstruct the more standard way of understanding Spinoza's thought that has been consolidated in the past decades of readings. The hope of this project is to use this hermeneutic deconstruction to reveal new potential paths and resources concealed in Spinoza's texts and not yet fully exploited or appreciated. On the one hand, we hope to show that by adopting a 'relational' account of autonomy it is possible to reconsider several crucial features of Spinoza's philosophy and to reassess several problems opened by his moral and political thought, as well as by his conceptions of action, body and mind. On the other hand, we aim to show that Spinoza's philosophy can form the basis of a constructive but critical engagement with contemporary debates regarding relational autonomy by suggesting new approaches and adding novel research questions to the contemporary agenda.

Thinking of Spinoza as a 'noble ancestor' of a relational account of autonomy might sound awkward. A well-established 'rationalistic' reading insists that, according to Spinoza, the individual can achieve freedom only through a 'therapeutic' use of adequate knowledge and rationality, which aims to progressively overcome the passions and imagination. Spinoza's model of a rational free individual has often been understood as the paradigm of a perfectly self-sufficient agent, and as a consequence, his conception of autonomy has been treated in a rather dismissive way. Unlike other classical authors revived by contemporary moral and political philosophers (e.g. Aristotle by Alasdair MacIntyre, Rousseau by Charles Taylor or Kant by John Rawls), Spinoza has not yet played any significant role in orienting contemporary debates. The chapters included in this collection aim to challenge such a reading and correct this oversight.

Addressing the question of autonomy in Spinoza's corpus requires grappling with several interpretive and conceptual issues. In fact, proposing a relational reading of Spinoza's philosophy cannot consist in merely discussing some specific aspect of his system. Rather, a relational reading entails a complete reassessment of crucial issues of Spinoza's thought, from the metaphysical and ontological ground of his notions of 'individuality' and 'activity' to the moral, psychological and political consequences of his account of the emotions or affects. For instance, one of the central commitments of recent relational approaches to autonomy is to rethinking the atomistic, rights-bearing individual of the liberal tradition. On some readings of Spinoza, he offers an alternative conception of individuality that challenges the dichotomy between individual autonomy and relationally conceived identity or even 'transindividuality' (to use the term introduced by Balibar). Spinoza's idea that individual autonomy may be enhanced by the right kinds of social and political relationships suggests a rethinking of entrenched dichotomies between independence and dependence, self and other, separation and connection.

Spinoza's insistence on the embodiment of the mind leads to the requirement to address physical vulnerabilities and well-being as relevant to individual autonomy. In this way, a Spinozistic perspective directs attention to the material supports necessary to developing the capacity for autonomy and so avoids excessively rationalistic (i.e. mentalistic and internalist) interpretations of autonomy. Spinoza's moral psychology grounds the mind's ideas and beliefs in its fundamental striving for acting and increasing its power. Insofar as the mind strives to cope with the environment in which it exists and operates, it devises different *strategies* to resist potentially destructive interactions with others and with external causes and adapt as much as possible to its environment. From this point of view, Spinoza's moral psychology can offer unexpected resources to engage with the issue of adaptive preferences, which affect and may significantly impair individuals' autonomy.

Spinoza's treatment of activity and passivity allows us to consider the contribution that external things make to individual's power to act more autonomously, and leads us to rethink our notion of freedom. The pay-off of this relational interpretation is double. On the one hand, the chapters of this collection show that a relational reading of Spinoza fits better with several of Spinoza's claims – concerning autonomy, freedom and the necessity of social life – that are otherwise difficult to understand or have been treated in deflationary ways. On the other hand, insofar as Spinoza's thought is understood as a powerful defence of a relational account, it reveals its great potential for generating new research questions and providing a challenging agenda for the contemporary debate.

If a relational reading is to advance the discussion of autonomy, the editors have shared the conviction that this collection must encompass readings representing an exceptionally wide range of philosophical approaches and traditions. It must countenance a meaningful conversation with 'the French reception' and with 'continental' readings of Spinoza, including the important work of Gueroult, Matheron, Zac, Deleuze, Balibar and Negri amongst others. These readings have often attended most closely to the implications of the idea of relational identity and transindividuality. But it is equally important to engage interpretations of Spinoza by feminist thinkers like Gatens and Butler, and by thinkers within broadly 'analytic' traditions of thought who have put forward challenging and suggestive rereadings of matters such as agency, the status of individuals, the nature of mind, and the 'parallelism' doctrine. However, the contributions in this collection do not put forward one single reading of Spinoza, or one overarching view of autonomy as relational. The authors not only represent a wide range of philosophical methods and traditions, they represent a wide range of interpretative possibilities; and they are brought together with the aim of exploring a theme through diverse voices. The aim of this collection is to foster conversation across the gulfs that continue to challenge and divide philosophical conversations.

2. Contents Outline

In Chapter 1, Catriona Mackenzie provides an overview of the current debate on relational autonomy. Despite fairly widespread agreement in liberal democracies about the normative value of autonomy, exactly what the concept means and entails is disputed. Over the last two decades, relational theories of autonomy have marked a new intervention in philosophical debates about autonomy. Relational theories are responsive to feminist critiques of substantively individualist conceptions of autonomy and seek to refigure the concept of autonomy as socio-relational. A particular concern of relational theories is to explain the autonomy-impairing effects of social oppression. Relational autonomy is, however, an 'umbrella term'. In order to develop a better understanding of relational autonomy, Mackenzie maps out the various positions in debates within the recent literature. A central challenge facing relational theories is to negotiate the 'agency dilemma'. This is the challenge of recognising and explaining the ways in which social oppression can impair or constrain the autonomy of members of socially subordinated groups, without impugning and disrespecting their agency or licensing paternalistic interference in their lives. The rival positions in debates about relational autonomy theory over the last two decades have been staked partially in response to this challenge. In the final section of the chapter, Mackenzie proposes that the agency dilemma can be negotiated, and we can move beyond some of the impasses in the current debate, if we understand autonomy as a multidimensional rather than a unitary concept. In outlining her own multidimensional theory of relational autonomy, Mackenzie proposes that autonomy comprises three distinct but causally interconnected dimensions: self-determination, self-governance and self-authorisation. The aims of this proposal are to do justice to the complexity of the concept, to reconcile what are usually taken to be competitor positions in the debate, and to show how a multidimensional approach can answer the agency dilemma.

In Chapter 2, Ursula Renz focuses on Spinoza's account of the individual mind. Recent Spinoza scholarship has emphasised the value of conceptions such as 'trans-subjectivity', 'intersubjectivity' and the 'social nature of minds'. In her contribution, Renz argues that notions of transindividuality, however important, do not wholly subsume individuals as subjects or agents. Renz claims that many interpreters have overlooked that, in some respects, Spinoza irreducibly relies on an individualistic idea of the perfection of knowledge and individual minds. In this chapter, Renz discusses the question of the respect in which Spinoza (and Kant) sticks with Descartes' epistemic individualism. She argues that one can make a strong case for a reading that goes for a sort of individualism accommodating Spinoza's views on both the social nature of thought and the irreducibility of dependency in human existence. Renz's historical reconstruction is also a source of critical insight that contextualises Spinoza's views of individuals as 'modes' and Spinoza's sense of this notion.

In Chapter 3, Martin Lenz contends that Spinoza holds a relational view of the human mind, according to which the content of ideas is crucially determined by the ideas of others. What is it then that determines the content of my ideas? According to Lenz, Spinoza defends the view that mental content is determined intersubjectively. If one has the idea that the cat is on the mat, the content of her thought is not only determined by other ideas in her own mind, but also by the ideas of others. This view, Lenz submits, clearly flows from Spinoza's conception of relationally determined individuals. Thus, Lenz argues for the claim that Spinoza holds an intersubjectivist view of mental content and shows how it is rooted in his metaphysics.

If correct, Lenz's interpretation is at odds with the common picture of Spinoza's view of the mind. Many philosophers writing in the wake of Descartes defend an individualist view of the human mind. One's own mind, one's own mental states and volitions seem to be the starting point for investigations in theoretical and practical philosophy. The common interpretations of Spinoza are no exception. Given the centrality of the principle of self-preservation, the *conatus* principle, Spinoza's *Ethics* (E) seems to lend itself clearly to an individualist account of the mind as well as to egoism in ethics.

Although this general picture has been challenged by a number of commentators, it still pervades our understanding of Spinoza's theory of knowledge and intentionality. What is missing is a study that shows how Spinoza's intersubjectivist view of the mind is grounded in his related philosophical positions. This chapter tries to contribute to this larger project by investigating the relation between his view on intentionality and his relational account of individuals.

What then is it that determines the content of my ideas, according to Spinoza? It is helpful to begin by noting that Spinoza introduces ideas in degrees of adequacy: depending on how ideas are embedded in a given mind, they are more or less adequate. This has an unfortunate consequence for human minds. A central thesis in Spinoza's theory of the human mind is that most ideas are inadequate. Taken as individual modes, we are only part of the causal and conceptual network, and thus our grasp of things is equally partial and inadequate.

Although this thesis is fairly complex, it gives rise to a convenient holistic interpretation (Brandom, Della Rocca, Perler, Renz) of ideational content: while the content of an idea is adequately determined by all other ideas in God's mind, the content of the idea as it is in my mind is partial and relative. The problem with this interpretation is that it explains content through two static perspectives (the divine or human). In doing so it disregards the *dynamic nature of ideas and their adequacy*, that is, the fact that our ideas can become more or less adequate depending on our conative attitudes towards them.

In Chapter 4, Matthew Kisner examines how Spinoza's relational theory of autonomy is grounded in his metaphysics, specifically in his view of natures. Spinoza's view of natures in some ways sides with Descartes' view, most notably by identifying extension as the nature of substance, which provides some footing for a mechanistic explanation of the physical world. Indeed, Spinoza extends Cartesian mechanism by providing the basis for a mechanistic account of the natures of individual bodies. Yet, in other ways, Spinoza returns to a more Aristotelian view. In particular, Spinoza conceives of individual natures as *conatus*, which sides with Aristotelians in conceiving of individual natures as intrinsic, active powers. Consequently, Spinoza also sides with Aristotelians – at least with many scholastic Aristotelians – in emphasising that individual things are active when their natures determine them to particular changes and effects.

Attending to this view sheds light on two ways that Spinoza provides a metaphysical basis for a relational account of autonomy. First, Spinoza's more Aristotelian conception of natures indicates a relatively unexplored way that he provides such a basis. Spinoza's conception of natures implies that people can be active in the sense that their natures determine them to particular effects, even in cases where the people are also passive, that is, where they are affected by others and where they work cooperatively with others to bring about some effect. Consequently, this account of natures provides Spinoza with the resources to explain how people can be self-determining or autonomous in virtue of their social relationships, where they are affected by others and are cooperative.

Second, the examination sheds light on another way that Spinoza provides a basis for a relational theory of autonomy, one that has been more widely discussed in the literature. Spinoza offers an unorthodox theory of individuals, according to which individuals are formed whenever things work together to bring about some effect. This entails that any person belongs to multiple individuals formed from any sort of collective action. On this theory, it is impossible to understand individuals atomistically, that is, in isolation from their broader social and political context. This is a central commitment of relational theories of autonomy. Kisner's examination shows that this unorthodox account of individuals has some basis in Spinoza's theory of natures, more specifically in his effort to extend and shore up Descartes' mechanistic approach to explaining bodies.

In Chapter 5, Heidi M. Ravven argues that Spinoza's understanding of the third kind of knowledge, the source of the greatest human satisfaction, entails the achievement of a form of independence of mind consistent with and even dependent upon ever increasing relatedness to and within the world. In interpreting the aim of human striving in this way, Spinoza owes a debt to Maimonides' Aristotelian conception of theoretical contemplation, and ultimately to Aristotle's notion of the activity of thinking in which the mind's own mental act becomes one with the activity of nature naturing. Hence for Spinoza the ever increasing relation of one's mind and body within nature and a person's independence of mind are mutually constitutive rather than in conflict. This is the case because, in Maimonides, what was the autonomy of the mind via its transcendence of the mundane world of the singular and the body toward the universal and rational, becomes, instead, in Spinoza's reworking, the transcendence of the local and durational via the mind–body's active understanding and enacting of its infinite constitutive relations. Hence the asymptotic relationality of agency, and especially moral agency, according to Spinoza.

In Chapter 6, Caroline Williams argues that freedom and autonomy are polysemic concepts that are shaped in part by the world in which they appear as well as the underlying philosophical systems that give them meaning. Spinoza's philosophy shatters modern Enlightenment, arguably instrumental, conceptions of freedom based on a free will because it challenges the ontological foundation of the will itself. At first glance, the philosophical opposition between freedom and necessity, and the strong commitment to the latter, appears to offer few resources for thinking about a robust conception of autonomy that may inform contemporary philosophy and politics. However, Spinoza's primary attention to freedom (and bondage) leads many Spinoza scholars to understand such an opposition to merely cover over the deeper sense of freedom buried within his thought. Williams suggests that it is a close examination of the malleable and somewhat plastic form of some of Spinoza's central concepts that elicits a novel understanding of autonomy. In particular, Williams claims that when Spinoza's concept of *conatus* is examined as a force or power of *all* things, this engenders in turn a sense of relationality that ties human communicative power and freedom to non-human others and things. Spinoza's dynamic conceptions of imagination and affect are shown to deepen this understanding. This reading of Spinoza's philosophy entails a reflection upon *degrees* of autonomy, as well as the political stakes of Spinoza's reframing and repositioning of human power.

In Chapter 7, Justin Steinberg aims to shed light on Spinoza's conception of the relationship between the citizen and the state by examining two interpretative questions: (1) Is the state an individual? (2) What grounds Spinoza's claim that the human individual ought always to comply with civil laws? Several scholars, whom he refers to as Restrictive Individualists, have worried that answering (1) in the affirmative would entail an intolerable understanding of (2), according to which the human individual would be engulfed in the functioning of the state. Steinberg argues that (1) should be answered affirmatively and that the worries of the Restrictive Individualists are unfounded. He then proposes a way of answering (2) that is consistent with the normative priority of the human individual.

Restrictive Individualists place two conditions on higher-order individuality: (1) the laws that govern the activity of higher-order individuals must be *more basic* than those that govern the activity of lower-order individuals; (2) higher-order individuals, like all other individuals, must have 'intrinsic' conative power, a power that is not reducible to the power of its constitutive parts. On the Restrictive Individualist account, the state is at best a mere aggregate, since its laws are rooted in the more basic laws of human psychology and its power is derived entirely from the power of its constituent members. Steinberg argues that Spinoza would reject both of these conditions.

According to Steinberg, the worry that if a state were an individual, the normative priority of the human individual would be compromised is misplaced. On Spinoza's account, normative priority is indexed to a particular striving. The supposition that one could subordinate the pursuit of one's own good to the good of another is at odds with the core features of Spinoza's moral psychology. Consequently, we need not worry that state individualism threatens normative priority.

This last point, however, raises a new worry: if Spinoza is indeed committed to the normative priority of the human individual, why does he insist that human individuals should always seek to comply with civil law? It does not require much imagination to devise scenarios in which one's own personal welfare could be strengthened by non-compliance.

One way of approaching this problem is to see it as a special case of altruism. This is how Michael Della Rocca addresses the issue. He claims that Spinoza adopts a scalar version of the identity of indiscernibles on the basis of which he can maintain that a rational individual will pursue the good of those who agree with her because, to the extent that they agree with her, they literally *are* (numerically!) her. The same logic applies to compliance with the law: we agree not only with other citizens but also with the state itself and to that extent we will pursue their ends as ours.

Steinberg argues that there are good reasons to resist Della Rocca's interpretation, not least of which being that it fails to account for the special utility of civic relations or the way in which one's fellow citizens are uniquely useful to oneself. Nevertheless, Della Rocca is right to look to the concept of agreement (*convenientia*) to ground Spinoza's demand of civil compliance. Steinberg shows that in the *Political Treatise* Spinoza uses the concept of agreement to mean something more like cooperation – a literal coming together (*con-venire*) – with citizens functioning as parts of a single individual. Cooperative functioning is in turn mutually empowering, since by participating in larger social wholes, the causal capacities of the individuals are enhanced. Coming together with others thus provides conditions in which we can flourish individually.

In Chapter 8, Ericka Tucker argues that we can find Spinoza's theory of freedom in his discussions of power. To do this, Tucker shows, first, how Spinoza defines freedom in terms of power. Tucker traces Spinoza's definitions of power and freedom through the *Ethics* and political works and concludes that, for Spinoza, power and freedom are coextensive. Power, for Spinoza, plays the functional role of freedom – explaining what humans are able to do and be. Increases of power count as increases of freedom. Tucker goes on to show that, for Spinoza, individual power is relational. Tucker sets out Spinoza's view of individual power and shows how individual power is affected by other individuals. The power of individuals within a group is mediated by affects, ideas and desires of that group. The freedom of an individual is ineluctably tied to the power of the community of which that individual is a part. Spinoza's theory of relational power and relational freedom do not solve the libertarian problem of individual freedom in community; however, Tucker proposes that Spinoza's theory of power offers us a rich conception of the ways in which social, political and psychological forces shape individual and collective freedom.

In Chapter 9, Keith Green examines Spinoza's reasons for denying that penitence, humility, shame and abjection can possibly be virtues, even when these affects mediate obedience to rational moral rules. He argues that Spinoza's denial implies that what passes for autonomy according to proceduralist or 'neutralist' views fall short of autonomy, conceived as a capacity for moral self-direction through the powers of one's own mind. The reason is that these emotions, as well as blaming or motivational liability to blame, even without overt compulsion (that amounts to what Spinoza calls 'force'), reflect a condition that Spinoza calls 'weakness of spirit' (*impotentia animi*). And 'weakness of spirit' is a condition under which a subject/agent is moved to grasp and obey reasonable moral rules by causes beyond their own 'strength of mind'. Yet, acting from 'strength of mind', Spinoza believes, moves 'agents' to desire genuine goods for themselves that also redound to the good of any other individual with a nature that 'agrees' (in Spinoza's sense of *convenientia*) in relevant ways. The upshot is that those who are able to seek their own perseverance and flourishing from 'strength of mind' act 'from' genuine self-love but also follow what amounts to the love commands – one loves one's neighbour as oneself. This means that genuine self-love (as opposed to what Spinoza calls pride) is a necessary and perhaps sufficient condition for autonomy. But loving oneself genuinely and necessarily entails acknowledging and sustaining the 'plenum' of relationships that sustain individual autonomy.

In Chapter 10, Andrea Sangiacomo implements Spinoza's account of autonomy to deal with the use and legitimacy of paternalistic interferences. Paternalism is often invoked to prevent certain subjects from acting in a self-harming way, although their choices appear to be both free and voluntary. To justify paternalistic interventions, it is commonly argued that agents acting in a self-harming way are not really autonomous but rather forced to behave in such a way by visible forms of exploitation or simply by some kind of 'adaptive preference'. In this chapter, Sangiacomo argues that by adopting a Spinozistic approach to relational autonomy we can develop a rather different approach to paternalism. Sangiacomo contends that Spinoza's moral philosophy not only develops an account of (constitutive) relational autonomy, but it also introduces a further distinction between a quantitative dimension of autonomy (i.e. the capacity of an agent to be more or less autonomous) and a qualitative dimension of autonomy (i.e. the capacity of an agent to develop better or worse forms of autonomy). Sangiacomo argues that this distinction is important to deal with particularly hard cases that are addressed in the contemporary debate. The chapter focuses on the case study provided by prostitution and interventions intended to combat it. Sangiacomo argues that these interventions should not be designed to remedy a 'self-harm' but rather to provide the agents with better resources to improve their own autonomy.

1

Relational Autonomy: State of the Art Debate

Catriona Mackenzie

1. Relational Autonomy: Overview

Autonomy is a highly prized value in liberal democratic societies, a value associated with liberalism's emphasis on the normative importance of the individual and of freedom. Reflecting this value, the concept of autonomy has come to play an increasingly central role in a wide range of debates in contemporary social and political philosophy and in bioethics.

Autonomy is both a status and a capacity concept. Understood as a status concept, it refers to the idea that individuals are entitled to exercise self-determining authority over their own lives, an entitlement that can only be infringed under specified constraints, such as if its exercise causes harm to others.[1] What underpins this entitlement is the idea that competent adult individuals should be presumed to have the capacity for rational self-governance; that is, the capacity to make decisions about matters of importance to their lives, informed by their own reflectively held values and commitments.

Yet despite fairly widespread agreement in liberal democracies about the normative value of autonomy, exactly what the concept means and entails is far from straightforward. The brief definition given above raises a host of complex questions about what self-determination means and about the conditions under which an individual's entitlement to exercise self-determining authority can legitimately be infringed. Addressing these questions takes us to the heart of debates in social and political philosophy about the nature and limits of individual freedom. Similarly complex questions arise about the nature of the capacities required for self-governing agency and the processes involved in critically reflecting on one's values and commitments. Addressing these questions takes us to the heart of debates in moral philosophy and moral psychology about the nature of agency. Given the complexity of the conceptual terrain, it should therefore come as no surprise that, despite agreement about the value of autonomy, both within philosophy and in public discourse there is a range of competing conceptions of autonomy, which provide different answers to these questions.[2]

Over the last two decades, relational theories of autonomy have marked a new intervention in philosophical debates about autonomy.[3] Relational theories are motivated in part by feminist critiques of classical liberal conceptions of the individual and of autonomy.[4] One strand of the feminist critique focuses on conceptions of self-determination, charging that within liberalism autonomy has been implicitly coded as masculine. Feminist critics have claimed that the notion of individual self-determination assumes a socially atomistic conception of persons, which gives normative primacy to ideals of individualism and substantive independence and devalues relations of interpersonal dependency, care and connection that historically have been associated with women. Within this masculinist framework, self-determination is thus conceptualised as freedom from any form of dependence on others and from the constraints of social bonds.

A related strand of the feminist critique targets the role played by the rhetoric of autonomy within contemporary liberal polities. Legal theorist Martha Fineman (2008, 2010), for example, criticises what she refers to as the 'liberal subject' model of citizen–state relations and its associated 'myths' of autonomy and personal responsibility. The liberal subject construct, she argues, is based on a flawed conception of persons as self-interested, substantively independent, rational contractors, and ignores the facts of human vulnerability and dependency. Further, the associated rhetoric of autonomy and personal responsibility functions to mask social injustice, structural inequality and disadvantage, and shifts the onus for redressing these problems away from the state and onto individuals.[5]

A rather different strand of feminist critique focuses on the notion of self-governing agency, charging that, as interpreted within the Enlightenment tradition, the notion of self-governance is overly rationalistic, assuming a false conception of agents as self-transparent and psychically unified, and failing to account for the emotional and embodied dimensions of agency.

In the wake of these critiques, relational theorists seek to refigure the concept of autonomy in several ways. First, in response to the charge that autonomy as self-determination assumes a socially atomistic conception of persons, relational theories reject social atomism and take as their starting point a socio-relational ontology of persons. According to relational theories, persons are both causally and constitutively relational and social beings. Causally, because developmentally we only become persons through embodied social interaction with other persons with whom we exist in various relations of dependency. Constitutively, persons are relational because our identities and our sense of self are constituted through social relationships and through processes of enculturation into specific linguistic, political and historical communities. Given this commitment to a socio-relational conception of persons, relational theorists hold that an adequate conception of autonomy must be responsive to the facts of human vulnerability and dependency, and must be consistent with social relations of care.

Relational theorists thus reject substantive individualist conceptions of autonomy. Nevertheless, while rejecting substantive individualism, relational theories uphold the normative value of individual or personal autonomy. They are therefore committed to a form of normative individualism. Normative individualism is the view that the rights, welfare, dignity, freedom and autonomy of individuals matter and impose normative constraints on the claims of social groups or collectives.[6] The distinction between normative and substantive individualism is critical for understanding the underlying aim of relational theories, which is to articulate a conception of autonomy that upholds the normative significance of individuality and individual autonomy while rejecting social atomism.

Second, in response to the feminist charge that the notion of self-governance is overly rationalistic, relational theories seek to provide a richer characterisation of individual identity and of the requirements for self-governing agency. Relational theories acknowledge that our individual identities are shaped by the historical, social and relational contexts in which we are embedded, and by intersecting determinants of gender, culture, class, religion, ethnicity and race. An adequate conception of autonomy must therefore be premised on a thick socio-historical conception of individual identity. It must also recognise that our motives and commitments are often not transparent to us. The self-knowledge required for self-governing agency thus requires social interaction and dialogue with others as much as it requires introspective reflective skills. Moreover, relational theories recognise that since we are emotional, embodied, feeling, as well as rational creatures, self-governing agency involves the exercise of imaginative and emotional competences, not just practical rationality.[7] In line with the commitment to a socio-relational ontology of persons, relational theories understand self-governing agency as a complex competence, the development and exercise of which requires ongoing interpersonal, social and institutional scaffolding.

This last point connects to the third way in which relational theories seek to refigure the concept of autonomy, namely by focusing attention on the role of the interpersonal and social environment in shaping our agency. A particular concern of relational theories is to identify the characteristics of an autonomy-enabling social environment, as well as to explain how oppressive social environments can impair autonomy. While emphasising the crucial role of interpersonal and social dynamics in shaping agency and our self-identities, relational theories also identify the ways that some social relationships, such as those characterised by domination, abuse, coercion, violence or disrespect, provide hostile conditions for autonomy. In addition, they focus attention on broader social and political structures, and the ways these can undermine or defeat individuals' efforts at self-determination, for example through curtailing important freedoms or restricting opportunities. Relational theories are thus responsive to the concerns about social injustice, structural inequality and disadvantage that animate Fineman's critique of the 'autonomy myth'.

Relational autonomy is, however, an 'umbrella term' (Mackenzie and Stoljar 2000b). While the foregoing discussion has provided a broad overview of some of the central concerns and commitments of relational theories, it has glossed over important differences among these theories. To develop a better understanding of relational autonomy it is important to map out the various positions in debates within the literature over the last two decades. A central challenge facing relational theories is to negotiate the 'agency dilemma' (Khader 2011; Mackenzie 2014b). This is the challenge of recognising and explaining the ways in which social oppression can impair or constrain the autonomy of members of socially subordinated groups, without impugning and disrespecting their agency or licensing paternalistic interference in their lives. The rival positions in debates about relational autonomy theory over the last two decades have been staked in response to this challenge. One way to map out the differences between rival positions is to distinguish broadly between internalist and externalist theories (see e.g. Johnston 2017). Another way is to distinguish between procedural and substantive theories (see e.g. Mackenzie and Stoljar 2000b). In outlining the debates in the following section I refer to both distinctions, proposing that the procedural/substantive distinction should be understood as marking out differences among varieties of internalist theories.

In the third section, I propose that the agency dilemma can be negotiated, and we can move beyond some of the impasses in the current debate, if we understand autonomy as a multidimensional rather than a unitary concept. In outlining my own multidimensional theory of relational autonomy, I propose that autonomy comprises three distinct but causally interconnected dimensions: self-determination, self-governance and self-authorisation. To be self-determining is to have the freedom and opportunities necessary for determining the direction of one's own life. To be self-governing is to have the competences necessary for making authentic decisions about one's life. To be self-authorising is to regard oneself, and to be regarded by others, as normatively authorised to determine the direction of one's life and competent to govern oneself. I have already briefly introduced the concepts of self-determination and self-governance in this section in providing an overview of the concerns and commitments of relational theories. However, these concepts are not usually distinguished, either from each other or from the concept of self-authorisation. Rather, autonomy is taken to be equivalent to the unitary concept of self-governance. I suggest that this is a mistake and that we can bring greater clarity and some resolution to the debate by understanding these concepts as highlighting different dimensions of the concept of autonomy.

2. Relational Autonomy: State of the Debate[8]

The debate between internalist and externalist relational theorists centres on whether the necessary and sufficient conditions for autonomy, and the social dimensions of autonomy, can be adequately articulated solely with reference to the internal structure of an agent's will or motivational set. Internalists, as the name suggests, think that autonomy, or self-governance, depends solely on factors internal to the psychology of the agent. Most non-relational theories of autonomy, such as the influential hierarchical theories discussed below, are also internalist. What differentiates relational internalist theories is that they explicitly recognise the ways in which individual identity and agency are socially constituted. Thus they recognise that an agent's identity and the elements of her motivational set – her preferences, values and commitments – are shaped by social relationships and by the broader social environment. They also acknowledge that the competences required for self-governing agency are socially scaffolded. Nevertheless, they think the necessary and sufficient conditions for autonomy, and the sense in which autonomy is social depend on factors internal to the agent. Externalist theories, in contrast, argue that autonomy, or self-governance, is not just a matter of how agents' wills or psychologies are internally structured; it also requires that certain external, social, structural conditions be in place. It is thus not possible to explain the sense in which autonomy is social, or how social oppression can thwart autonomy, by focusing only on features internal to the agent.[9]

Procedural theories of autonomy are internalist. They seek to identify the necessary and sufficient conditions for a particular preference, commitment or value to count as autonomous by appealing to a critical reflection procedure of some kind. So long as an element of a person's motivational set meets the critical reflection test, she is autonomous with respect to it, regardless of the specific content of her preferences, commitments or values. Substantive theorists object that procedural theories are insufficient to explain how social oppression impairs autonomy. To explain the autonomy-impairing effects of oppression, they propose additional substantive constraints, either on the content of autonomous preferences, values or commitments, or on the self-reflexive attitudes required for self-governing agency.

Relational theorists who favour a procedural approach claim that a strong reason for preferring procedural theories is that their commitment to content-neutrality is socially and politically inclusive and respectful of agents' first-person perspectives (Friedman 2003). These theorists often invoke the 'agency dilemma' against substantive relational theories, charging that substantive theories may license disrespect towards the perspectives of socially oppressed agents and paternalistic forms of interference in their lives (see e.g. Christman 2004; Holroyd 2009; Sperry 2013). Note that substantive theories are also internalist, however, insofar as their analysis of the conditions for self-governing agency is restricted to elements internal to an agent's psychology, such as preferences, values, competences or self-reflexive attitudes.

In what follows, I first sketch out in more detail the conditions for autonomy proposed by procedural theorists, before outlining the contours of the debate that has been generated by the objections of substantive theorists. I then briefly discuss and provide qualified support for externalist theories. It is important to note that externalist theories do not discount the relevance of the conditions for self-governance proposed by internalist theories. Their argument is rather that these conditions are not sufficient to explain either the sense in which autonomy is social or the impacts of social oppression on autonomy.

2.1 Proceduralism

Procedural theorists hold that an agent is autonomous with respect to a decision, preference, value or commitment so long as that decision, or the relevant element of the agent's motivational set, is authentically her own. To count as authentic, the decision or element must pass some kind of critical reflection test. Many theorists therefore follow John Christman (2009) in distinguishing two broad kinds of procedural conditions for autonomy: authenticity and competence. Authenticity conditions specify the necessary and sufficient conditions for appropriate critical reflection, and hence for a person's decisions, preferences, commitments or values to count as authentically her own. Competence conditions specify the underpinning competences that agents must possess and exercise to be capable of appropriate critical reflection. In seeking to articulate the sense in which autonomy is relational and to explain the impacts of social oppression on autonomy, procedural relational theorists have significantly extended and reinterpreted mainstream understandings of both authenticity and competence.

2.2 Authenticity

The accounts of authenticity proposed by relational theorists arise from critiques of mainstream hierarchical theories (see e.g. Dworkin 1988; Frankfurt 1971; Watson 1975). Hierarchical theories distinguish between first-order elements of an agent's motivational set (e.g. desires or first-order preferences) and second-order reflective preferences or values. They hold that an agent is autonomous if her first-order motivations are in accord with her second-order reflective preferences or values; that is, if in light of second-order reflection she endorses her first-order motivations. Hierarchical reflective endorsement procedures therefore explain autonomy in terms of structural features of the agent's will at the time of reflection and action, specifically internal psychic coherence between second-order reflection and first-order elements of the agent's motivational set.

Relational theorists charge, however, that mainstream hierarchical theories overlook the social dimensions of identity and agency. The reflective endorsement procedures proposed by hierarchical theories therefore fail to account for the autonomy-impairing effects of social oppression. In one of the original discussions in the literature, Marilyn Friedman (1986) uses an example of a conflicted 1950s housewife to make this point. Friedman's housewife has internalised prevailing social norms that a good wife and mother should stay at home and put her own needs secondary to those of her husband and children. At the second-order level, she endorses these norms. However, she is frustrated and unhappy and frequently experiences what she regards as wayward first-order preferences and emotions in conflict with these norms. Friedman argues, contra hierarchical theories, that these apparently wayward first-order desires and emotions may be more expressive of the woman's authentic wants and values than any reflection she engages in at the second-order level, which may simply reinforce her oppressive social conditioning.[10]

A further problem with hierarchical theories, revealed by this example, is that the requirement of internal coherence between second-order reflection and first-order elements of the agent's motivational structure seems to set the bar for self-integration unrealistically high and to equate autonomous agency with psychological rigidity. Frankfurt, for example, regards ambivalence as a 'disease of the will' (1999: 100). Now while too much unresolved ambivalence and psychic fragmentation can impair autonomy, as in the case of Friedman's housewife, as

J. David Velleman (2002) has argued, ambivalence and some degree of inner psychic conflict or fragmentation are not only inescapable aspects of individual identity formation but may also be necessary for psychological health. Further, as Diana Meyers (2000) argues, intrapsychic tension and ambivalence are characteristic features of intersectional identity. The notion of intersectional identity (see e.g. Crenshaw 1991) is a metaphor used by feminist and critical race theorists to characterise the way experiences of social subordination across multiple identity categories, such as gender, race, class or sexual orientation, constitute identities as complex and often internally conflicted.

In the wake of this critique, relational procedural theorists have sought to develop analyses of authentic critical reflection that acknowledge the complexities of individual identity formation. Friedman (1986, 2003) proposes an *integration* test according to which reflective endorsement is authentic and autonomous when lower-order preferences and higher-order normative commitments are integrated in a person's motivational set as a result of two-way processes of bottom up and top down reflection.[11] In rejecting top down analyses of self-governing agency, Friedman highlights the way that social oppression shapes not only our preferences but also our self-conceptions and normative commitments. She also highlights the importance of emotionally informed self-knowledge for authentic critical reflection.

Christman (1991, 2009) identifies two additional problems with mainstream hierarchical theories, and develops an alternative procedural test for authentic critical reflection that seeks to remedy these problems. First, he argues that hierarchical theories cannot account for the autonomy-impairing effects of social oppression because they take a time slice approach to agency and focus solely on the structure of an agent's motivations at the time of deliberation and action. In so doing, they fail to attend to the historical processes of practical identity formation; that is, the historical processes by which an agent acquired her preferences, values and commitments. However, it may be the case that if an agent were to reflect on the historical processes by which she acquired these elements of her motivational set, she would reject them as inauthentic, for example, because she realises that they are the result of oppressive relationships or social conditioning. Christman's focus on the importance for autonomy of reflecting on the historical processes of identity formation may suggest that he assumes a rather unrealistic picture of autonomous agency as requiring both self-transparency and continuous conscious critical reflection about our personal histories. Earlier formulations of Christman's view (e.g. Christman 1991) are certainly vulnerable to this objection. However, in his later work (e.g. Christman 2009) he acknowledges that we are often not motivationally transparent to ourselves, and that critical reflection need not be a sustained, deliberate, conscious process.

Second, Christman argues that the notions of identification and endorsement are too strong. To be autonomous with respect to a preference, value or commitment only requires that we are not alienated from it. Christman's historical, counterfactual, *non-alienation* test thus specifies that an element of a person's motivational set is authentically her own if, *were* she counterfactually to engage in reflection on the historical processes of its formation, she would not repudiate or feel alienated from that element (2009: 155). The notion of non-alienation is weaker than the notion of endorsement and acknowledges that there are elements of one's motivational set that one may not endorse but nevertheless accepts as authentically one's own.

Unlike hierarchical theories, Friedman's and Christman's theories are explicitly premised on a socio-historical conception of persons, which takes account of the way our identities, values and commitments are shaped by social relationships and our personal histories. Like hierarchical theories, these theories are nevertheless internalist, insofar as the integration test and the counterfactual non-alienation test provide criteria for autonomy that focus wholly on the internal structure or ordering of elements within the agent's psyche, rather than on any conditions external to the agent.

2.3 Competence

Competence conditions have received less attention than authenticity conditions in philosophical debates about autonomy. The reverse is true in bioethics, where concerns about the conditions for informed consent have focused discussions about autonomy primarily on competence rather than authenticity. In bioethics, competence is understood quite minimally, as having sufficient rational competence to understand the information relevant for making an informed choice (for example about treatment options), and the ability to communicate this choice effectively to others (see e.g. Beauchamp and Childress 2012). Philosophical accounts of competence typically focus on capacities for rationality, self-control, and freedom from psychopathology and systematic self-deception. However, relational autonomy theorists, influenced by the work of Diana Meyers (1989), argue the need for a much richer conception of what Meyers calls *autonomy competence*.

According to Meyers, autonomous self-governance involves a repertoire of complex competences (1989: 76–91). This repertoire includes reasoning and communication skills. Importantly, however, it also includes interpersonal skills of social cooperation, emotional skills, such as the capacities to interpret and regulate one's emotions, as well as the imaginative skills required for understanding the implications of one's decisions and envisaging alternative possible courses of action. Autonomous self-governance, in her view, also requires capacities to reflect critically on social norms and values. Each of these skills may be developed to greater or lesser degrees. On this picture, then, a person is autonomous, and her choices are authentically her own, to the degree that she has developed the relevant skills and can exercise them to understand herself (self-discovery), define her values and commitments (self-definition), and direct her life (self-direction).

Meyers' focus on competence provides an alternative procedural approach to the problem of how to distinguish authentic from inauthentic critical reflection in contexts of social oppression. Her account of autonomy competence is procedural or content-neutral, because in Meyers' view whether or not a person is autonomous does not depend on the specific content of the person's preferences, values and commitments, but rather on whether or not she exercises the necessary reflective skills to develop and express an authentic self-conception. Meyers' notion of autonomy competence is relational because she foregrounds the extensive social scaffolding required to develop and exercise the competences required for authentic critical reflection. She emphasises that these competences are developed through the socialisation process and exercised in the context of social relationships, thus the extent to which an agent is autonomous is significantly dependent on the character of her social environment. An autonomy enhancing social environment is one that supports individuals to develop and exercise the full repertoire of autonomy skills required for developing a dynamic, authentic self-portrait. An autonomy inhibiting social environment, in contrast, selectively stunts the development or truncates the exercise of these skills. Meyers argues that traditional gender socialisation, for example, tends to encourage in girls the development of emotional skills that are important for self-discovery, but thwarts the development and exercise of some of the skills required for self-definition and self-direction. She also distinguishes several different levels at which agents can exercise autonomy competence, and suggests that because traditional gender socialisation discourages women from developing self-defining and self-directed plans and goals, it can hinder their global autonomy, or their autonomy with respect to their lives overall.

By bringing into focus the interpersonal and social scaffolding required for autonomy, Meyers' theory significantly advances our understanding of the relational constitution of autonomy. Despite its emphasis on the social scaffolding of autonomy competence, however, her theory can nevertheless be characterised as internalist because the extent to which an agent is autonomous, in her view, is determined solely by the extent to which the agent possesses and exercises the relevant competences, and not by any additional external structural factors, such as whether she is socially subordinated. Of course, Meyers acknowledges that being socially subordinated is likely to have negative impacts on an agent's autonomy competence. One of the aims of her theory is to explain the processes by which this occurs. However, she rejects the claim, made by some externalist theories, that social subordination is incompatible with autonomy.

2.4 Substantivism

Substantive theorists accept the importance of both critical reflection and autonomy competence for self-governing agency. However, they reject procedural theorists' commitment to content-neutrality, arguing that to explain the autonomy-impairing effects of oppressive socialisation, relational theories must identify more substantive constraints either on the content of autonomous preferences, values and choices or on agents' self-evaluative attitudes. Some theories that have been labelled 'substantive', such as Marina Oshana's (2006) socio-relational theory, are in my view better understood as externalist, as I explain below. I will therefore reserve this term for theories that propose additional substantive internal constraints on autonomous agency.

A distinction is often drawn in the literature between strong and weak substantive theories (see e.g. Mackenzie and Stoljar 2000b; Benson 2005; Stoljar 2013). Strong substantive theories reject content-neutrality because they hold that genuinely autonomous preferences or decisions must satisfy certain normative constraints; specifically, they must be guided by true rather than false norms (see e.g. Benson 1991; Stoljar 2000). According to this view, the reason that Friedman's housewife and other agents who have internalised oppressive social norms and stereotypes are not autonomous with respect to them is because these norms and stereotypes are false. Moreover, the internalisation of false norms and stereotypes typically disables agents' capacities to subject them to critically reflective scrutiny. Thus, decisions and behaviour guided by them cannot be autonomous. Natalie Stoljar (2000) discusses the example of women who seek multiple abortions as a result of repeated failure to take contraceptive precautions. Drawing on Kristin Luker's (1975) interview-based studies with women in this situation, Stoljar argues that these women fail to act autonomously with respect to their own sexual activity because they have internalised oppressive sexual double standards. Their failure to take contraceptive precautions is motivated by their (self-deceived) self-conceptions as the kind of women who do not have sex outside marriage. Stoljar claims that insofar as this behaviour and their self-conceptions are guided by false social norms, these women are non-autonomous with respect to the specific norms in question and the choices and actions that flow from them.

One of the motivations for strong substantive theories is to account for the phenomenon of adaptive preference formation and its impact on autonomous agency. Adaptive preferences are preferences that are formed in response to severely constrained or unjust social environments, which deny freedoms or block opportunities to members of socially oppressed groups or subject them to prejudicial stereotypes and oppressive social norms. The notion of adaptive preference formation refers to the way that agents in these kinds of social environment adapt their preferences and beliefs to the constraints of their situation. These kinds of adaptation can take different forms, including (often unconsciously) eliminating or failing to form preferences and goals one cannot hope to satisfy (Stoljar 2014a), being unable to imagine one's life being otherwise (Mackenzie 2000) or making strategic trade-offs among one's preferences (Khader 2011). Strong substantive theorists claim that because adaptive desires and beliefs are deformed or distorted by the agent's oppressive social environment they lack agential authority (see e.g. Superson 2005; Cudd 2014). While not disputing the reality of adaptive preferences, critics object that strong substantive theorists fail to recognise the range of reasons people might have for complying with oppressive norms (Khader 2011; Sperry 2013) or conflate autonomy with substantive independence (Christman 2004), thereby falling foul of the 'agency dilemma'. In the following section I will suggest that a multidimensional approach to autonomy is useful for illuminating what is correct about the positions on both sides of this debate.

Weak substantive theories arise from concern that while proceduralism is insufficient to explain the autonomy-impairing effects of social oppression, strong substantivism imposes requirements on autonomy that are too stringent. In particular, weak substantivists reject the strong substantivist claim that to count as autonomous an agent's behaviour and choices must be guided by true rather than false norms and beliefs. Rather than holding that to count as autonomous an agent's preferences, beliefs and values must satisfy certain normative constraints, weak substantivists propose other constraints on self-governing agency. Some theorists suggest that to be autonomous, agents must hold appropriate self-reflexive attitudes, in particular attitudes of self-respect, self-trust, and self-esteem or self-worth (see Benson 1994, 2000; Govier 2003; Anderson and Honneth 2005; Mackenzie 2008). Self-respect involves regarding oneself as the moral equal of others, as having equal standing to have one's views and claims taken seriously. Self-trust is the capacity to trust one's own convictions, emotional responses and judgments. Self-esteem or self-worth is an evaluative attitude towards oneself, which involves thinking of oneself, one's life and one's undertakings as meaningful and worthwhile.

Weak substantivists point out that one of the insidious effects of social oppression, which is not captured by procedural theories, is the way that experiences of injustice, discrimination and prejudicial stereotyping can erode these attitudes, thereby impairing one's sense of oneself as normatively authorised to determine the direction of one's life and competent to govern oneself. In a related vein, Benson (2005, 2014a) proposes that autonomous agency is characterised by a sense of ownership of one's choices and actions. It involves regarding oneself as positioned, and as having the appropriate authority, to speak and answer for oneself.[12] One of the effects of internalised oppression on this account is that it impairs autonomy by impairing a person's sense of herself as having a legitimate voice, and as competent and authorised to speak or answer for her values and commitments. Weak substantivist views therefore bring out a further aspect of the sense in which autonomy is relational. Specifically, they highlight the importance of social recognition for developing and maintaining the self-evaluative attitudes that underpin autonomous agency, and for regarding oneself as having the *status* of an autonomous agent, or as entitled to determine the direction of one's life and competent to govern oneself. In the following section, I will propose that this aspect of autonomy is best understood as a distinct dimension of the concept, which I term 'self-authorisation'.

2.5 Externalism

Proceduralism, strong substantivism and weak substantivism are all varieties of internalist theory. Externalists argue that the problem with internalist theories is that their exclusive focus on agents' psychologies fails to identify the impact of external constraints on autonomy, including social relations of domination and subordination, structural injustices, restricted freedom and opportunities, discrimination and stereotyping.

To better understand the motivation for externalist theories, it is useful to consider an example discussed by Jennifer Warriner (2014). Warriner's argument is addressed specifically to weak substantive theories such as Benson's, but it has broader implications for internalist theories more generally. Her example is of women who belong to Christian Evangelical churches, who have thoroughly internalised oppressive gender norms according to which women's subordination to male authority is normatively required by their religious commitments. Despite willingly accepting their subordinated status, such women are nevertheless likely to have a strong sense of ownership of their actions and choices because within their community they are still 'expected to regard themselves as having agential authority and are expected to authorize their agency' (2014: 37). Thus they seem to satisfy Benson's requirements for autonomous agency. However, it seems counterintuitive to say these women are autonomous, because their agential authority can only be exercised within the constraints of a social script of male dominance and female subordination, the reasons for which they are not permitted to question or challenge. Warriner argues that this example shows that genuine autonomy requires external, not just internal conditions; in particular, it requires socio-relational equality.

This is the view most influentially articulated in Marina Oshana's (2006; 2014b) socio-relational theory of autonomy. Oshana's theory is often characterised as a strong substantive view, perhaps because she presents her theory as an account of self-governance. However, I suggest that this is misleading, and that Oshana's view should be understood as externalist because she thinks that a person's socio-relational status is the crucial determinant of autonomy. In her view, agents who stand in relations of subordination, subservience, deference, or economic or psychological dependence, cannot be autonomous, even if they meet the conditions for autonomy proposed by procedural or substantive internalist theories. This is because such agents, by virtue of their subordinated position, lack the authority and power to exercise effective practical control over important aspects of their life that is the hallmark of autonomous agency.

Critics of Oshana often invoke the 'agency dilemma' against her view, arguing that it disrespects the autonomy of agents who have managed to lead self-governing lives despite being subject to crushing forms of oppression (Christman 2004). Such critics cite examples, such as Martin Luther King Jr or Rosa Parkes, and others like them, who seem to be prime exemplars of autonomous agency in their struggles against the racial oppression and injustice to which they were subject. At times Oshana suggests that, rather than demonstrating the implausibility of the socio-relational account, such heroism 'should rather serve as an example of an *exception* to the socio-relational account' (2014b: 11). At other times she bites the bullet, suggesting that, despite their heroism, King and Parkes were not autonomous because of their subordinated status in an unjust social hierarchy. In either case, the objections to Oshana arise because she presents her theory as an account of the conditions for self-governing agency and hence critics interpret her theory as internalist. The criticism that her theory impugns the competence and agency of persons subject to oppression therefore seems justified. However, if her theory is interpreted as externalist, it becomes clear that her focus is less on agents' psychologies and capacities and more on how oppressive socio-relational structures constrain self-determination.

The debates between procedural and substantive, and internalist and externalist theories have certainly advanced the development of relational conceptions of autonomy and enhanced our understanding of the social dimensions of autonomy. However, in my view these debates have now reached something of an impasse, suggesting the need to rethink the conceptual terrain. The problem, as I see it, is that autonomy is a complex concept. As we have seen, it refers to both status and capacity; it is also conceptually interconnected with a range of related concepts, such as freedom, authenticity, competence and agential authority. Moreover, the enabling and constraining social conditions for autonomy are also complex. This conceptual complexity may explain why our philosophical intuitions are pulled in different directions by examples that highlight different aspects of the concept. For example, if autonomy is understood as a status concept allied to the concept of freedom, Oshana seems correct in pointing out that Martin Luther King Jr's ability to lead a self-determining life was highly restricted, since as an African American in the Jim Crow era he did not enjoy the socio-relational status of a free and equal citizen entitled to be treated with respect by others. However, if autonomy is understood as a matter of having an authentic voice and a sense of agential authority, and if we focus on King's heroic defence of the rights of African Americans to equal treatment and his persistence in the face of brutal oppression, he seems an exemplar of self-governing, self-authorising agency.

My proposal is that to do justice to this complexity it would serve us better to understand autonomy as a multidimensional, rather than a unitary concept, comprising three distinct but causally interconnected dimensions or axes: self-determination, self-governance and self-authorisation (Mackenzie 2014a). To be self-determining is to have the freedom and opportunities necessary for determining the direction of one's own life. To be self-governing is to have the competences necessary for making authentic decisions about one's life. To be self-authorising is to regard oneself, and to be regarded by others, as normatively authorised to determine the direction of one's life and competent to govern oneself. In seeking to explain the autonomy-undermining effects of social oppression, the different relational theories discussed in this section highlight different dimensions of the concept: externalist theories focus on self-determination; internalist procedural and strong substantive theories focus on self-governance; weak substantive theories focus on self-authorisation. Rather than understanding these theories as competitor explanations, I suggest we should think of them as analysing a range of different mechanisms of social oppression, some of which function as external constraints on autonomy, while others shape agents' psychologies in potentially autonomy-impairing ways. In the following section, I explain this proposal in more detail. I also identify areas where further conceptual work needs to be done to explicate each dimension more fully in order to further advance debates about relational autonomy.

3. Relational Autonomy: A Multidimensional Theory

3.1 Autonomy as Self-determination

The notion of self-determination articulates one of the central roles that the concept of autonomy plays in liberal moral and political discourse: namely to define the entitlement of each individual to determine the direction of one's life, and to exercise control over important domains of one's life. To be self-determining requires being free from domination and undue interference by others as well as having the freedom and opportunities required to exercise this kind of control. The self-determination axis thus points to the interconnections between the concepts of autonomy, freedom and opportunity. Freedom is necessary for autonomy because people's abilities to lead self-determining lives can be severely curtailed if they are denied important political and personal liberties, and if they are subject to social and political domination. Opportunity is important for autonomy because opportunities translate formal liberties into substantive freedom. A person who has formal access to political and personal liberties but lacks access to an adequate array of genuine opportunities will find it difficult to lead a self-determining life. Poor education, limited employment opportunities, poverty and social marginalisation can all undermine a person's ability to exercise control over important domains of her life. This is why externalist theorists insist on the importance of external, structural conditions for autonomy.

Freedom and opportunity are contested concepts, however, so which conceptions of freedom and opportunity are most amenable to relational theories of autonomy? This question has received insufficient attention in the literature, mainly because the debate has focused on the conditions for self-governing agency, rather than on the conditions for self-determination. Here I can only gesture towards an answer to this question. However, I would suggest first that a relational approach to self-determination entails a rejection of libertarian conceptions of freedom as negative liberty; and second, that the conceptual connections between relational autonomy and neo-republican theories of freedom are worth investigating further.[13] I would also suggest that capabilities theory provides a fruitful vocabulary for articulating the notion of opportunity that is relevant for self-determination.

On the first point, I have suggested that self-determination requires both freedom and opportunity. Freedom is required because it is difficult for a person to live a self-governing life if political or personal restrictions prevent her from making choices about matters that are important to her life. However, living a self-determining life seems to require more than being free from restrictive interference by others or the state. It also seems to require access to genuine opportunities, or to a range of significant options (Raz 1986), which means access to social goods such as education, health care, housing and social support; adequate nutrition, sanitation and personal safety; opportunities for political participation and paid or unpaid employment; and some degree of mobility. These goods require complex social, economic and political infrastructures.

Different theories weight the values of freedom and opportunity differently, however. Libertarian conceptions of freedom as negative liberty give undue weight to the importance of liberty, understood as non-interference by others or the state, while overlooking the importance for self-determination of access to social goods and opportunities. Further, libertarian conceptions pay insufficient attention to whether or not the social distribution of opportunities is equitable, and whether or not some individuals require more social assistance than others in order to be able to lead self-determining lives. Libertarian conceptions of freedom are thus inconsistent with the central concerns of relational theorists, which is to identify and address the impacts of social oppression on individuals' abilities to lead self-determining lives.[14]

On the second point, republican theories of freedom claim that self-determination is not secured simply by absence of interference, but rather requires freedom from domination and from subjection to arbitrary forms of power and interference, or what Pettit refers to as 'freedom of undominated status' (2012: 88). On the republican view, even if a person is not actually and presently subject to domination by another, she is not self-determining if, by virtue of her social status, she is vulnerable to domination. Thus, from a republican perspective, to ensure equal status, the basic liberties must be legally, politically and socially entrenched and resourced. Further, these liberties must be equally accessible to, and equally able to be enjoyed by, all members of a society.[15] As I argued in the previous section, externalist theorists such as Oshana similarly claim that socially subordinated agents are not autonomous because they lack the authority and power to exercise effective practical control over important aspects of their lives. This suggests that there may be fruitful connections, worth investigating further, between republican theories of freedom and relational theories of autonomy.[16]

Finally, in articulating the importance of opportunity for autonomy, externalist theorists such as Oshana have drawn mainly on the work of Joseph Raz (1986), who argues that autonomy requires access to an adequate array of significant opportunities, or what he refers to as options. Although access to options requires certain freedoms, in the form of basic rights and liberties, Raz also rejects the libertarian conception of freedom as negative liberty and minimally constrained freedom of choice, arguing that it conflates self-determination with license (1994). While I am broadly sympathetic to Raz's account of significant options, in my view capabilities theory also provides a promising vocabulary for articulating the opportunity conditions for self-determination, because it combines a focus on the importance of individual self-determination with attention to the social and political constraining and enabling conditions for self-determination. The theory recognises, on one hand, that different people will value different capabilities, and hence argues that a just society ought to ensure equality of access to a wide range of opportunities but leave it to individuals to choose which particular capabilities to realise beyond the threshold. On the other hand, capability theorists, like theorists of relational autonomy, are also sensitive to the role of the social environment and social, political, legal and economic institutions in enabling or constraining individual self-determination (Sen 1992, 2009).[17]

By identifying self-determination as a distinct dimension of autonomy, the multidimensional analysis points to important conceptual links between relational autonomy theory and recent work in political philosophy on freedom and justice. More work needs to be done, however, to investigate in detail the fruitfulness of these links for relational autonomy theory.

3.2 Autonomy as Self-Governance

Whereas the self-determination axis identifies external, structural or sociopolitical conditions for autonomy, the self-governance axis identifies conditions for autonomy that are internal to the agent. To be self-governing is to have the competences necessary for making authentic decisions about one's life, decisions that express or cohere with one's deeply held values and commitments. As discussed in the previous section, much of the debate in the relational autonomy literature has focused on analysing the necessary and sufficient conditions for self-governance and explaining how these conditions can be thwarted by social oppression. However, by locating the autonomy-impairing effects of structural social and political constraints wholly within agents' psychologies, this exclusive focus on self-governance makes relational theories vulnerable to the agency dilemma. Distinguishing self-determination from self-governance, as I propose, makes it possible to explain how agents whose capacities for self-determination are severely constrained by oppressive social environments may nevertheless still be self-governing in important respects, thus avoiding the agency dilemma.

A further virtue of distinguishing these two dimensions of autonomy is that it helps to explain the causal interaction between social and political structures and individual agency. For if, as relational theorists hold, persons are socially constituted, then external conditions (social relationships, political, legal and economic structures, available opportunities) must shape the historical processes of individual identity formation – both who a person is, or the authentic *self* of self-governance, and the development and exercise of the skills and competences required for *governing* the self. Explaining how the internalisation of social subordination and restricted freedom and opportunity can impair self-governing agency is a complex question. Recent discussions have focused on the phenomenon of adaptive preference formation (see e.g. Stoljar 2014a; Cudd 2014; Mackenzie 2014b), and the ways that oppressive social scripts which are ascribed third-personally by others become internalised in agents' self-conceptions, thereby impairing their psychological freedom (see e.g. Oshana 2005; Stoljar 2014b). These recent discussions draw not only on theoretical work on oppression in feminist philosophy and critical race theory, but also on research in social psychology on stereotype threat and implicit bias. The large body of empirical research in social psychology on the psychological effects of injustice and oppression is of increasing interest to philosophers, and is likely to be of ongoing benefit to relational theorists in explaining the processes by which the internalisation of structural injustice and oppression can impair self-governing agency.

Relational theory might also benefit from a renewed focus on its positive agenda of developing a richer conception of agency. As discussed in the previous section, relational theorists argue that autonomy competence and capacities for critical reflection encompass a range of agential skills, including emotional and imaginative skills, not just reasoning skills. They therefore pose a challenge to mainstream autonomy theories that typically understand critical reflection in terms of reasons-responsiveness and think of emotions as elements of our psychologies with respect to which we are passive. Nevertheless, the role of emotions and imagination in critical reflection and self-governing agency remains a relatively under-explored topic in the literature. There has been a resurgence of philosophical interest in the emotions over the last two decades. Much of this work has challenged traditional conceptions of the emotions as cognitively impenetrable biological mechanisms or mere bodily feelings, proposing instead that emotions are crucial to reasoning and cognition.[18] The sophisticated analyses of the emotions that emerge from this recent literature provide a fruitful resource on which relational theorists could draw to explicate both the epistemic role of emotions in self-knowledge and self-governing agency and the role of emotion regulation or reflective self-monitoring in critical reflection.[19]

3.3 Self-authorisation

The *self-authorisation* axis illuminates the connections between autonomy, self-reflexive attitudes and social recognition that are of concern to weak substantive theorists. To be self-authorising is to regard oneself as having the normative authority to take ownership of, or responsibility for, one's values, decisions and one's life. It also involves regarding oneself as an equal participant in reciprocal accountability relations – as able to account for oneself to others and also to hold others to account. Thinking of oneself in this way involves holding appropriate attitudes of self-respect, self-trust and self-esteem. These psychological attitudes are inherently social, because they are developed and sustained through intersubjective social relations and normative structures and practices of social recognition. One of the insidious effects of social subordination is that persistent messages of social inferiority and unworthiness, embedded in everyday social interactions and conveyed through demeaning stereotypes, can be internalised in feelings of shame and humiliation, of diminished self-respect, self-trust and self-esteem, and of social invisibility.

Rather than understanding these attitudes as conditions of self-governance, however, the multidimensional analysis proposed here suggests that they should be understood as a separate axis of autonomy. As mentioned above, recent developments in social epistemology on epistemic injustice, and in social psychology on implicit bias and stereotype threat, have expanded the conceptual resources for understanding the various mechanisms by which social oppression can be internalised and thereby can threaten what I am calling self-authorising agency. Relational theorists have recently begun to investigate the potential impact of epistemic injustice on agents' autonomy. Beate Roessler (2014), for example, takes up Miranda Fricker's (2007) work on testimonial injustice, or the injustice of one's views and utterances being given less credibility by virtue of identity prejudice (due to factors such as race, class or gender) on the part of hearers. Roessler argues that repeated experiences of testimonial injustice can give rise to autonomy-impairing harms, specifically a damaged sense of self-worth, and potentially crippling self-doubt with respect to one's epistemic capacities, especially one's capacities to deliberate and make up one's own mind about what one believes. Benson (2014b) draws on the literature in social psychology on stereotype threat and 'belonging uncertainty' to provide empirical support for the claim that social oppression can impair self-worth and a person's sense of themselves as a self-authorising agent.[20]

4. Conclusion

My aim in this chapter has been to provide an overview of current debates in the literature on relational autonomy. Inevitably any survey such as this will overlook many of the finer details of various positions in the debate. Hopefully, however, it provides a sufficiently comprehensive overview for readers who are new to the literature. I have also sketched out a preliminary outline of my proposal that autonomy should be understood as a multidimensional concept. The aims of this proposal are to do justice to the complexity of the concept, to reconcile what are usually taken to be competitor positions in the debate, and to show how a multidimensional approach can answer the agency dilemma. By distinguishing different dimensions of autonomy, we can see why the claim that social subordination constrains people's capacities to lead autonomous lives in the self-determination sense does not manifest disrespect towards socially subordinated persons, nor does it imply that such persons lack capacities for self-governance or self-authorisation. At the same time, the multidimensional analysis draws on the important insights of relational autonomy theorists into the ways that the internalisation of social oppression can (but need not) impair capacities for self-governance and an agent's sense of herself as self-authorising. Much work remains to be done to flesh out the conceptual details of each dimension of autonomy, but hopefully enough has been said to persuade readers of the intuitive plausibility of the multidimensional account.

Notes

1. This constraint, known as the harm condition, is due to J. S. Mill (1962).
2. Within contemporary philosophy these competing conceptions derive, to some extent, from different historical sources, most notably Mill and Kant. While Mill's liberalism links autonomy to notions of individual self-expression and freedom from undue interference, Kant understands autonomy as a capacity of the rational self-governing will.
3. For an overview of relational conceptions of autonomy see Mackenzie and Stoljar (2000a). Two recent volumes that significantly advance debates about relational autonomy are Veltman and Piper (2014) and Oshana (2014a).
4. For a detailed discussion and response to several variants of these critiques, see Mackenzie and Stoljar (2000a).

5. See Mackenzie (2014c) for a detailed response to Fineman's critique of the 'autonomy myth'. In that paper I agree with Fineman's critique of the minimal state and associated rhetoric, but argue that Fineman conflates autonomy with libertarian conceptions of autonomy.
6. For a detailed analysis of normative individualism, see Anderson (2009).
7. For discussion of the imaginative and emotional competences involved in autonomous agency see Meyers (1989) and Mackenzie (2000, 2002).
8. The structure of the argument and some of the text in this section draws on material in some of my previously published work, especially Mackenzie (2017) and Mackenzie (forthcoming).
9. In the following section, I propose that externalist theories are better understood as concerned with the conditions for self-determination, rather than self-governance.
10. The character of Laura Brown in Michael Cunningham's novel *The Hours* (1999) provides a vivid fictional characterisation of such a woman.
11. Meyers argues that the notion of integration is too static to capture the dynamic process of authentic self-definition, suggesting that this process should be understood as 'akin to improvisational orchestration' (2000: 172). I discuss Meyers' view below.
12. See also Westlund (2009) who argues that autonomy requires normative and dialogical competence to take responsibility, or answer for oneself.
13. See for example Pettit (1997, 2012).
14. For more detailed discussion of these objections to libertarian conceptions of freedom and autonomy see Mackenzie (2014c, 2015).
15. My discussion draws here on Pettit (2012: Ch. 2).
16. In Mackenzie (2016), I have begun to sketch out some of these connections in an analysis of Mary Wollstonecraft's work. In that paper I argue that Wollstonecraft's analysis of women's subjection draws on a republican conception of freedom as non-domination. Drawing on my multidimensional theory of autonomy, I also argue that her work anticipates contemporary relational theories of autonomy.
17. The concerns of feminist capabilities theorists, such as Elizabeth Anderson (1999, 2010) and Ingrid Robeyns (2003, 2010) in particular, overlap with the concerns of relational autonomy theorists. In Mackenzie (2014c), I outline in a bit more detail the potential fruitfulness of capabilities theory for articulating the opportunity conditions for autonomy.
18. The literature is too voluminous to cite here. However, one of the most influential contributions to the recent literature is de Sousa's (1987) quasi-perceptual theory of the emotions.
19. See Tappolet (2014) for a recent discussion of these issues. The concept of reflective self-monitoring is due to Jones (2003).
20. The term 'belonging uncertainty' refers to anxiety experienced by members of stigmatised social groups who are subject to stereotype threat that they do not belong in certain privileged environments, for example in university. Note that the term 'self-authorisation' is mine, not Benson's.

Works Cited

Anderson, Elizabeth (1999), 'What is the Point of Equality?', *Ethics* 109(2): 287–337.
Anderson, Elizabeth (2009), 'Towards a Non-Ideal, Relational Methodology for Political Philosophy', *Hypatia*, 24(4): 130–45.

Anderson, Elizabeth (2010), 'Justifying the Capabilities Approach to Justice', in Harry Brighouse and Ingrid Robeyns (eds), *Measuring Justice: Primary Goods and Capabilities*, Cambridge: Cambridge University Press, pp. 81–100.

Anderson, Joel and Axel Honneth (2005), 'Autonomy, Vulnerability, Recognition and Justice', in John Christman and Joel Anderson (eds), *Autonomy and the Challenges to Liberalism*, Cambridge: Cambridge University Press, pp. 127–49.

Beauchamp, Tom and James Childress (2012), *Principles of Biomedical Ethics*, 7th edn, New York: Oxford University Press.

Benson, Paul (1991), 'Autonomy and Oppressive Socialization', *Social Theory and Practice*, 17: 385–408.

Benson, Paul (1994), 'Free Agency and Self-Worth', *Journal of Philosophy*, 91: 650–68.

Benson, Paul (2000), 'Feeling Crazy: Self-Worth and the Social Character of Responsibility', in Catriona Mackenzie and Natalie Stoljar (eds), *Relational Autonomy: Feminist Perspectives on Autonomy, Agency and the Social Self*, New York: Oxford University Press, pp. 72–93.

Benson, Paul (2005), 'Taking Ownership: Authority and Voice in Autonomous Agency', in John Christman and Joel Anderson (eds), *Autonomy and the Challenges to Liberalism*, Cambridge: Cambridge University Press, pp. 101–26.

Benson, Paul (2014a), 'Feminist Commitments and Relational Autonomy', in Andrea Veltman and Mark Piper (eds), *Autonomy, Oppression, and Gender*, New York: Oxford University Press, pp. 87–113.

Benson, Paul (2014b), 'Stereotype Threat, Social Belonging, and Relational Autonomy', in Marina Oshana (ed.), *Personal Autonomy and Social Oppression: Philosophical Perspectives*, New York: Routledge, pp. 124–41.

Christman, John (1991), 'Autonomy and Personal History', *Canadian Journal of Philosophy*, 21: 1–24.

Christman, John (2004), 'Relational Autonomy, Liberal Individualism and the Social Constitution of Selves', *Philosophical Studies*, 117: 143–64.

Christman, John (2009), *The Politics of Persons: Individual Autonomy and Socio-Historical Selves*, Cambridge: Cambridge University Press.

Crenshaw, Kimberle (1991), 'Mapping the Margins: Intersectionality, Identity Politics, and Violence against Women of Color', *Stanford Law Review*, 43(6): 1241–99.

Cudd, Ann (2014), 'Adaptations to Oppression: Preference, Autonomy and Resistance', in Marina Oshana (ed.), *Personal Autonomy and Social Oppression: Philosophical Perspectives*, New York: Routledge, pp. 142–60.

Cunningham, Michael (1999), *The Hours*, London: Fourth Estate.

De Sousa, Ronald (1987), *The Rationality of Emotions*, Cambridge, MA: MIT Press.

Dworkin, Gerald (1988), *The Theory and Practice of Autonomy*, New York: Cambridge University Press.

Fineman, Martha (2008), 'The Vulnerable Subject: Anchoring Equality in the Human Condition', *Yale Journal of Law and Feminism*, 20(1): 1–23.

Fineman, Martha (2010), 'The Vulnerable Subject and the Responsive State', *Emory Law Journal*, 60: 251–75.

Frankfurt, Harry (1971), 'Freedom of the Will and the Concept of a Person', *The Journal of Philosophy*, 68(1): 5–20.

Frankfurt, Harry (1999), *Necessity, Volition and Love*, Cambridge: Cambridge University Press.

Friedman, Marilyn (1986), 'Autonomy and the Split-Level Self', *Southern Journal of Philosophy*, 24(1): 19–35.

Friedman, Marilyn (2003), *Autonomy, Gender, Politics*, New York: Oxford University Press.
Fricker, Miranda (2007), *Epistemic Injustice: Power and the Ethics of Knowing*, Oxford: Oxford University Press.
Govier, Trudy (2003), 'Self-Trust, Autonomy, and Self-Esteem', *Hypatia*, 8: 99–120.
Holroyd, Jules (2009), 'Relational Autonomy and Paternalistic Interventions,' *Res Publica*, 15(4): 321–36.
Johnston, Rebekah (2017), 'Personal Autonomy, Social Identity, and Oppressive Social Contexts', *Hypatia*, 32(2): 312–28.
Jones, Karen (2003), 'Emotion, Weakness of Will, and the Normative Conception of Agency', in Anthony Hatzimoysis (ed.), *Philosophy and the Emotions*, Cambridge: Cambridge University Press, pp. 181–200.
Khader, Serene (2011), *Adaptive Preferences and Women's Empowerment*, New York: Oxford University Press.
Luker, Kristin (1975), *Taking Chances: Abortion and the Decision Not To Contracept*, Berkeley: University of California Press.
Mackenzie, Catriona (2000), 'Imagining Oneself Otherwise', in Catriona Mackenzie and Natalie Stoljar (eds), *Relational Autonomy: Feminist Perspectives on Autonomy, Agency and the Social Self*, New York: Oxford University Press, pp. 124–50.
Mackenzie, Catriona (2002), 'Critical Reflection, Self-Knowledge, and the Emotions', *Philosophical Explorations*, 5(2): 186–206.
Mackenzie, Catriona (2008), 'Relational Autonomy, Normative Authority and Perfectionism', *Journal of Social Philosophy*, 39: 512–33.
Mackenzie, Catriona (2014a), 'Three Dimensions of Autonomy: A Relational Analysis', in Andrea Veltman and Mark Piper (eds), *Autonomy, Oppression, and Gender*, New York: Oxford University Press, pp. 15–41.
Mackenzie, Catriona (2014b), 'Responding to the Agency Dilemma: Autonomy, Adaptive Preferences and Internalized Oppression', in M. Oshana (ed.), *Personal Autonomy and Social Oppression*, New York and London: Routledge, pp. 48–67.
Mackenzie, Catriona (2014c), 'The Importance of Relational Autonomy and Capabilities for an Ethics of Vulnerability', in Catriona Mackenzie, Wendy Rogers and Susan Dodds (eds), *Vulnerability: New Essays in Ethics and Feminist Philosophy*, New York: Oxford University Press, pp. 33–59.
Mackenzie, Catriona (2015), 'Autonomy', in John Arras, Elizabeth Fenton and Rebecca Kukla (eds), *Routledge Companion to Bioethics*, New York and London: Routledge, pp. 277–90.
Mackenzie, Catriona (2016), 'Mary Wollstonecraft: An Early Relational Autonomy Theorist?', in Sandrine Berges and Alan Coffee (eds), *The Social and Political Thought of Mary Wollstonecraft*, Oxford: Oxford University Press, 2016, pp. 67–91.
Mackenzie, Catriona (2017), 'Feminist Conceptions of Autonomy', in Ann Garry, Serene Khader and Alison Stone (eds), *Routledge Companion to Feminist Philosophy*, New York and London: Routledge, pp. 515–27.
Mackenzie, Catriona (forthcoming), 'Relational Autonomy', in Kim Hall and Asta Sveinsdottir (eds), *The Oxford Handbook of Feminist Philosophy*, Oxford: Oxford University Press.
Mackenzie, Catriona and Natalie Stoljar (eds) (2000a), *Relational Autonomy: Feminist Perspectives on Autonomy, Agency and the Social Self*, New York: Oxford University Press.
Mackenzie, Catriona and Natalie Stoljar (2000b), 'Introduction: Autonomy Refigured', in Catriona Mackenzie and Natalie Stoljar (eds), *Relational Autonomy: Feminist*

Perspectives on Autonomy, Agency and the Social Self, New York: Oxford University Press, pp. 3–31.

Meyers, Diana (1989), *Self, Society and Personal Choice*, New York: Columbia University Press.

Meyers, Diana (2000), 'Intersectional Identity and the Authentic Self: Opposites Attract', in Catriona Mackenzie and Natalie Stoljar (eds), *Relational Autonomy: Feminist Perspectives on Autonomy, Agency and the Social Self*, New York: Oxford University Press, pp. 151–80.

Mill, John Stuart [1859] (1962) *On Liberty*, in J. S. Mill, *Utilitarianism, On Liberty and Other Essays*, ed. M. Warnock, London: Fontana, pp. 126–250.

Oshana, Marina (2005), 'Autonomy and Self-Identity', in John Christman and Joel Anderson (eds), *Autonomy and the Challenges to Liberalism*, New York: Cambridge University Press, pp. 77–97.

Oshana, Marina (2006), *Personal Autonomy in Society*, Aldershot: Ashgate.

Oshana, Marina (2014a), *Personal Autonomy and Social Oppression: Philosophical Perspectives*, New York: Routledge.

Oshana, Marina (2014b), 'Is Socio-Relational Autonomy a Plausible Ideal?', in Marina Oshana (ed.), *Personal Autonomy and Social Oppression: Philosophical Perspectives*, New York: Routledge, pp. 3–24.

Pettit, Philip (1997), *Republicanism. A Theory of Freedom and Government*, Oxford: Oxford University Press.

Pettit, Phillip (2012), *On the People's Terms: A Republican Theory and Model of Democracy*, Cambridge: Cambridge University Press.

Raz, Joseph (1986), *The Morality of Freedom*, Oxford: Clarendon Press.

Raz, Joseph (1994), 'Multiculturalism: A Liberal Perspective', in *Ethics in the Public Domain: Essays in the Morality of Law and Politics*, Oxford: Clarendon Press.

Robeyns, Ingrid (2003), 'Sen's Capability Approach and Gender Inequality: Selecting Relevant Capabilities', *Feminist Economics*, 9(2–3): 61–92.

Robeyns, Ingrid (2010), 'Gender and the Metric of Justice', in Harry Brighouse and Ingrid Robeyns (eds), *Measuring Justice: Primary Goods and Capabilities*, Cambridge: Cambridge University Press, pp. 215–35.

Roessler, Beate (2014), 'Autonomy, Self-Knowledge, and Oppression', in Marina Oshana (ed.), *Personal Autonomy and Social Oppression: Philosophical Perspectives*, New York: Routledge, pp. 68–84.

Sen, Amartya (1992), *Inequality Reexamined*, Cambridge: Cambridge University Press.

Sen, Amartya (2009), *The Idea of Justice*, Cambridge: Cambridge University Press.

Sperry, Elizabeth (2013), 'Dupes of Patriarchy: Feminist Strong Substantive Autonomy's Epistemological Weakness', *Hypatia*, 28(4): 887–904.

Stoljar, Natalie (2000), 'Autonomy and the Feminist Intuition', in Catriona Mackenzie and Natalie Stoljar (eds), *Relational Autonomy: Feminist Perspectives on Autonomy, Agency and the Social Self*, New York: Oxford University Press, pp. 94–111.

Stoljar, Natalie (2013), 'Feminist Perspectives on Autonomy', *Stanford Encyclopedia of Philosophy*, <http://plato.stanford.edu/entries/feminism-autonomy/> (last accessed 5 November 2018).

Stoljar, Natalie (2014a), 'Autonomy and Adaptive Preference Formation', in Andrea Veltman and Mark Piper (eds), *Autonomy, Oppression and Gender*, New York: Oxford University Press, pp. 227–52.

Stoljar, Natalie (2014b), '"Living Constantly at Tiptoe Stance": Social Scripts, Psychological Freedom, and Autonomy', in Marina Oshana (ed.) *Personal*

Autonomy and Social Oppression: Philosophical Perspectives, New York: Routledge, pp. 105–23.

Superson, Anita (2005), 'Deformed Desires and Informed Desire Tests', *Hypatia*, 20: 109–16.

Tappolet, Christine (2014), 'Emotions, Reasons, and Autonomy', in Andrea Veltman and Mark Piper (eds), *Autonomy, Oppression and Gender*, New York: Oxford University Press, pp. 163–80.

Velleman, J. David (2002), 'Identification and Identity', in Sarah Buss and Lee Overton (eds), *Contours of Agency: Essays on Themes from Harry Frankfurt*, Cambridge, MA: MIT Press, pp. 91–123.

Veltman, Andrea and Mark Piper (eds) (2014), *Autonomy, Oppression and Gender*, New York: Oxford University Press.

Warriner, Jennifer (2014), 'Gender Oppression and Weak Substantive Theories of Autonomy', in Marina Oshana (ed.), *Personal Autonomy and Social Oppression: Philosophical Perspectives*, New York: Routledge, pp. 25–47.

Watson, Gary (1975), 'Free Agency', *Journal of Philosophy*, 72(8): 205–20.

Westlund, Andrea (2009), 'Rethinking Relational Autonomy,' *Hypatia*, 24(4): 26–49.

2

Epistemic Autonomy in Descartes, Spinoza and Kant: The Value of Thinking for Oneself

Ursula Renz

In the past few years, philosophers have made a considerable effort towards a reinterpretation of the epistemological tradition between early modern philosophers and Kant, claiming that many of the accounts we find in this period are far less individualistic than usually assumed. Criticising the picture cultivated since Anthony Coady's (1992) seminal book on testimony, they claimed that there was a lot of social epistemology in early modern philosophy even before Thomas Reid, who has long been portrayed as the only early modern philosopher who accepted testimony as source of knowledge.[1]

There is a lot to be said about this. Generally, it is always a good thing to provide a more nuanced reconstruction of historical answers to questions and problems debated in contemporary philosophy, and I agree that the picture of early modern philosophy as cultivated in the testimony debate calls for a correction. Yet, I am not convinced by the suggestion that not only Reid and perhaps Crucius, but also Locke, Hume and – most important – Spinoza and Kant defended views that turn them into the avant-garde of contemporary 'social' or 'communitarian epistemology'. This is not to deny that they had a sense of the social nature of human thought. On the contrary, fighting public restrictions suppressing freedom of speech, philosophers engaged in the historical Enlightenment were quite aware of the fact that individual thought is deeply influenced by all sorts of social conditions. I am nonetheless suspicious of this interpretive effort. Rather, we should examine the charge of individualism itself, or, if it is used merely polemically, criticise it. Yet, the problem is that we still have a blurred view of the precise role played by individual subjects in epistemic processes. Thus, the question to be addressed in early modern philosophy is this: *Why did so many early modern philosophers adopt the view that certain epistemic acts are, or must be, the domain of individuals rather than of communities?*

Thus I suggest examining early moderns for their reasons for maintaining epistemic individualism. In particular, we should focus on those accounts that are most likely to provide good reasons for individualism, and these are to be found, I think, in the rationalist rather than the empiricist tradition. (The reason for this preference will become clear in the discussion of Kant's account.) Thus, today I suggest examining Spinoza's (section 2) and Kant's views (section 3) for their comprehension of the problem of epistemic autonomy of individual subjects. To set the scene, however, and to give some background, I will also have to look briefly at Descartes (section 1), as the very character of his epistemology is missed in many standard depictions of his account. In particular, I will focus on his reasons for individualism as advocated in the *Rules for the Direction of the Mind*. This text puts forward one of the most radical versions of early modern individualism, yet it is one of the clearest when it comes to the reasons for adopting individualism. As such, it certainly constitutes a crucial background against which later philosophers articulate their mostly moderate approaches.

In the end, it will turn out, perhaps somewhat surprisingly, that both Spinoza and Kant, while adopting a rather critical stance toward the Cartesian notion of concept formation, remained loyal to what may be considered Descartes' reasons for his epistemic individualism.

1. Individualism and *Scientia* in the Young Descartes

Descartes is certainly among the first figures that come into one's mind when one thinks about epistemic individualism in early modern philosophy. His ideas on human learning and science had a profound influence on the epistemological debate of the seventeenth and eighteenth centuries. Examining his approach, one soon discovers that more than by the alleged suspicion concerning any empirical sources of knowledge, Descartes' approach is shaped by a deeply dismissive attitude toward testimonial beliefs.[2] But why was Descartes so sceptical about the epistemic value of testimony as a source of knowledge? To understand the reasons for his scepticism, rather than focusing on the *Meditations* or the *Discourse*, I propose to look at his methodological views as discussed in the fragmentary treatise on the *Rules for the Direction of the Mind*. There, in Rule III, he advocates the view that science can only be acquired where the objects in question are either clearly and evidently intuited or deduced from such intuition.[3] What this rule requires is well known. We should, Descartes claims, begin our search for knowledge by grasping concepts that are evident and leave no doubt about the very nature of the objects of our inquiry. The question remains why Descartes assumes that knowledge can only be acquired if we employ this rigid method.

At this point, it is important to note that in Rule III the aim of inquiry is not referred to as knowledge, or *cognitio*, but as science, *scientia*. To see why this matters, note that the seventeenth-century term *scientia* had a somewhat different sense than our notion of 'science'. It is helpful, for instance, to consult Goclenius' *Lexicon philosophicum*. Published in 1613, this lexicon is just a few years older than Descartes' *Rules*, the first draft of which is dated 1619. The entry on *scientia* establishes the basic sense of *scientia* in terms of the Aristotelian notion of *habitus*. Considered ontologically, *scientia* is thus an *attitude* that we adopt when we come to know things in a certain manner, as well as the *disposition* we thereby acquire. In any case, it is neither reduced to an 'objective stock of knowledge' available to us, nor simply the special status conferred on some of our beliefs.

The question remains what sort of *habitus scientia* consists in. Goclenius addresses this question by differentiating several ways in which we may come to know things. In particular, he distinguishes between a proper and an improper sense of *scientia*.[4] In the proper sense, *scientia* denotes that *habitus* which we acquire when we know things in a demonstrative manner, for example when we see how some thing follows from some other thing. In the improper sense, *scientia* subsumes those intellectual attitudes brought about by all other sorts of acts of knowledge; this is what allows Goclenius, in the rest of the entry, to engage in a discussion of several different divisions between senses of *scientiae*, such as universal versus particular *scientia*; theoretical versus practical *scientia*; and *scientia* of simple versus *scientia* of complex things.

One might say here that these are inherited concepts that need not correspond with Descartes' views. In fact, some have argued that in the *Rules*, Descartes rejects the notion of *scientia* being a *habitus*.[5] And indeed, in the chapter on Rule I, which Rule claims that '[t]he aim of [one's] studies should be to dispose the mind to form true and solid judgments about whatever comes before it',[6] Descartes points out that 'they wrongly compare the sciences, which consist wholly in knowledge acquired by the mind, with the arts, which require some usage and disposition of the body' (*habitus corporis*).[7]

Descartes here explicitly rejects the parallel between the sciences and the arts, which were also seen as *habitus corporis*. Yet, his point is not that *scientia* should not be conceived in terms of a *habitus* at all, but he argues that, other than the *habitus corporis*, which requires a division of labour, the mental disposition, or mental perfection, constituting *scientia* must be such that one singular subject can in principle acquire and display it, however different the objects are to which it is employed. Descartes' point, in other words, is that the intellectual disposition, the acquisition of which is the final aim of study and which only enables the mind to 'form true and solid judgments', is essentially one, or indivisible. This is corroborated a little bit later by the claim that

> all sciences [*scientiae*] are nothing but human science [*scientia humana*], which always remains one and the same, however different the subjects to which it is applied, it being no more altered by them than sunlight is by the variety of things it illuminates.[8]

We can conclude that the goal of Descartes' individualist methodology is not simply to propose a reliable procedure for scientific inquiry in the modern sense of the term, nor is science merely a matter of knowing the essences of things, as it is sometimes purported. Instead, we have to understand Descartes' approach in light of the overall goal to provide guidance for human learning, so that the mind acquires a capacity for 'true and solid judgment', the having of which eventually improves our epistemic balance.

Now, one might think that this brings Descartes' individualist approach into a rather weak argumentative position. For does not all its plausibility depend now on whether or not one accepts the somewhat old-fashioned idea that scientific learning *is* essentially a matter of the acquisition of intellectual capacities?

Perhaps this is a questionable premise, but it nonetheless exhibits perspicuously why epistemological individualism is so plausible and intuitively appealing to many. For even if we do not adhere to the notion that science is an intellectual *habitus*, we usually assume that knowledge has some sort subjective aspect, or outcome. This is what distinguishes intuitive notions of knowledge from the notion of truth. We seem to think that knowledge only exists where it is instantiated in some particular subject. And my point is just that: once we focus on this subjective aspect, individualism is just the natural preference.

This may also help to defend Descartes' approach. For this much is clear: if we define the aim of *scientia* in terms of the disposition to form only solid and true judgments, that is, if the goal of scientific cognition and study is, ontologically speaking, seen in the acquisition of a special capacity by individual subjects, then it is naturally the acts of these very same individuals that matter. It is simply not comprehensible how someone can acquire a mental disposition by the acts of another subject.

At this point, two questions already seem to lurk in the background. First, one might wonder whether this train of thought does not eventually rely on a descriptive metaphysics, in which it is always and only singular human minds that constitute individual subjects. Is not, in other words, the very credibility of Descartes' epistemological individualism dependent on his substance metaphysics according to which different people are to be comprehended as wholly separate entities? What happens, in contrast, if we operate within a framework where the term 'individual' is used for all sorts of entities, including the body of communities and states?

Second, one might say that my reconstruction of Descartes' approach provided only a conditional argument. That we should focus on the acts of individuals is argued for under the condition that we in fact see the aim of scientific cognition and study in the acquisition of the disposition to form solid and true judgments. But why should we define the aim of scientific cognition and study in these terms? Is it really a meaningful end to acquire the disposition to form solid and true judgments? Why not just accumulate as many true beliefs as possible and make them available to as many people as possible?

Unfortunately, Descartes himself does not address this question explicitly. And in fact, if the entry on *scientia* in Goclenius' *Lexicon* expresses an understanding that was still alive in the seventeenth century, there was no need to do that. Still, one can presume that in the aftermath of Descartes' *Meditations*, or, more generally, in the Enlightenment, the problem of the value of individual thought and knowledge became a more prominent issue. It is against the background of this presumption that I shall discuss Spinoza's and Kant's views on individualism in the remaining sections.

2. Individualism and Perfectionism and the Mature Spinoza

Since the appearance of Alexandre Matheron's seminal book *Individu et Communauté chez Spinoza* in 1969, Spinoza's philosophy has become a frequent point of reference for reflection about all sorts of concerns related to the idea of transindividuality.[9] These interpretations have a clear fundament in Spinoza's texts. Given the definition of *res singularis* as articulated in E2def7 and the wide range of application of the term *individuum* as suggested in the definition of the physical digression following E2p13s, Spinoza advocates a rather revisionary notion of individuality. He allows for quite different kinds of bodily entities to count as individuals, whether small or large, simple or complex, amorphous or systematically organised. Moreover, regarding the way in which the term is used in E4p18s, there is no doubt that Spinoza considered political bodies as individuals in the defined sense of the word. Why, therefore, not assume that epistemic subjects may consist in groups, societies or other sorts of collective entities? What prevents us from embracing the view that Spinoza is committed to some form of social or communitarian epistemology, according to which communities, societies or states are real epistemic subjects?[10]

To my mind, despite the seemingly obvious textual evidence, differentiation is required here, for several reasons. First, Spinoza's metaphysics of individuation is certainly less individualistic, than, say, Aristotelianism or Cartesianism. But this is simply the consequence of his substance monism. Once the traditional equation of substances with singular things is given up, we are in need of another criterion for deciding whether or not some object counts as an individual, and not surprisingly without the backing from the notion of substance this will amount to a more relativistic view on individuation.

Second, note that the textual situation is more complex that one might think at first. Notably, it was Matheron himself who pointed this out in a paper from 2003, which he wrote for the *Festschrift* of the German Spinoza scholar Manfred Walther. In this paper, Matheron responds to Balibar's, among others, quite nuanced proposal from 2001, and he does so by slightly refining the views from his seminal book from 1969. In a nutshell, his view is this: while states and similar bodily complexes may count as individuals in the strict sense for Spinoza (Matheron 2003: 132), the case is far more difficult with respect to the mental parallels of bodily entities (ibid.: 133ff.). In particular, he shows, Spinoza almost always uses adverbs such as *quasi*, or *veluti*, when he talks of the (one) mind of groups or states.

It is against this background that, in my reconstruction of Spinoza's philosophy of mind, I defended the view that what may be called 'group minds' in contemporary terminology are not really Spinozistic individuals in their own right.[11] I admitted, of course, that they may be called so in a derivative way, namely insofar as they are about bodily individuals. But this is only a weak unifier. It allows for several kinds of strong internal divisions and tensions, which, unlike in the case of divisions in bodily individuals, are not accidental, but essential. Or more to the point: it is essential that divisions arise in 'group minds' for Spinoza, but where precisely the fractures are running may be subject to contingent influences.

Let me illustrate this point by an example. Imagine a group of students assembled in a lecture hall. There is a fixed proportion of motion and rest as well as a settled arrangement of bodies, thus the group apparently forms one bodily individual in Spinoza's sense of the word. The minds of the particular members of the group, however, are less organised and unified. Perhaps they are all thinking of the same subject matter, for example if they are attending a lecture on Spinoza's concept of the individual. At the same time, the minds of the students represent different portions of the world, and this is not just a matter of metaphysics, but it has a psychological effect. The mind of student A, for example, is perhaps just noticing that he is getting tired, whereas the mind of student B is busy with understanding the Latin of E3p6. If I was the speaker in the hall, I would, perhaps, struggle with pronouncing the English language properly. Clearly, these minds have a different focus of attention, and this necessarily so. Since even if I could, contrary to the facts, use the tongue of any native speaker in the same room instead of mine, my mind would still be about the clumsy tongue in my mouth, not about the tongues of the audience.[12] So while this group of people do constitute, for the time of the lecture in question, one Spinozistic bodily individual in the strict sense, their minds are not unified in the same way.

To conclude, we can assume that even within Spinoza's account, the individuation of minds is a more complex affair than the individuation of bodies. Taking this at face value, we can ascribe the view to Spinoza that our minds remain isolated to a certain degree, even when our bodies are unified. And this is crucial for our concern: if we want to understand Spinoza's ideas of epistemic subjects, we have to consider his thoughts about the mental aspect of our existence, not about the physical arrangement of our bodies. Thus, in order to know what individuality means with regard to epistemic subjects, we must consult Spinoza's views on the individuation of minds, not of bodies.

Let me come to a third point, which is the main reason why I am sceptical about the view that Spinoza embraced the notion of collective epistemic subjects. As we all know, the term 'knowledge' is usually taken to be a normative predicate. When we ascribe knowledge to someone, we do not simply ascribe some cognition or mental content to her, but we acknowledge that the cognition in question meets some standard, however the nature and origin of this standard may be explained. Note that this is not contrary to Spinoza's account. As I have argued in some detail in several papers on Spinoza's epistemology, there is a normative dimension in his views of knowledge.[13]

The question is how this affects the notion of epistemic subjects. The answer is easy, I think: when we ascribe knowledge to someone, our implicit evaluation is not just a matter of the content of her belief, but it reaches out to the question of whether or not she has got the belief in a legitimate way or on a legitimate ground. This is what contemporary analytic epistemology discusses under the label of justification or reliability and so on. In the rationalists, this was often discussed as a matter of whether or not a subject has the intellectual capacity to adopt a belief in the right way, which is perhaps why contemporary epistemologists began to think about classical rationalism as some form of virtue epistemology.[14]

To illustrate this, let me quote Descartes again:

We shall never become mathematicians, even though we know other people's demonstrations by heart, unless we were also capable, out of our own mind, to solve any given problem; or philosophers, even though we have read all the arguments by Plato and Aristotle, if we cannot make a solid judgment on matters which come up for discussion: in this case what we would seem to have learnt would not be science, but history.[15]

In the same spirit, in his discussion of the first kind of knowledge in E2p40s2, Spinoza invokes the example of the knowledge of merchants. Merchants, he says, can solve a given mathematical problem, because 'they have not forgotten what they heard from their teacher without any demonstration'.[16] This shows on the one hand that, unlike Descartes who dismisses testimonial belief as useless for the acquisition of *scientia*, Spinoza accepts it as a form of knowledge. On the other hand, however, provided the normative dimension at the bottom of his distinction between the three types of knowledge, we can assume that Spinoza considered testimonial belief as far less reliable and epistemically valuable than knowledge constituted by common notions or intuitive cognition.[17]

This indicates that Spinoza's departure from Cartesian epistemology does not concern the assumption that our epistemological vocabulary entails a normative dimension. But where, then, is the point of disagreement between the two? I think that what Spinoza must have been most opposed to, were Descartes' fundamentalist views about concept formation. Contrary to Descartes, Spinoza is a holist with regard to mental content, and this precludes that we can form ideas along the lines of the Cartesian concept of intuition. Forming a concept, we simply cannot begin from scratch. Instead, we must use all sorts of representational items in our mind to come to terms with reality.[18] Still, in our epistemic search we must evaluate our ideas upon the way in which we cognise them. And while all sorts of true cognitions may be useful, in a pragmatic manner, in our search for wisdom, we must try to employ mainly those of our cognitive capacities that bring us closer to epistemic perfection or of the having of *scientia intuitiva*. Thus, while perhaps useful in a merely pragmatic respect, learning by testimony does not really contribute to our epistemic perfection.

To conclude, we can say that even in Spinoza's account, the ascription of knowledge is an evaluative affair that measures cognitions upon their contribution to some ideal epistemic end. This ideal end, moreover, is a matter of an individual reaching epistemic perfection or having and employing the right epistemic capacities. This shows that like Descartes, Spinoza is committed to some sort of epistemic perfectionism, and this commitment is the more significant, as he accepts that, considered on a pragmatic level, a huge amount of our daily beliefs derive from the testimony of others. Thus, paradoxically, it is just the ubiquity of testimonial belief in human thought which requires a metaphysics of epistemic subjects that allows for drawing distinctions between minds, which have and employ, and minds, which don't have and employ the right capacities in their search for knowledge.

There are thus good reasons to doubt the validity of communitarian readings of Spinoza's epistemology. Now, perhaps, some might think that this is a very theoretical, abstract reconstruction which misses how deeply Spinoza's social philosophy, and thus his views about the problem of the division of cognitive labour, is rooted in his doctrine of affects, which theory in fact pays a lot of attention to the intersubjective dimensions of both human thought and feeling.

I would refute this objection. It is true that Spinoza is deeply concerned with the intersubjective roots of our emotions,[19] and this has indeed a major impact on his views on the contents of our ordinary way of thought.[20] I would be the last to deny this.[21] However, this does not change the basic metaphysical picture, but it only explains why, when our imagination is at work, we may think of ourselves as parts of group minds or a larger epistemic subject.

At this point, let us take a closer view at letter 17 (in *Epistolae* [Ep]), which Spinoza wrote to his friend Pieter Balling, after the latter had lost his son. In this letter, after a few words of consolation, Spinoza answers his friend's question, who wanted to know what it meant that his son was sighing at a time, when he was still healthy. Spinoza refutes the notion that this was an omen of the later illness by pointing out to Balling that this 'was not a true sigh, but only your imagination'.[22] To explain this statement, he refers, among others, to the following example:

> To take an example like yours, a father so loves his son that he and his beloved son are, as it were, one and the same. According to what I have demonstrated on another occasion, there must be in thought an idea of his son's essence, its affections, and its consequences. Because of this, and because the father, by the union he has with his son, is a part of the reminded [*memorati*] son, the father's soul must necessarily participate in the son's ideal essence, its affections, and consequences ... Also, since the father's soul ideally participates in what follows from the son's essence, he can sometimes imagine something of what follows from [the son's] essence very vividly, as if he had it in its presence.[23]

This example is very instructive, but we must take care to get things right. First, as in many similar formulations, Spinoza enters the adverb *quasi* before *unus, idemque*, qualifying thus his talk of a union between father and son as merely metaphorical. Next, consider what Spinoza is in fact doing here: he is suggesting a genetic explanation for the vivid impression we may have of some imagined affection of our beloved. This is not metaphysics, but cognitive psychology! Finally, note that the cognitive psychological explanation he's providing here only applies to the father's soul; it has no implications with respect to the mind of the son, nor does it allege the existence of some other, larger, 'epistemic subject'.

Perhaps some might think that this example is problematic, as it thematises the union between minds as it shows up in the imagination of individual persons. But, they might object, it does not concern the union which is formed when people cooperate in a state or a community of rational citizens. The critical question is of course: isn't it rather this ideal, or rational, union which is at stake, when communitarian epistemologists praise the division of cognitive labour in groups? And isn't it one of Spinoza's most important insights that the more we cooperate as if we were one rational subject, the stronger we are?

I would again respond by distinguishing several points. It is true that Spinoza has a high opinion of the community of rational minds, and even though this is perhaps merely an ideal term, which is never really instantiated, he certainly assumes that communities are more effective in both political and epistemological concerns, the more they come close to this ideal.[24] Evidence for this can be found in both the *Ethics* as well as in his political writings, in particular the *Political Treatise*.[25] The question, however, is why Spinoza maintains this. What are his reasons for this assumption?

To my mind, the rationale for this claim derives not from any commitment to the metaphysical notion of 'larger subjects' (as Martin Lenz has recently argued, ignoring, unfortunately, the discussion that has been taking place since the publication of Matheron 1969).[26] Rather, Spinoza's point is that when we live together in society as if we were all rational, this strengthens our individual epistemic powers, and this increases our common knowledge and power, which in turn has an impact on our individual strength. Moreover, existing in a rational society allows more individuals to develop attitudes such as generosity and confidence and to avoid anti-social affects. Thus, it is, somewhat paradoxically perhaps, the reinforcement of individuals as individuals that strengthens the community, but they do not merge into a larger epistemic subject. Living together with (other) rational minds, in other words, touches upon the balance of objective knowledge available to the individual, but does not change the metaphysics of the epistemic subject.

To conclude, we can therefore say that neither Spinoza's cognitive psychology, nor his epistemology, nor even his metaphysics of individuation allow for the conclusion that he rejected Descartes' individualism in favour of a social or communitarian epistemology. Moreover, considering his epistemic perfectionism, he remained loyal to Descartes' reasons for individualism. If he did not treat individual cognising in the same manner as a prerequisite for any process of learning, as Descartes did it, this was because he had a different view on the formation of ideas. Unlike Descartes, Spinoza was a holist with regard to the determination of mental content, and this explains why he also had such a lively grasp of both the dangers threatening our epistemic autonomy and the chances contained in human communication of thoughts and emotions. Still, that epistemic autonomy is a perfection of individuals, or an ideal goal of their epistemic development, is a conviction which Spinoza, to my mind at least, would never have given up.

3. Individualism and Enlightenment in the Late Kant

In the first section, I agreed with Descartes that, if we see the aim of scientific cognition and study in the acquisition of the disposition to form solid and true judgments by individual subjects, then it is naturally the acts of the very same individuals that matter. In the previous section, I agreed with Spinoza that even within a metaphysical framework, where social entities such as communities or states are considered as individuals in their own right, it is the achievement of the minds of particular human subjects that matters for epistemic perfection.

The question remains, however, why we should stick with this perfectionist perspective in epistemology. Why should we define the aim of human learning in terms of the acquisition of some ideal epistemic *habitus* by individuals? Or put in Cartesian terms: Why is it the disposition to form solid and true judgments that we should strive for in our study?

Unfortunately, Descartes' answer to this question is only halfway satisfying, as it eventually leads back to his epistemological fundamentalism. His basic point seems to be that it is only in virtue of this capacity that we can develop axiomatic systems of knowledge. Spinoza departs from Descartes on this point, yet for him, the value of the acquisition of intellectual capacities seems to derive from his conception of happiness, according to which knowing things in the right way just makes us happy. Let me emphasise that I consider this a very attractive idea; still, for now it remains to be stated that neither his, nor Descartes', approach provide us with a clear grasp of why individual epistemic perfectioning, or, say, the acquisition of solid judgment, could be an epistemic (and not moral) end in itself. It is to clarify this problem that I shall consider Kant's views on the value of people's thinking for one-self in this section.

Some might question whether this is really a good choice, as Kant famously makes considerable concessions with respect to the validity of testimonial belief. For example, in the Jäsche-Logik, he claims that

> subject-matters of belief are no objects of empirical knowledge. The so-called historical belief cannot be properly called belief and opposed to [real] knowledge, as it can itself be knowledge. Accepting upon testimony is neither in degree nor in kind different from acceptance through one's own experience.[27](Translation my own)

Kant explicitly dismisses here any categorical distinction between empirical and historical knowledge; remarkably, he even denies any difference with regard to their respective degree of certainty. This is the more noteworthy, as it distinguishes Kant from his predecessors. That historical and empirical knowledge differ in their degree of certainty is an assumption that cannot only be found in Georg Friedrich Meier's (1752) 'Einleitung in die Vernunftlehre', which was the model of Kant's *Lectures on Logics*, but also, and perhaps more importantly, in Christian Wolff 's (1996) *Discursus Praeliminaris de Philosophia in Genere*. Although Wolff subsumes here empirical and historical knowledge under one single basic category, he characterises the latter as less certain. Not so Kant. Unlike Meier and Wolff, he takes testimony to be of an equal epistemic value as one's own perception.

Yet, despite this appraisal of testimony as a source of knowledge, Kant is nonetheless far from advocating a social epistemology, as Axel Gelfert has recently suggested.[28] First, remember that for following the First Critique, both sensation and understanding are required for a posteriori knowledge in Kant. Unless Kant had dramatically changed his mind about this, one can presume that he assumed testimony to play the role of sensation, but not of sensation and understanding together. The crucial question is thus not whether testimony is an equally valuable source of knowledge as one's own experience, but whether the part played by the higher faculties in the First Critique could be delegated to others according to Kant.

To clarify this question I suggest considering his maxims of common reason (or common sense) which are invoked in several of his writings. These maxims famously require, '1. To think for oneself; 2. To think in the position of everyone else; 3. Always to think in accord with oneself.'[29] It is, of course, the first maxim that interests me most here, which maxim Kant also refers to as the maxim of understanding or as the principle of enlightenment. So, he writes in the *Critique of Judgement*: 'One can say: the first of these maxims is the maxim of understanding, the second of judgment, the third of reason.'[30]

In the same vein, he says in the essay 'What Does It Mean to Orient Oneself in Thought': 'To think for oneself requires that the highest touchstone of truth be searched in oneself (i.e. in one's own reason); and the maxim to always think for oneself is enlightenment.'[31]

Despite the high esteem Kant expresses here for the individual thinker, it has been suggested that these maxims are the very proof of Kant's commitment to some form of social epistemology. Elaborating on them, Onora O'Neill, for example, ascribes the view to Kant that public use of reason is not just prerequisite for free talk and writing, but also for any sort of rational thought. She concludes that '[t]he option of solitary thinking is not open, in Kant's view. Even solitary uses assume some plurality.'[32]

This calls for differentiation, I think. It is true that for Kant the idea of common sense, which he also circumscribes as a communal sense, requires that we judge things in agreement with general human reason.[33] Moreover, as the discussion of the second maxim shows, it is crucial for any progress in enlightenment that, after having rejected all implausible prejudice, one also sets one's 'subjective, private conditions of judgment' aside, and adopts a general standpoint.[34] Thus, I agree with O'Neill that Kant's views as expressed in those maxims invite the idea of public reason.

This said, I think she goes too far in dismissing the option of solitary thinking altogether. We should keep two things apart: it is one thing to say, as Kant in fact does, that only those thoughts may be considered the object of reason which are in principle valid for all and are to be affirmed from the perspective of any rational subject. Generalisability and communicability are thus conditions of rationality, as it were. Yet, it is another thing to say that this precludes the option of solitary thinking. Unless one requires solitary thinking to consist in solipsist contemplation, this conclusion doesn't hold.

The question remains of what role individual or solitary thought might play in Kant's approach. Two points need to be emphasised here. First, note that there is a determinate relationship between the three maxims, respectively the acts they require. While it must be possible, for Kant, to follow the first maxim without following the second or the third maxim, we can simply not follow the second maxim without following the first. Likewise, we cannot follow the third maxim, without following the first and the second. There is thus an asymmetrical relation between these maxims: we can realise the ideal of thinking for oneself without realising the ideals expressed by the other maxims, but the reverse is not possible. That this is in fact Kant's view is clear from the way in which he associates these maxims with manners of thinking, or *Denkungsarten*. If we follow just the first maxim, without proceeding to the second, this may result in a stubborn *Denkungsart*. Perhaps this is not something we should strive for, but it is an entirely possible phenomenon.

Second, and perhaps more important here, is Kant's emphasis on the notion of *Denkungsart* itself. His explanation for his usage of this term is this: whether or not we follow the maxims of common sense, is not, he declares, a question of having certain natural faculties, but of how we employ them. *Denkungsarten* are thus dispositions or habits we may acquire by a repeated, regular observance of these maxims; they constitute different *habitus* as it were. This also shows why it is a necessary condition for all reasoning that we think for ourselves. The same intuition was already underlying Descartes' individualism: acquiring a *habitus* is essentially a matter of individual training; it cannot be imposed on other minds. O'Neill's conclusion misses this point.

Coming back to our initial question, with which I started this third part, one might think that this is rather a disenchanting result. It may seem that our reading of Kant has not really brought us any further; it has not provided us with an answer to the question we started with. At this point, however, it might be helpful to consider two differences between Kant's and Descartes' approach. First, note that contrary to what happens in Descartes, Kant's focus is on the habit of right employment of natural capacities, not on the capacities themselves. He thus seems to think that having the right natural capacities is not sufficient, but we must learn to use them, or else they decline. This is perhaps most obvious from his description of the first maxim as 'the maxim of a never passive reason'.[35] Reading this against the background of his cognitive psychology, we may ascribe the view to Kant that any acceptance of concepts from others requires activity on the part of the individual subject. It is not possible to acquire concepts simply from hearsay.

Second, and perhaps more importantly, note that Kant's interest here is not in the conditions of the possibility of knowledge, but of enlightenment. In particular, he is concerned with problems arising mostly in situations, or with regard to subject matters, where knowledge is not available, but only more or less rationally grounded opinions. He thus alleges that it is in situations of general ignorance where individual epistemic autonomy matters most, and not, of course, in cases where objectively grounded knowledge can be acquired in principle. This emphasis is no mere coincidence, but it expresses a deep insight, I think. Facing a situation of general ignorance, reason is often challenged and needed for legitimation. Yet, if this is so, the imperative that anyone first and foremost has to think for him- or herself, might simply express the need for 'reason's self-preservation', to use another circumscription of Kant.[36]

Some might say that this looks like a rather weak argument, too weak for many. I am afraid I have nothing stronger to offer. But perhaps this is neither Kant's nor my fault, but is precisely how things must be. Or wouldn't it be self-refuting if we expected to be provided with a stronger reason for the value of our own epistemic autonomy?

Notes

1. See for example Lenz (2010, esp. 437–519) for Locke, and Lenz, in this volume, on Spinoza; Welbourne (2002), Gelfert (2010, 2017), Traiger (2010), and Wilson (2010) for Hume; Scholz (2001a, 2001b) on Crusius; and Scholz (2004) and Schmitt and Scholz (2010) for a survey on early modern epistemology.
2. Note that even those doubts raised about the reliability of the senses in the beginning of the *Meditations* are directed at both sensory perception and testimonial belief. This is clear from the *Conversation with Burman*, where Descartes explains that by the phrase *per sensus*, 'through the senses', he meant those beliefs which we learn from our parents or teachers by hearing. See the following quotes from the *Meditations*: 'Whatever I have up till now accepted as most true I have acquired either from the senses or through the senses' (*The Philosophical Writings of Descartes* (CSM) II: 12); 'Nempe quidquid hactenus ut maxime verum admisi, vel a sensibus, vel per sensus accepi . . .' (*Œuvres de Descartes* (AT) VII: 18)); and the *Conversation with Burman*: 'From the senses, i.e. from sight, by which I have perceived colours, figures and all the like ; besides this, I have accepted through the mediation of the senses, or by hearing, for thus I have learnt and accepted what I know from my parents, teachers and other men' (translation my own); 'A sensibus, id est visu, quo colores, figuras et similia omnia percepi; praeter illum autem accepi reliqua per sensus, vel per auditum, quia ita parentibus, praeceptoribus aliisque hominibus accepi et hausi ea quae scio' (AT V: 146).
3. Rule III says: 'Concerning the objects proposed, we ought to investigate what we can clearly and evidently intuit or what we can deduce with certainty. For "scientia" cannot be attained otherwise' (translation my own). 'Circa objecta proposita non quid alii senserint, vel quid ipsi suscepimur, sed quid clare et evidenter possimus intueri vel certo deducere quaerendum est; non aliter enim scientia acquiritur' (AT X: 366). For reasons that will become clear shortly, I leave the term *scientia* untranslated here. As, for interpretive reasons, my translation regularly deviates from the one provided in CSM, I only mention AT here.
4. 'Science is taken in two ways: in a proper way for the *habitus* we acquire through demonstration . . . [and] in an improper way for any other intellectual *habitus*' (translation my own). 'Scientia duobus modis accipitur: Proprie pro eo habitu, quem per demonstrationem acquirimus. . . . Improprie accipitur pro quibusuis aliis habitibus intellectivis' (Goclenius 1980: 1009–10).
5. This was, famously, Jean-Luc Marion's (1975) claim in his study of the relation between Cartesian *scientia* and Aristotelian *episteme*.
6. 'Studiorum finis esse debet ingenii directio ad solida et vera, de iis omnibus quae occurrunt, proferenda judicia' (AT X: 359).
7. 'Ita scientias, quae totae in animi cognitione consistent, cum artibus, quae aliquem corporis usum habitumque desiderant' (AT X: 359).
8. '[S]cientiae omnes nihil aliud sint quam humana scientia, quae semper una et eadem manet, quantumvis differentibus subjectis applicata, nec majorem ab illis

distinctionem mutuatur, quam solis lumen a rerum, quas illustrate, varietate, ...'
(AT X: 359).
9. Using the term 'transindividual', I simply refer to all non-individualistic readings. Thus I consciously overlook that this notion has been introduced by Etienne Balibar (2001: 128) to express the notion that in collective entities of all sorts thought is a transindividual process. As I read it, though, Balibar's interpretation is strikingly individualist and liberal in my sense of the word.
10. Martin Lenz (n.d.) suggests this in an unpublished manuscript. His contribution to the present volume is more cautious in, first, distinguishing between ideas and beliefs, and, second, concluding only that Spinoza 'holds an interactive account of ideas in that their affirmative force is explained in virtue of contrariety'. Note that this latter claim does not conflict with my reading.
11. Renz (2010: 64–78, esp. 72ff.; 2018: 51–61, esp. 58ff.; forthcoming).
12. This example is a variation of a thought experiment I frequently employed to illustrate the point of my reconstruction of Spinoza's definition of the human mind, see also Renz (2011: 111–12).
13. Renz (2009, forthcoming).
14. See in particular Sosa (2012).
15. 'unquam ... Mathematici evaderemus, licet omnes aliorum demonstrations memoria teneamus, nisi simus etiam ingenio apti ad quaecumque problemata resolvenda; vel Philosophi, si omnia Platonis et Aristotelis argumenta legerimus, de propositis atume rebus stabile judicium ferre nequamus: ita enim non scientias videremur didicisse, sed historias' (AT X: 367).
16. 'Haec omnia unius rei exemplo explicabo. Dantur ex. gr. tres numeri, ad quartum obtinendum, qui sit ad tertium ut secundus ad primum. Non dubitant mercatores secundum in tertium ducere et productum per primum dividere; quia scilicet ea, quae a magistro absque ulla demonstratione audiverunt, nondum tradiderunt oblivioni ...' (Spinoza, *Ethics*, English translation in Curley (C) 1: 478. Latin version in Gebhardt (G) ii: 122).
17. The example with the merchant shows clearly what reliability is for Spinoza. For a merchant who has only this sort of knowledge is, in comparison with knowers equipped with more adequate knowledge, (1) less certain about the reach of the truth of the idea in question, (2) she has less causal understanding of why the idea is true, and (3) she is less determined to effectively affirm the idea.
18. See Della Rocca (1996: 68–84) and Renz (2010: 101–2) for Spinoza's holist conception of ideas.
19. See in particular Moreau (2011) for this.
20. See also Lenz in this volume.
21. See my reading of his theory of imagination in Renz (2010: 215–40).
22. 'As for the omens that you mention – that when your child was still healthy and well, you heard sighs like those he made when he was ill and shortly afterwards passed away – I should think that this was not a true sigh, but only your imagination' (C1: 352). 'Quantum omina, quorum mentionum facis, attinet, nempe quod infante tuo adhuc sano, & valente tales gemitus audiveris, quales edebat quum aegrotabat, & Paulo post satis concedebat; Existimarem eg, hanc verum non fuisse gemitum, sed non nisi tuam imaginationem' (G iv: 76).
23. C1: 353–4: '[N]empe, pater (ut tui simile adducam exemplum) adeo filium suum amat, ut is, & dilectus filius quasi unus, idemque sint. Et quoniam (juxta id, quod alia occasione demonstravi) filii essentiae affectionum, & quae inde sequuntur, necessario

in cogitatione dari debet idea, & pater, ob unionem, quam cum filio suo habet, pars memorati filii est, etiam necessario patris anima de essentia ideali filii, & ejusdem affectionibus, & iis, quae inde sequuntur, participare debet . . . Porro, quoniam patriis anima idealiter de iis, quae essentiam filii consequuntur, participat, ille (ut dixi) potest interdum aliquid ex iis, quae ejus essentiam consequuntur, tam vivide imaginary, ac si id coram se haberet' (G iv: 77–8). Note that the given translation departs from Curley's by rendering the word *memorati* as 'reminded', and not as 'said'. To my mind, the addition of 'said' is useless, as that the son has just been mentioned in the first part of the sentence. In contrast, if it is translated as 'reminded', it may be taken to indicate that the explanation given here operates on a cognitive psychological, and not a metaphysical, level.
24. Therefore, it doesn't matter whether the application of *individuum* to the community of rational men in E4p18s was merely as analogical, or whether it is meant in a strict sense, as Matheron had it.
25. See in particular TP2.13; and E4p18s.
26. Lenz n.d.
27. 'Sachen des Glaubens sind [also] keine Gegenstände des empirischen Erkenntnisses. Der sogenannte historische Glaube kann daher eigentlich auch nicht Glaube genannt und als solcher dem Wissen entgegengesetzt werden, da er selbst ein Wissen sein kann. Das Fürwahrhalten auf ein Zeugniß ist weder dem Grade noch der Art nach vom Fürwahrhalten durch eigene Erfahrung unterschieden' (Kant 1999 (AA) IX: 69).
28. Gelfert (2010), but see earlier Gelfert (2006).
29. 1. 'Selbstdenken; 2. An der Stelle jedes andern denken; 3. Jederzeit mit sich selbst einstimmig denken' (AA V: 294. cf. also AA XV: 188; or AA VII: 201).
30. 'Man kann sagen: die erste dieser Maximen ist die Maxime des Verstandes, die zweite der Urteilskraft, die dritte der Vernunft' (AA V: 295).
31. 'Selbstdenken heißt den obersten Probierstein der Wahrheit in sich selbst (d.i. in seiner eigenen Vernunft) suchen; und die Maxime jederzeit selbst zu denken, ist die Aufklärung' (AA VIII: 150).
32. O'Neill (2001: 42). See O'Neill 2006 for some background.
33. 'Unter dem sensus communis aber muß man die Idee eines gemeinschaftlichen Sinnes, d. i. eines Beurteilungsvermögens verstehen, welches in der Reflexion auf die Vorstellungsart jedes anderen in Gedanken (a priori) Rücksicht nimmt, um gleichsam an die gesamte Menschenvernunft sein Urteil zu halten und dadurch der Illusion zu entgehen, die aus subjektiven Privatbedingungen, welche leicht für objektiv gehalten werden könnten, auf das Urteil nachteiligen Einfluss haben würde' (AA V: 293).
34. 'Allein hier ist nicht die Rede von Vermögen des Erkenntnisses, sondern von der Denkungsart, einen zweckmäßigen Gebrauch davon zu machen; welche, so klein auch der Umfang und der Grad sei, wohin die Naturgabe des Menschen reicht, dennoch einen Mann von erweiterter Denkungsart anzeigt, wenn er sich über die subjektiven Privatbedingungen des Urteils, wozwischen so viele andere wie eingeklammert sind, wegsetzen kann und aus einem allgemeinen Standpunkte (den er dadurch nur bestimmen kann, dass er sich in den Standpunkt anderer versetzt) über sein eigenes Urteil reflektiert' (AA V: 295).
35. 'Die erste ist die Maxime einer niemals passiven Vernunft' (AA V: 294).
36. 'Sich seiner eigenen Vernunft bedienen will nichts weiter sagen, als bei allem dem, was man annehmen soll, sich selbst fragen: ob man es wohl tunlich finde, den Grund, warum man etwas annimmt, oder auch die Regel, die aus dem, was man annimmt,

folgt, zum allgemeinen Grundsatze seines Vernunftgebrauchs zu machen? Diese Probe kann ein jeder mit sich selbst anstellen; und er wird Aberglauben und Schwärmerei bei dieser Prüfung alsbald schwinden sehen, wenn er gleich bei weitem die Kenntnisse nicht hat, beide aus objektiven Gründen zu widerlegen. Denn er bedient sich bloss der Selbsterhaltung der Vernunft' (AA VIII: 150–1).

Works Cited

Balibar, Etienne (2001), 'Potentia multitudinis, quae una veluti mente ducitur', in Marcel Senn and Manfred Walther (eds), *Ethik, Recht und Politik bei Spinoza. Vorträge des 6. Internationalen Kongresses der Spinoza Gesellschaft*, Zürich: Schulthess, pp. 105–37.

Coady, C. A. J. (1992), *Testimony: A Philosophical Study*, Oxford: Oxford University Press.

Della Rocca, Michael (1996), *Representation and the Mind-Body Problem in Spinoza*, Oxford: Oxford University Press

Gelfert, Axel (2006), 'Kant on Testimony', *British Journal for the History of Philosophy*, 14: 627–52.

Gelfert, Axel (2010), 'Kant and the Enlightenment's Contribution to Social Epistemology', *Episteme*, 7: 79–99.

Gelfert, Axel (2017), '"Keine gewöhnlichere, nützlichere und selbst für das menschliche Leben notwendigere Schlussart": Ein neues Bild von David Hume als Theoretiker menschlichen Zeugnisses', in Matthias Däumer, Aurélia Kalisky and Heike Schlie (eds), *Über Zeugen: Szenarien von Zeugenschaft und ihre Akteure*, Paderborn: Wilhelm Fink Verlag, pp. 195–211.

Goclenius, Rodolphus [1613] (1980), *Lexicon philosophicum*, Frankfurt: Hildesheim and New York: G. Olms.

Kant, Immanuel (1999), *Kant's Gesammelte Schriften* 'Akademieausgabe', Berlin: Königlich Preußische Akademie der Wissenschaften.

Lenz, Martin (2010), *Lockes Sprachkonzeption*, Berlin: De Gruyter.

Lenz, Martin (n.d.), 'Intersubjectivity in Early Modern Philosophy: Spinoza and the Division of Cognitive Labour', unpublished.

Marion, Jean-Luc (1975), *Sur l'ontologie grise de Descartes: science cartesienne et savoir aristotelien dans les Regulae*, Paris: J. Vrin.

Matheron, Alexandre (1969), *Individu et Communauté chez Spinoza*, Paris: Minuit.

Matheron, Alexandre (2003), 'L'état, selon Spinoza, est-il un individu au sens de Spinoza?', in Michael Czelisnki et al. (eds), *Transformationen der Moderne. Zur Gegenwärtigkeit der theoretischen und praktischen Philosophie Spinozas*, Würzburg: Könighausen & Neumann, pp. 127–45.

Meier, Georg Friedrich (1752), 'Einleitung in die Vernunftlehre', in Immanuel Kant, *Gesammelte Schriften*, Akademie-Ausgabe, vol. XVI, pp. 50–872.

Moreau, Pierre-François (2011), 'Imitation of the Affects and Interhuman Relations', in Michael Hampe, Ursula Renz and Robert Schnepf (eds), *Spinoza's Ethics. A Collective Commentary*, Leiden: Brill, pp. 167–78.

O'Neill, Onora (2001), 'Kant's Conception of Public Reason', in Volker Gerhardt, Rolf-Peter Horstmann and Ralph Schumacher (eds), *Kant und die Berliner Aufklärung, Akten des IX. Internationalen Kant-Kongresses*, Vol. 1, Berlin: De Gruyter, pp. 35–47.

O'Neill, Onora [1993] (2006), 'Vindicating Reason', in Paul Guyer (ed.), *The Cambridge Companion to Kant*, 17th edn, Cambridge: Cambridge University Press, pp. 280–308.

Renz, Ursula (2009), 'Spinozas Erkenntnistheorie: Eine naturalisierte Epistemologie?', *Deutsche Zeitschrift für Philosophie* 57: 419–32.

Renz, Ursula (2010), *Die Erklärbarkeit von Erfahrung. Realismus und Subjektivität in Spinozas Theorie des menschlichen Geistes*, Frankfurt: Klostermann.
Renz, Ursula (2011), 'The Definition of the Human Mind and the Numerical Difference between Subjects', in Michael Hampe, Ursula Renz and Robert Schnepf (eds), *Spinoza's Ethics. A Collective Commentary* Leiden and Boston: Brill, pp. 98–118.
Renz, Ursula (2018), *The Explainability of Experience: Realism and Subjectivity in Spinoza's Theory of the Human Mind*, New York: Oxford University Press.
Renz, Ursula (forthcoming), 'Spinoza's Epistemology', in Don Garrett (ed.), *The Cambridge Companion to Spinoza*, 2nd edn, Cambridge: Cambridge University Press.
Schmitt, Frederick F. and Oliver Robert Scholz (2010), 'The History of Social Epistemology', *Episteme*, 7(1): 1–6.
Scholz, Oliver Robert (2001a), 'Autonomie angesichts epistemischer Abhängigkeit. Kant über das Zeugnis anderer', in Volker Gerhardt, Rolf-Peter Horstmann and Ralph Schumacher (eds), *Kant und die Berliner Aufklärung. Akten des IX. Internationalen Kant-Kongresses*, Vol. 2. Berlin: De Gruyter, pp. 829–39.
Scholz, Oliver Robert (2001b), 'Das Zeugnis anderer. Prolegomena zu einer sozialen Erkenntnistheorie', in Thomas Grundmann (ed.), *Erkenntnistheorie. Positionen zwischen Tradition und Gegenwart*, Paderborn: Mentis, pp. 354–74.
Scholz, Oliver Robert (2004), 'Zeuge. Zeugnis', in Joachim Ritter, Karlfried Gründer and Gottfried Gabriel (eds), *Historisches Wörterbuch der Philosophie* vol. 12, W–Z, Basel: Schwabe, 1317–24.
Sosa, Ernest (2012), 'Descartes and Virtue Epistemology', in Kelly James Clark and Michael Rea (eds), *Reason, Metaphysics, and Mind. New Essays on the Philosophy of Alvin Plantinga*, Oxford: Oxford University Press, pp. 107–27.
Traiger, Saul (2010), 'Experience and Testimony in Hume's Philosophy', *Episteme*, 7: 42–57.
Welbourne, Michael (2002), 'Is Hume Really a Reductivist?', *Studies in History and Philosophy of Science*, 33: 407–23.
Wilson, Fred (2010), 'Hume and the Role of Testimony', *Episteme*, 7: 58–78.
Wolff, Christian (1996), *Discursus Praeliminaris de Philosophia in Genere. Einleitende Abhandlung über Philosophie im Allgemeinen*. Historisch-kritische Ausgabe, Günter Gawlick und Lothar Kreimendahl (ed. and trans.), Stuttgart: frohmann-holzboog.

3

Spinoza on the Interaction of Ideas: Biased Beliefs

Martin Lenz

Spinoza famously holds that we standardly believe whatever it is that is perceived or goes through our mind, unless we hold stronger beliefs to the contrary (E2p17). So if you see a winged horse on your lawn, you will also believe that there is a winged horse on the lawn, unless you have strong beliefs excluding the existence of winged horses. Let's call this the principle of the priority of belief. Couched in the terminology of the seventeenth century, Spinoza holds that we cannot merely contemplate ideas, but that every idea involves at least an affirmation. Countering Cartesian as well as scholastic positions, he claims that ideas are not merely considered and *then* affirmed or denied in virtue of the will. In this sense, ideas are what we now call beliefs, and believing is, as it were, the default mode of thinking. Spinoza's principle has been well acknowledged in the literature: Edwin Curley, Jonathan Bennett, Michael Della Rocca and Ursula Renz, for instance, present extensive discussions of Spinoza's doxastic involuntarism, and some of the contemporary psychological literature even credits Spinoza with inventing a promising account of thinking as believing.[1]

However, it is rarely considered how this principle is coupled with what could be called the principle of exclusion: we believe something *unless* a certain thought is excluded by beliefs we already hold. But if we tend to embrace what coheres with previous beliefs, we don't just believe anything. Rather we might say that our minds are governed by what could be called a constant confirmation bias, that is, a tendency to confirm existing beliefs (E3p12). This raises the question of what governs this bias. Why don't we believe in winged horses? In other words, what is the foundation of including certain beliefs and excluding others? To answer this question we need to consider Spinoza's understanding of ideas and the exclusion principle. A promising answer is of course that ideas must ultimately be explained in virtue of the *conatus*, that is, the self-preservation drive. But although the *conatus* doctrine has been readily cited to explain the power of ideas,[2] it remains underdetermined so long as we do not account for the mechanisms that govern the exclusion and inclusion of ideas. These mechanisms, I submit, cannot be understood so long as we merely look at individual minds. Rather, the exclusion principle should be seen as rooted in the assumption that things (and thus also minds) are of a contrary nature. Accordingly, I shall argue that Spinoza holds an interactive account of ideas in that their affirmative force is explained in virtue of contrariety. Only when considering opposing ideas (and minds) can we understand why ideas exclude one another in their contrary striving. Here, it might seem natural to think of contrariety as an intramental relation, such that we might hold contrary beliefs, for example in thinking that a man is healthy and that he is ill. But as we will see, contrariety is crucially used to refer to an *intermental relation* between ideas, such that it is contrariety that makes ideas belong to different minds. Having introduced the assumption that all finite things have a *conatus*, Spinoza writes: 'An idea that excludes the existence of our body cannot be in our mind, but is contrary to it' (E3p10).

This proposition suggests that contrariety marks off the difference between minds, such that thinking a thought contrary to one's body's existence would mean to have an idea of another mind. Thus, for instance, the affirmation that I have a cold or worse seems to be an affirmation that is endorsed, not by myself but by something contrary to my mind. This will need some unpacking in due course.

Analysing Spinoza's interactionism of ideas requires us to focus on the question of what it means for ideas to have a *conatus*. What does it mean to say that the ideas themselves strive to persevere, rather than the cognitive agents who have ideas? In view of this focus, I will begin by exploring the question of why we believe what we believe in the light of the principles of the priority of belief and the exclusion principle. As will become clear, it is the exclusion principle that turns our ideas into biased beliefs (section 1). Taking ideas to be biased raises the question of what governs the striving of ideas in the first place. After assessing some individualist answers, I will show that it is not any single *conatus* but the interaction of ideas, set off by contrariety, that governs the striving and determines which beliefs are held. We shall see that the exclusion principle that founds our biases is not a merely logical notion but rooted in the contrary nature of things (section 2). Understanding interaction in terms of contrariety, however, will give rise to a number of objections, the discussion of which will shed some light on the details of contrary interaction among ideas (section 3). Finally, I will try to situate the emerging account with a view to current philosophical approaches and show how the exclusion principle lends itself to an understanding of ideas in terms of confirmation bias (section 4).

1. Two Principles: Priority of Belief and Exclusion

As is well known, Spinoza's *Ethics* endorses the assumption that we hold most beliefs without knowing why we do. As he points out in various places, humans are often ignorant of what causes their beliefs, which is why they are often like 'conclusions without premises' (E2p28dem). Therefore, one of the most pressing questions Spinoza tries to answer is *why do we believe what we believe?* While we might assume that we consider and weigh the evidence in favour of this or that thought or this or that course of action, we are in fact driven by beliefs we already hold. This ignorance, he explains, remains often unnoticed, because, instead of the premises unknown to us, we take our own conscious beliefs to be the causes of further beliefs, volitions or actions: 'men think themselves free, because they are conscious of their volitions and their appetite, and do not think, even in their dreams, of what moves them to wanting and willing' (E1app). In this sense, much of the *Ethics* can be read as an analysis of what in fact structures and causes our beliefs. Before we dive deeper into this issue, however, we should begin by explaining Spinoza's notion of belief, for not only does Spinoza think that we misunderstand the causes of our beliefs, he also urges a new understanding of what a belief is.

What is a belief then? Terminologically speaking, Spinoza's crucial step is to use the term 'idea' for what we might call beliefs. Structurally speaking, a belief is the mental counterpart to what can be expressed by a statement. It means to think that something is the case or to predicate some thing of something. So the talk of the 'idea of a green apple', for instance, should be taken as talk of the 'belief that apples are green', which, in turn, can be expressed by the statement 'apples are green'. In the scholastic tradition as well as among early modern philosophers it is common to distinguish between different mental operations in relation to different logical units. Accordingly we may distinguish both on the level of the thought and language between terms, statements and inferences, such that inferences presuppose statements and statements presuppose terms. According to this order, beliefs are judgments expressible by statements. Commenting on Aristotle's *De anima*, scholastics often distinguish between *acts of apprehension* yielding concepts and *acts of judgment* yielding propositions that are combinations of concepts. The distinction between perception and judgment is often construed in a similar fashion in that perception is taken to be a mere consideration or exposure to information. Although talking of ideas rather than concepts and propositions, authors following Descartes' coinage of the term 'idea' still retain a distinction that mirrors the distinction between apprehension and judgment. Descartes distinguishes between 'ideas' as images or representations of things, on the one hand, and affirmations and other modes of thought, on the other. While apprehension generally counts as a mere consideration or grasping of the concept, it is the judgment that can be true or false.[3] For our purposes it is crucial to see that the traditional order prioritises the formation of concepts or the mere consideration of an idea over the formation of a judgment. A simple example might illustrate this: before I can judge that apples are green, I first have to form the idea of apple and of green. Some late scholastic authors such as Francisco Suárez and Martinus Smiglecius have already raised doubts about this order of explanation,[4] but we still find Descartes adhering to it when he claims that judgment requires an act of the will. In stating that ideas involve affirmations, Spinoza turns this order explicitly upside-down: 'They look on ideas, therefore, as mute pictures on a panel, and preoccupied with this prejudice, do not see that an idea, insofar as it is an idea, involves an affirmation or negation' (E2p49s).

This is, then, what I call the principle of the priority of belief. As is well known, this position follows from Spinoza's denial of the distinction between will and intellect. Whereas Descartes assumes in the *Fourth Meditation*[5] that we can look at ideas like at mute pictures, before willingly deciding to affirm or deny, Spinoza urges that there is no such difference. 'For what is perceiving a winged horse other than affirming wings of the horse?' (ibid.) The upshot is a denial of 'mere' perception or consideration. There is no idea without an affirmation or denial. And since human minds consist of ideas (E2p11), everything that goes on in my mind involves a belief. Of course, this view raises an immediate problem. Do we really believe everything we think? Do we, to use Spinoza's example, believe in winged horses just because reading about them in this chapter might trigger an idea of a winged horse? Spinoza has a straightforward answer to this question. We believe everything we perceive, *unless* we have another idea that excludes the existence of the thing perceived (ibid.). It is, inter alia, this kind of reply that renders Spinoza's notion of belief *holistic*. Obviously, beliefs are held so long as they agree with one another. So if I know nothing or just very little about horses, I might embrace the belief that horses have wings as true right upon reading or hearing it. But if most of my beliefs about horses imply that horses do not have wings, then my mind excludes the belief that horses have wings. Thus certain ideas are ruled out by what I have called the *principle of exclusion*: if we have ideas that exclude certain other ideas, these other ideas will not be held. It is crucial to see, however, that the exclusion principle works on the basis of predominant beliefs. It's not that our mind first considers and then rejects or embraces an idea. Everything is believed unless it is excluded. Spinoza formulates this clearly in E2p17:

> If the human body is affected with a mode that involves the nature of an external body, the human mind will regard the same external body as actually existing, or as present to it, until the body is affected by an affect that excludes the existence or presence of that body.

In other words, perceiving is believing. As Spinoza goes on to point out, this fact explains also 'how it can happen (as it often does) that we regard as present things that do not exist' (E2p17s). If I perceive a flying pig, my mind will believe it to exist, unless it holds beliefs to the contrary. Accordingly, Spinoza thinks that the mind 'does not err from the fact that it imagines, but only insofar as it is considered to lack an idea which excludes the existence of those things which it imagines present to it' (ibid.). In other words, the error does not lie in the belief of a flying pig, but in my lack of ideas that exclude the existence of flying pigs.

While Spinoza's holism of ideas is widely acknowledged in the wake of Michael Della Rocca's work,[6] the exclusion principle shows that ideas are to be seen as standing in exclusive or inclusive relations to one another. A set of ideas can include or exclude another idea or set of ideas. This means that we only hold such beliefs as can be included by our mind. Although believing is the default mode of our mind, not every idea can enter. This is why our ideas turn out to be biased on Spinoza's account. While the exclusion principle provides an answer to the question of whether we do not simply believe everything, it raises new questions. What is the criterion for exclusion and inclusion? Is exclusion a logical notion, as Diane Steinberg suggests, or is it rooted in Spinoza's metaphysics?[7] As we will see, the relations of exclusion and inclusion are crucial for understanding the dynamics among ideas.

2. The *Conatus* of Ideas

Let's take stock of Spinoza's central points again: if we were to ask Spinoza why we hold the beliefs we do, he could direct us to the thesis of the *priority of belief*. Unlike Descartes suggests, we do not contemplate and decide to believe or reject a thought; rather every idea is a belief. Asking further why we hold certain beliefs rather than others, Spinoza could reply by pointing to the *exclusion principle*: we embrace those ideas that are not excluded by the ideas we already have.

However, the exclusion principle gives rise to a refined version of the original question: why is it that we hold certain beliefs *in the first place*? In other words, what is the foundation of our biases? It is not enough to say that we believe that p because we already believe that q and r. If it's true that we form the *new belief that p* on the basis of a *previous set of beliefs that q and r*, we should also say why we believe that q and r in the first place. Of course, we might just say that we acquired these beliefs on the basis of an even earlier set of beliefs. But if we want to avoid a vicious regress or the mere claim of an initial set of beliefs as a brute fact, we should be able to point to some guiding principle that is not itself a mere belief or set of beliefs.

Moreover, if the exclusion principle is in place, we cannot just hold any old set of beliefs. Rather, there must be a tendency to hold certain sets of beliefs over others. Either I believe in a universe that does contain winged horses or in one that doesn't. So what explains the dominance of certain beliefs over others? Of course, a first answer might lie in the fact that we grow up in societies that sanction certain beliefs. As Spinoza points out in the appendix to the first part of the *Ethics*, many if not all humans grow up with a number of prejudices that seem to be common among humans. So we might, for instance, be exposed to the belief that there is a god who designed the universe in accordance with our needs or that we are free to act whichever way we decide. Thus, we might be inclined to agree to assumptions about the teleological structure of the universe or about our free agency. It seems natural to assume, then, that such beliefs are consolidated in our minds. However, even societies hold quite contrary beliefs. So the social context alone seems too coarse-grained a measure to determine initial sets of beliefs. What then governs our belief sets? In order to answer this question, we need to know (1) how initial sets of ideas might take hold in our minds and (2) what it is that constitutes the agreement or disagreement between sets of ideas.

A rough and ready answer to both questions seems to lie in the *conatus* principle that we already touched on above. Spinoza writes that 'the mind, as far as it can, strives to imagine those things that increase or aid the body's power of acting' (E3p12). Thus, I hold not just any old belief set, but those beliefs that contribute to my self-preservation or at least *seem* to contribute to my self-preservation. And it is ideas matching those self-preserving ideas that get included. However, as pointed out earlier, minds or ideas making up minds should not be seen as striving for the sake of something else; rather it is the *ideas themselves that have a conatus*. Although this point has been made before, it is unclear what this means. Thus, I would like to address this tenet head-on and discuss individualist as well as interactionist readings of this tenet. It will turn out that Spinoza is committed to an interactionist view that is grounded in contrary strivings of ideas.

2.1 Individualist Answers

What does it mean to say that ideas have a *conatus*? Although much has been written on Spinoza's theory of ideas, very few commentators explicitly acknowledge that Spinoza is committed to this view.[8] Spinoza does not assert the claim as such, but he does discuss the claim with regard to *certain* ideas, most notably with regard to human minds, which *are* ideas. Nevertheless, the claim neatly falls out of Spinoza's commitments. So let's briefly see how it might be established from the crucial passages of the *Ethics*.

As is well known, Spinoza asserts that 'each thing, as far as it can by its own power, strives to persevere in its being' (E3p6). This is the so-called *conatus* doctrine. In the demonstration of this proposition we are told that 'singular things are modes by which God's attributes are expressed in a certain and determinate way'. If we accept what is called the *parallelism* of the attributes of thought and extension (E2p7), it follows that these things, when conceived as modes under the attribute of thought, are to be seen as ideas. So if we can say that each *thing* has a *conatus*, we can legitimately say that each *idea* has a *conatus*. But what does this mean? We might imagine that everything has a *conatus*. We might also reach a viable understanding of the assumption that everything can be considered under the attribute of thought, in the sense of, for instance, some version of pan-conceptualism. But in what sense can we say that ideas have a *conatus*? Isn't this just an obvious consequence of parallelism? Spinoza answers this question clearly when he explains that, when 'this striving is related only to the mind, it is called will; but when it is related to the mind and the body together, it is called appetite' (E3p9s). So if a mind is to be seen as an (highly complex) idea, as E2p11 suggests, this means that the *conatus* of such an idea is what we call the mind's will.

What then does it mean for the mind to have that will? Michael LeBuffe, for instance, claims that Spinoza does not clarify what it means for a mind to strive.[9] But it is exactly this question we need to pursue now. As I see it, Spinoza does not address this point directly in the *conatus* argument, but spells it out in his discussion of the will as an affirmation. The will is a 'faculty of affirming and denying' (E2p48). So an idea's *conatus* is the will of an idea, which is in turn an affirming (or denying). This carries over nicely to Spinoza's assumption that the mind is an idea of the body, which in turn can be taken as the claim that the mind's will amounts to an affirmation that the body exists. Accordingly, Spinoza writes that 'since the first thing that constitutes the essence of the mind is the idea of an actually existing body, the first and principal [tendency] of the striving of our mind (by p 7) is to affirm the existence of our body' (E3p10). In other words, the *conatus* of an idea is what we today would call a propositional attitude or force.[10] In this sense, Spinoza renders the *conatus* of the mind as an affirmation of the existence of its object, that is, the existence of the body.

In the light of these remarks it might indeed seem apt to call Spinoza a psychological individualist or even egoist: an individual human mind would always will its own perseverance. But this interpretation would only make sense if individual human minds were somehow special in opposition to other individuals. Yet, what we have seen so far is that individual human minds are not special in having a *conatus*. Rather there is no reason not to assume that *every* idea – whether it exists in my mind or somewhere else in another human or non-human being – has a *conatus*. Thus, humans would have no special status; rather every passing thought would be egoistic in the sense that it wills the existence of its content. You may call this egoism if you like, but I don't see how it would explain anything. Rather, my mind should be seen as consisting of a vast set of thoughts, all of which strive for *their perseverance*, not just for the perseverance of my mind. In other words, we should not ascribe the *conatus* to (human) minds but to ideas at every level, no matter whether they constitute a mind or merely part of a mind.[11]

But now you might object that, although it might make sense to say of my mind that it has a will, this does not have to carry over to each individual idea. What is true of the whole (mind), does not have to be true of its constituents. Yet, this is exactly what Spinoza claims when he explains his thesis of the unity of will and intellect (E2p49c–d): 'The will and the intellect are nothing apart from the singular volitions and ideas themselves ... But the singular volitions and ideas are one and the same.' So besides specifying that ideas are volitions (= affirmations), Spinoza makes it clear that he doesn't think of a mind's will as anything over and above the individual volitions. Thus we can conclude that, when Spinoza talks about the *conatus* of the mind, he sees himself as talking about the *conatus* of individual ideas (that happen to make up a mind). This does not mean that larger units of ideas, such as whole minds or groups of mind, cannot have a *conatus*, too. The point is rather that we have to accept that any idea, however complex or simple, can be said to have a *conatus*. Thus, we have to take Spinoza as being committed to the assumption that ideas have a *conatus*, meaning that ideas strive to affirm whatever they are ideas of.

Now if indeed every idea has a *conatus* and strives to affirm the existence of its object, one pressing question arises immediately. What governs the striving of ideas? A straightforward answer seems to be that the ideas' striving is a *function of the mind that they are part of*. So the ideas that constitute your mind strive for the benefit of your mind, while the ideas in my mind strive for the benefit of my mind. Such an interpretation has been suggested by Michael Della Rocca. Taking ideas as actions, he concludes that, if

> a mind does something in virtue of having an idea, that idea and the effects stemming from it must somehow be a manifestation of the agent's striving.

Thus all causation by an idea in an agent's mind must in some way be directed to the good of the agent.[12]

But although this answer might seem natural, it is not available to Spinoza. Of course, insofar as the mind is an idea, it strives to persevere. After all, it is the 'first and principal' tendency of the mind to affirm the body's existence (E3p10). The mind does indeed strive for self-preservation and is conscious of that striving (E3p9). And this would mean that at least part of the ideas constituting my mind *strive in unison* with the more complex idea that is my whole mind. So we might conclude that, for instance, the idea that affirms the existence of my right foot, strives in unison with other ideas that affirm the existence of other parts of my body. In view of what Spinoza says about the composition of individuals (E2p13l5), we can think of the mind as composed of smaller individuals and as embedded in the whole intellect that makes up the whole of nature. In this sense, we might consider the mind a functional union in the way that is suggested in the 'physical interlude' (see especially the definition following E2p13): parallel to the individual parts that form the body of a human being, the individual ideas strive in unison and affirm the existence of my whole body. At the same time, then, my mind affirms the existence of my whole body and even tries to imagine things that increase its power of acting (E3p12).

However, while the ideas that constitute my mind might be said to strive in unison and while my mind might be said to strive for its perseverance,[13] we cannot conclude that these individual ideas strive *for the sake* of my mind. In other words, although my mind can be rightly called an individual, the ideas making up my mind are individuals, too. And there is no reason to suppose that smaller individual modes strive for the sake of larger individual modes. Why? Although Spinoza singles out human minds for consideration in part two of the *Ethics*, this does not mean that these kinds of minds were privileged in the sense that those ideas constituting human minds were teleologically ordered to maintain the whole. So the question of what governs the striving of ideas should not be seen as a teleological issue. It would be wholly un-Spinozistic to say that certain individuals are designed to strive for the sake of the greater whole. This crude kind of teleology is clearly ruled out in the appendix to the first part of the *Ethics*. Just as it would be merely superstitious to assume that things in nature are arranged for the sake of humans, it would certainly be equally superstitious to assume that individual ideas are made for the sake of a human mind.[14]

Moreover, as Diane Steinberg has pointed out, while most ideas that my mind affirms are partly constitutive of my mind, they are also affirmations of external things that affect my body. Therefore, some ideas cannot be a function of my *conatus* and might even prove harmful for me. Now what conclusion can be drawn from this analysis? Steinberg claims that 'not every idea can be a belief' for Spinoza. This conclusion would indeed allow us to make good sense of the fact that some ideas are supposed to be overpowered by others. When thinking of winged horses, we normally do not believe in their existence. If not every idea is a belief, then we now have an explanation for this fact.[15] However, this does not sit well with the fact that Spinoza assumes *every* idea to involve an affirmation. To say that some ideas are not beliefs would require a distinction between kinds of ideas that Spinoza does not provide.

Therefore, I would like to suggest a different conclusion. Steinberg obviously ties her analysis of ideas to an individualistic understanding of the mind. But not every idea is a belief *of the agent in question*. This means that not every idea in my mind needs to be affirmed in virtue of *my conatus*. This reading makes good sense of all too common experiences: I can be simply mistaken about what is beneficial for me or I can be possessed by harmful ideas. And in this sense quite a number of ideas that impress my mind are not a function of my *conatus*. So while I agree that not all ideas are a function of my *conatus*, I don't think that these ideas are states without attitudes, that is, not beliefs. Rather, they should be seen as manifestations of different *conatus*. Not every idea that enters my mind has to be seen as *my* belief. External ideas can strive to take hold of what is commonly called my mind, and these might either lose out or overpower me.[16] A weak belief is still a belief. Strictly speaking, however, neither my ideas nor external ideas should be said to be a function of an agent or a greater unit. Rather, ideas can strive in unison or against one another.

But if all ideas strive in unison or against one another, while their striving is not governed by greater units of ideas (minds), what does govern the striving of ideas? A second option seems to be that the *object of the idea* governs the striving of the idea. After all, Spinoza asserts that the idea constituting my mind affirms the existence of my body. So we might conclude that my body governs the idea's striving, which does manifest itself in the act of affirmation. But if 'to govern' should be taken to mean 'to cause', this move would be blocked by Spinoza's rejection of any causal interaction between the attributes (IE3p2). It does not come as a surprise, then, that Spinoza explicitly states that 'the cause of the mind's affirming the body's existence is not that the body has begun to exist' (E3p11s). So although the mind affirms the body's existence, this affirmation or striving is not caused by the body's existence.

But what, then, governs the striving of ideas? Spinoza does tell us that the striving of modes *is* their actual essence (E3p7), but he does not say what it is that governs or causes the striving. But whatever it is, it must be what also is responsible for marking off the *identity* of the striving thing. After all, there must be something that marks off the difference between an individual idea that does strive for its perseverance and an idea that would not be said to strive for its perseverance. And if an idea's striving or willing or affirmation is its essence, the thing that governs the striving will also govern its identity.[17] Now that we have ruled out larger ideational units (e.g. minds) or the objects of ideas (the bodies that they are parallel to), there seems to be nothing left that governs or causes the striving. As will become clear shortly, there is indeed *no single item* that can be said to govern the striving. However, that doesn't mean that Spinoza did not provide an answer to this question. As I see it, the governing principle lies in the *interaction of ideas*.

2.2 An Interactionist Understanding

If we wish to understand what it is that governs the striving of ideas, we should turn to the exclusion principle once more. Exclusion of ideas, I submit, is rooted in the contrariety of ideas and things more generally. We can see this if we look at Spinoza's discussion of the constitution of the human mind in E3p10. Before telling us about the 'first and principal' tendency of the mind, Spinoza draws a distinction that marks off different minds, by explaining what can and cannot be 'in' the mind (E3p10): 'An idea that excludes the existence of our body cannot be in our mind, but is contrary to it.' Let's begin with a simple observation: Spinoza does not simply distinguish between the inside and outside of the mind but between the *inside and its contrary*. Moreover, what we introduced as the exclusion principle is now explicitly explained in terms of contrariety. Certain ideas are contrary to others, namely those that affirm and deny the existence of the same body. The insistence on contrariety gives us an important clue as to the character of the interaction of ideas. Let us look more closely at the notion of contrariety.

Like exclusion, contrariety is often taken in the sense of logical opposition. Thus, it does not come as a surprise that commentators such as Diane Steinberg and Yitzhak Melamed are inclined to interpret these relations accordingly.[18] Contraries seem to be first of all opposed predicates in propositions that are mutually inconsistent; they can both be false but not true at the same time ('Socrates is happy' versus 'Socrates is sad'). Yet in addition to this (1) logical consideration, contraries can also occur in a number of other kinds of oppositions. They can be seen as (2) opposed properties of elements or things, such as the property of heat or coldness or happiness and sadness, or as (3) opposed movements or even as (4) opposed wills.[19] Moreover, it is important to see that contraries are not merely ontologically or logically opposed items. Rather contraries are appealed to in identifying change and processes of change, such as generation and decay, or the transition of a substance from one state to another, such as healing or learning. In Aristotle's writings, contrary properties or powers play a fundamental role in physical and biological explanations. Likewise, natural philosophers in the middle ages and early modern period appeal to contrariety for explaining all kinds of processes.[20]

Now Spinoza clearly seems to draw on such traditional understandings in applying the opposition not only to ideas or linguistic items but also to 'things' more generally: things can only be destroyed through external causes (E3p4) and are 'of a contrary nature' (E3p5). What distinguishes things, also distinguishes ideas: contrariety.[21] The preceding talk of contrary things suggests, then, that 'contrariety' is not a mere logical relation between predicates such as 'healthy' and 'sick', but something that is rooted in the make-up of things. Moreover, contrary things are not solely opposed extremes, but seem to compete or fight and destroy each other. This suggests a dynamic and gradual understanding of contraries. When my injured foot heals, it does not heal all at once; rather it gradually changes from one state to another. As Gabbey has pointed out, there might be a general tendency in seventeenth-century physics to render 'interactions between bodies . . . as contests between opposing forces, the larger forces being the winners, the smaller forces being the losers'.[22] In the same vain, Andrea Sangiacomo convincingly argues that the *conatus* doctrine in the *Ethics* is developed out of a refinement of Descartes' understanding of contrarieties between moving bodies, and generally rephrased as a 'degree of agreement and disagreement in nature among things'.[23] An equally promising source is Francis Bacon's doctrine of appetites. According to Guido Giglioni's paraphrase, Bacon presupposes that 'the inner life of matter' results 'from the ultimate contrarieties of nature. Motions of desire are primordial, caused by original tensions between opposing forces.'[24] In view of this context it is no surprise, then, that Spinoza relies on the notion of contrariety to generally argue for the striving for self-preservation in all things. For in view of interacting contrary forces among finite things, a notion such as that of *conatus* seems required in order to safeguard some persistence of things, at least if you wish to avoid the assumption of a Heraclitean world of constant flux.

What I consider special in Spinoza with regard to our purposes is that he blends the opposition of physical forces into the contrariety of ideas, thus allowing for a metaphysically *conative* (rather than merely logical) understanding of contrary relations *between ideas*. One idea being contrary to another can now be read as one idea fighting or resisting another. This assumption is corroborated by Spinoza's assertion that contrariety can be attributed to *competing actions* (E5ax1), which in turn can be seen as competing ideas, since ideas are generally taken to be actions of the mind (E3dem3).

As is clear, contrariety is crucial for the explanation of change and motion in Aristotelian as well as in Cartesian natural philosophy. However, it remains an open question what exactly links this dynamic notion of contrariety to the theory of ideas. In this paper, I must confine myself to speculation, but an obvious link is provided in the discussion of emotions. As is evident, Spinoza combines his analysis of emotions with a specification of their ideational contents and the way they track conative states, going from love and hate to the respective contrary states of the *conatus*, which increases or decreases accordingly. As such, this connection is not new. Harking back to Aristotle's *Physics* V, Aquinas gives a detailed taxonomy of emotions in terms of contrariety.[25] The crucial step in Spinoza is to see emotions as ideas. 'Love', for instance, 'is nothing but joy with the accompanying idea of an external cause, and hate is nothing but joy with the accompanying idea of an external cause' (E3p13s). Equating ideas and emotions, then, allows analysing them as having all the required ingredients, that is, contrariety, conative force and intentional objects, for them to fulfil their roles under the principles of the priority of belief and exclusion. Moreover, like the principles of association that Spinoza appeals to, the connection between emotions and ideas provides us with an immediate understanding of how one idea might *cause* (and not just imply or entail) another idea, while reflecting and affecting the power of acting.

In view of this rich context regarding contrariety it is not surprising that Spinoza invokes this notion in his account of ideas in the *Ethics*, to which we will now return. A characterisation through contrariety always requires at least two items of the same kind; otherwise we could not sensibly talk about items being contrary to one another. Spinoza makes this point by distinguishing between things whose natures are entirely different as opposed to things that have something in common (E4p29). Only the latter can affect one another's power of acting: and this means that only the latter can 'agree' (to some extent) in their natures or be 'contrary' to one another (E4p31c).[26] Thus, contrariety requires first that things ought to have something in common, and in our case this means that they must at least belong to the same attribute, that is, the attribute of thought. But moreover these things ought to be contrary. That means it is not enough to have something in common; rather they must be opposed to one another in such a way that they disagree with regard to one another's nature. So the distinction between ideas through contrariety is not simply a distinction between a mind (= a complex idea) and an outside (be it another mind, another kind of mind or something extended), but between two kinds of ideas: between an idea that *denies* the existence of our body and an idea *affirming* this existence, as Spinoza puts it in E3p10. We might call the contrary relation between these ideas one of *competitive interaction*.

In the given context, the relation of competitive interaction provides the distinction between two sets of ideas, those affirming and those denying something's existence or affirming something contrary to that existence. Since Spinoza takes these relations not only as logical but as physical relations, it makes sense to assume that logical contradictions such as 'Socrates is healthy' versus 'Socrates is not healthy' can be taken as contrarieties such as 'Socrates is healthy' versus 'Socrates is sick'. The 'negation' of one's existence could then be 'performed' by any predication that indicates a decrease of one's power of acting or *conatus*. In any case, we might think, for example, of the contrast between an idea that affirms somebody's health or enhancement (an idea of something nourishing for example) and an idea that affirms somebody being weakened or even killed (an idea of something poisonous).

The attribution of competitive interaction to ideas finally provides an answer to the question of what governs the striving of ideas: contrariety. At the same time, the contrariety of ideas also bears on the question of identity of ideas. As we pointed out above, the *conatus* of ideas is their essence. How could something sensibly be said to strive, if it were not determinable that there is some possible opposition to this striving? In other words, how could there be sensible talk of affirmation without any possible negation? Thus it makes sense to assume that the identity of ideas is just as relational as their striving. Ideas, then, are determined through contrariety. To be sure, this understanding of ideas as rooted in contrariety should not be seen as a refutation of the holistic understanding of ideas, as urged for instance by Della Rocca; rather it provides a refinement of how this holism is taken to work. Since contrariety of ideas relies on the assumption that a competing idea cannot belong to the same mind (E3p10) and since contrariety does not in itself determine what it is that turns out to enhance or weaken another idea, the applicability of contrariety always requires more than one idea, and by extension, more than one mind. However, this reading does rule out an individualist understanding of ideas. If there were just one idea, it could not be contrary to anything and it could not be sensibly said to strive by affirming.

With regard to the overall question of what it means for an idea to have a *conatus* we can conclude that an idea's *conatus* consists in the affirmation of its object, and that the striving is governed by contrariety, such that every affirmation is contrary to another idea. This doesn't mean that every affirmation is contrary to every other affirmation, but that it is contrary to some other idea.[27] It is no surprise, then, that Spinoza assumes that the decline of an idea's striving is just as relational as the emergence of that striving. So a mind does not cease to affirm the body's existence because it might decide this or because the body might cease to exist. Rather the termination of an affirmation '*arises from another idea* which excludes the present existence of our body, and consequently of our mind, and which is thus contrary to the idea that constitutes our mind's essence' (E3p11s; emphasis added).

3. Problems for the Interactionist Account

While I think that the interactionist reading provides a succinct account of the *conatus* of ideas in the light of the principles of exclusion and the priority of belief, it also gives rise to some pressing questions. Given what Spinoza says in E3p10, contrary ideas have to be about the same body, but cannot be in the same mind. As is clear from E2p11, the prime object of one's mind is one's body, whose existence – as we have seen earlier – is affirmed by one's mind. So the ideas constituting one's mind are in some sense first and foremost about one's body. Now if one wants to form a contrary or contradictory idea to the affirmation 'a is F', where 'a' stands for a body and 'F' for a property of that body, the contrary idea has to be about the same body, a, as well. So a contrary idea to this affirmation might be 'a is G', but not 'b is G'. But if a is your body, that is, the body whose existence your mind is affirming, then the contrary idea negating a's existence cannot be in your mind. This is why contrary ideas have to be ideas that belong to different minds. But if contraries cannot be in the same mind, how do they ever arise?[28]

Let's spell out the problem. As should clear by now, in order for a contrariety to arise, there must be what I would like to call *triangulations about the same body*. We can, for instance, illustrate this with extremely opposed ideas, expressed by the sentences 'this body is alive' versus 'this body is dead'. That is, there must be a triangular scenario in which two different ideas relate to the same body:

Idea 1: 'This body is strong'   Idea 2: 'This body is weak'
↘   ↙
Body

So while these ideas triangulate over the same body, they are contrary to one another. Of course, in everyday life, we seem to have no problem with making contrary assertions about ourselves or our bodies, be it that we do so at different points in time or that we have conflicting states of mind. So we might say that we have been ill but are on the mend now, or we might feel overwhelmed by sadness and express suicidal thoughts as well as the will to live on. But as should be clear by now, for Spinoza, ideas are not internal musings or thoughts that we merely happen to entertain. Rather these ideas are fundamental affirmations of our physical existence that can be rendered as our striving to persevere. Pertinent contrary ideas, then, would be fundamental denials of our existence that should be rendered as a striving to destroy ourselves.

In view of such a triangular scenario, the problem of how contraries arise can be addressed by discussing the following two questions. (1) If the parallelism is true and if your ideas have your body as their object, then how can two ideas or minds ever relate to the *same* objects? (2) How can Spinoza account for the common experience that minds can have contrary thoughts?

(1) The first question concerns the relation between ideas and their objects and can be answered easily with reference to what is known as the *dual content* of ideas. Although the parallelism thesis and E2p13 seem to suggest that the intentional object or ideatum of my mind turns out, just by definition, to be my body, this is not the whole story. As is well known, Spinoza holds that our bodies are ceaselessly affected by other bodies. And when our minds form ideas of external things, these ideas have a dual content: they primarily indicate the state of one's own body as affected by the external bodies; secondarily they indicate the external body or bodies (see E2p16–17). In this sense, most of our ideas are confused and inadequate. So my idea of the sun primarily represents the light and heat my body undergoes; only secondarily it also represents the sun. With regard to our question, this means that bodies other than my own can very well be the object of my ideas. And these other bodies that affect my body can be both in agreement with my striving and contrary to my striving. Indeed, the affections are defined as ways of decreasing or increasing one's power of acting and thus defined by the degree to which they are competing or cohering with one's *conatus* (E3dem3). For both, ideas in agreement and contrary ideas, can triangulate about the same body in the same mind. In the latter sense I might, for instance, have the idea of something poisonous affecting my body. This idea is secondarily an idea of the poison, but at the same time it indicates my body as affected by it. Having this idea, my power of action is decreasing and my mind will hate the poison, strive to destroy it and to recollect things that exclude the poison's existence (E3p13). With regard to secondary indication, then, a mind can relate to external objects, and different ideas in different minds can triangulate over the same objects, even if these objects are external to most of the minds involved. Thus many human minds might hate the same poison or love this or that food, although it is as such not part of any human body.

(2) This account seems to provide an answer also to the second question, which concerns the relation between ideas. In allowing for contrary ideas in the same mind, Spinoza can explain the common experience of having contrary thoughts. On the one hand, I might have the idea of poison, countering my

existence; at the same time, I strive to destroy the poison. But this seems to fly in the face of Spinoza's assertion (in E3p10) that contrary ideas cannot be in the same mind. How then can the idea of something poisonous be in my mind? An answer to this question is that the talk of an idea being 'in one's mind' ought to be seen as ambiguous. A quick way to spell out the ambiguity would be to distinguish between an essential and a counter-essential understanding of an idea being in one's mind. Some ideas in our mind might be said to *constitute* the mind's essence or to *agree* to some extent with our mind's essence; they affirm our bodily existence or increase our power of acting (E3p3). But such agreement is of course a matter of degree. Just as our mind is said to strive for perseverance both with adequate and inadequate ideas, it can equally be said to act or undergo to some extent or to agree more or less with our essence (E3p1). Other ideas, then, might display a lesser agreement, and agree with our mind mainly in belonging to the attribute of thought, so that it makes more sense to say that they *disagree* with our essence and thus decrease our power of acting. These ideas, then, might still be said to be 'in our mind' in that they affect our mind, but they do not increase our power of acting and should thus be seen as *contrary* to our mind, at least to some extent. So the idea of something poisonous can be said to be 'in' my mind in the way that it in fact counters my mind, decreasing my power of acting. But so long as it does not overpower me completely, it competes with those ideas that are essentially in my mind. Spinoza famously introduces this kind of ideational competition by distinguishing degrees of activity and passivity in our ideas (E3dem2–3; E3p1). Being always passive to some degree, our minds are subject to ideas that are to some extent contrary to our mind. This way Spinoza can explain the quite common experience of having contrary ideas, in the guise of thoughts and emotions triangulating about the same body as well as external objects.

Although Spinoza clearly has the resources to explain how contrary ideas can arise even in the same mind, the focus on competitive interaction might give rise to yet another worry. Is interaction between ideas always competitive or antagonistic? As we saw earlier, the *conatus* of ideas is not a function of individual minds or the bodies whose existence they affirm. Rather, the *conatus* is 'set off', as it were, in the face of contrary ideas. In this sense, *competitive interaction* lies indeed at the heart of what explains ideational striving. To be sure, this does not mean that ideas are to be seen as wholly antagonistic units. Competition chiefly explains what motivates or directs the *conatus* of ideas, but it does not provide an exhaustive account of what governs the interactions. Since although minds can be of a contrary nature, their *contrariety is a matter of degree*. This means that, despite the disagreement, there is always some degree of agreement. Spinoza makes this abundantly clear when he speaks of the interactions of humans: '*insofar as men are torn by affects which are passions, they can be contrary to one another*' (E4p34), but 'insofar as men live according to reason, must they always agree in nature' (E4p35). With regard to the level of individual ideas, this means that their *conatus* or power of acting will be increased or decreased depending on the surrounding ideas. For illustration, you might think how certain mathematical or musical ideas thrive in some minds, while they wither away in others. The point is not only that certain minds are different from others, the point is that the *conatus* doctrine suggests considering ideas as having a life of their own, striving to persist and unite with ideas that enhance each other's power. The dynamics of cooperation and competition occur on all levels at which units can agree or disagree. As Hasana Sharp pertinently put it, because 'ideas, considered absolutely on Spinoza's terms, are indifferent to human flourishing, they survive, thrive, or atrophy on the basis of their relationship to ambient ideas'.[29]

Thus, contrariety should not solely be seen as a notion expressing competition, but also as capturing the gradual dynamics of ideational interaction. At the same time, this notion of contrariety unfailingly commits Spinoza to a non-individualistic account of ideas. This means that it would be hopeless to try and understand ideas, beliefs, emotions or the workings of the mind in general on the basis of individual beings or minds. Following on from Spinoza's holistic premises and especially from the assumption that individuals will never stop being *parts* of nature, an individual idea or even an individual mind is not explicable just by reference to itself. Even the perhaps most fundamental metaphysical assumption, the *conatus* doctrine, doesn't work on the level of single individuals. An individual does not simply strive for whatever is or seems best for its survival; the striving is 'set off' and directed by contrarieties. In order to understand the workings of things and thoughts, then, we need to look at contrarieties and the related agreements and disagreements. This is why an interactionist account is called for.

4. Conclusion: The Philosophical Impact of Spinoza's View

One can approach Spinoza's account of ideas through various historical and theoretical lenses. In addressing the philosophical impact of his doctrine I neither wish to 'actualise' his view, nor do I promote the assumption that the relevance of texts should be established by showing how they relate to present-day issues in philosophy.[30] Assuming that philosophical and historical study is a collaborative enterprise, I appreciate pluralist approaches that inform rather than exclude one another. In articulating the relation to present-day philosophy, then, I aim at explicating the particular genealogical lens that informs the choices in this chapter. This lens might be interesting in its own right in that it is dynamic and not a fixed perspective. Reconsidering Spinoza's theory of ideas in the light of the topic of relational autonomy, I began with the assumption that Spinoza's theory of ideas is primarily interesting in that it challenges our cognitive autonomy, that is, the assumption that subjects have control over what they believe, which is an aspect succinctly highlighted by Curley and Bennett.[31] While this is still true, the crucial role of the exclusion principle prompted the idea that Spinoza's account might speak more specifically to what is currently discussed under the heading of (confirmation) bias. Therefore, I would like to highlight briefly some general parallels to current topics and show in what way the issue of bias might be particularly pertinent.

First of all, Spinoza's account of ideas is indeed an enormous breach with the predominant tradition in the history of philosophical psychology in that it depicts believing as the 'default mode' of the mind. We have already seen that this view runs counter against most medieval and early modern positions. The traditional distinction between apprehension and judgment is reflected in the modern distinction between grasping or merely entertaining *content* and forming an *attitude* towards that content. According to such an account, I might merely grasp that horses have wings without affirming (or denying) it.[32] The view that belief states are prior to states of 'mere' consideration or doubting is famously attributed to philosophers of mind in the wake of Frege, certainly not to anyone before Kant.[33] However, as should be clear now, as already shown, Spinoza rejects the assumption that our minds entertain content without any attitude. But what is philosophically at stake?

In defending the priority principle, Spinoza's position could be said to be opposed to what, in the wake of Sellars (2000), is called the 'Myth of the Given', namely the assumption that our mind can grasp something like unmediated content or raw sense data without any conceptual activity, as is involved in forming a belief or judgment, and justify beliefs by reference to such supposed raw material.[34] While I did not intend to argue for this claim in this chapter, I think such an argument could be made by appealing to Spinoza's notion of ideas as holistic sets of beliefs. On Spinoza's view, most of our beliefs are tied to evaluative emotions and the mind cannot grasp content without an affirmative (or negative) attitude. Thus, for the human mind, there is no mere given. This is particularly true of one's own mental states, whose motivations, for Spinoza, are most of the time not available to the cognitive agent.

Relatedly, Robert Brandom famously credited Spinoza's theory of ideas with being *inferentialist* in that it prioritises inferential relations among ideas over representational relations between ideas and their *ideata*. At the same time, he noted that Spinoza focused too much on the causal aspects, ignoring the normative dimension of ideational relations. One might indeed hold that Spinoza's theory does not single out a set of normative practices to explain what governs the inferential relations between ideas. But this does not mean that he ignores the normative dimension. Arguably, the *conatus* doctrine provides the crucial source of normativity. Qua *conatus*, ideas strive for preservation, a striving that is spelled out as taking them as affirmative acts. Given that things (and ideas) strive for self-preservation, we might say that they are under normative pressure to the extent that they can strive *successfully* or *unsuccessfully*. If I want to survive, I *ought* to do certain things that promote this purpose, such as breathe for instance. Seeing my mind as a complex idea that strives to persevere, we can say that it ought to hold certain beliefs rather than others, namely healthy over harmful ones.[35] Additionally, I or the society around me might – rightly or wrongly – hold certain assumptions as to what *counts* as successful striving. If I want to survive, I *think I ought* to do certain things I think promote this purpose, such as buying foods of a certain brand for instance. Thus, we might rather say that Spinoza provides an account of causal mechanisms that could be undergirded by *several* and *disparate* normative practices. So in making belief the mind's default mode and grounding the affirmation of ideas in the *conatus* doctrine, Spinoza can also account for the normativity of ideas.[36]

However, while the *conatus* doctrine provides an account of how ideas strive, it raises the question of the subject of striving. *Whose* striving is it anyway? To a certain extent the answers seem compatible with an individualist account of striving minds. The existence that is affirmed and wanted in the affirmation of an idea could be the existence of an individual body and mind. Accordingly, the ideas in my mind affirm *my* existence. But as should have become clear, this picture cannot be right. In order to get a grip on Spinoza's account, we should take the assumption that ideas have a *conatus* quite literally: it's the ideas themselves that strive; and they don't strive for the sake of something else. Defying the assumption of individual minds as containers of thoughts or ideas, Spinoza's account should rather be seen as establishing an interactionist picture of ideas striving in agreement or disagreement. As Hasana Sharp has pointed out, the attribute of thought might be seen as a 'kind of ecosystem of ideas'.[37] In such an ecosystem, ideas strive more or less successfully, depending on whether they are surrounded by agreeing or disagreeing ideas. According to Sharp, this account lends itself to a *critique of ideology* in that it explains the flourishing of ideas not least in virtue of certain self-affirming illusions, such as the illusion that we are free and have control over our thoughts.

Seeing Spinoza's account as an 'ecosystem of ideas' seems to steer us in the right direction for an understanding of his interactionist view of ideas. However, rather than inquiring what *governs* the interaction, Sharp moves on to discuss means of overcoming ideologies through therapy. While this is an intriguing topic in itself, it leaves open the question of the mechanisms or forces that explain the interaction of ideas *independently* of our supposed desire for therapy. This is why stressing Spinoza's emphasis on the principle of exclusion is equally crucial. A key point of Spinoza's theory of ideas as an interactive ecosystem, then, is the assumption that believing is the default mode of the mind *unless* certain beliefs are excluded. As I see it, this point generalises: the way Spinoza introduces the exclusion principle could be seen as a paraphrase of what today is called *confirmation bias*. We are prone to go in for certain beliefs or ideologies because we believe without hesitation whatever *fits the beliefs already in place*. The idea of the winged horse, for instance, is not excluded from our minds on the grounds that we considered the case and gathered evidence speaking to the contrary, but rather because it does not agree with our other ideas about horses. The analogy to confirmation bias reveals a preliminary answer to the question at hand: why do we believe what we believe? We tend to believe what we believe because it agrees with prior beliefs.

Given these features of Spinoza's theory, it is perhaps not surprising that even recent psychological literature often distinguishes between *Cartesian* and *Spinozist kinds of minds*. Whereas Cartesian models of the mind construe beliefs as states that are under the control of the will and follow evaluation, Spinozist models put belief first.[38] Here, the question of why we believe what we believe is often addressed under the heading of 'belief fixation'. Arguably, Spinozistic models run into fewer problems when used to explain how beliefs get fixed and how implicit biases function. According to the psychologist Daniel Gilbert, who explicitly credits Spinoza with the invention of the proposed view, we generally believe what we perceive. Only in a second separate step can our mind intervene and question the belief already formed. A number of psychologists and cognitive scientists have picked up on Gilbert's Spinozistic theory of mind. Tests revealed that we even tend to believe nonsensical assertions such as 'a dinca is a flame'. This 'bias to believe' is taken to generalise to what is known as the confirmation bias, that is, the tendency to look for evidence confirming our beliefs. Worries to the effect that such a theory would underestimate the rational capacities of humans are often countered with arguments from cognitive economy. Believing simply requires less time and cognitive resources than explicit evaluation and decision. As experiments show, subjects tend to be even more accepting when under cognitive stress. Eric Mandelbaum even claims that we cannot contemplate any proposition without accepting it. This means that mere exposure to propositions makes us believe them. I might see or hear a sentence and cannot but believe it. Reinforced by association, beliefs are amplified and consolidated through the social contexts we are part of, while, at the same time, shared biases coordinate social behaviour. Arguably, a number of behaviours and beliefs, especially those where we accept propositions automatically and seemingly act on impulse, cannot be explained very well on the presupposition of the theory of a Cartesian mind, according to which we first consider the possibilities and then decide which proposition to believe.[39] Thus, the Spinozan thesis of the priority of belief appears to provide an explanatorily resourceful view of the mind.

Now like ideology, bias has a bad reputation, and confirmation bias is even counted as a fallacy. More often than not the priority of belief counts as an a-rational feature of the mental. On a closer look, however, the situation seems less clear. While many philosophers argue that biases are (morally) problematic and should be overcome, it is unclear whether bias is not rather an adaptive feature that allows for vital cognitive functions and, hence, for what we call rationality.[40] Although I do not wish to engage with the contemporary literature, three points of clarification seem to be called for. (1) Interestingly, much of the psychological studies take a Spinozan mind to be one that, initially at least, is prone to believe just anything one is exposed to. But as Hugo Mercier has pointed out, this way of rendering confirmation bias is problematic. He rather urges to take confirmation bias as a 'myside bias': that is, a tendency to support one's own views.[41] In view of Spinoza's account, we should urge for a similar refinement. Spinoza does not only endorse the priority principle but also the exclusion principle. The distinction between inclusion and exclusion would not account for believing anything but for believing whatever agrees with *previous* beliefs. (2) At the same time, however, we should note that the picture of an interactive ecosystem lends itself not to a confirmation of whatever it is that an individual mind believes; rather sets of ideas or minds are biased towards confirming *matching* sets of ideas. In other words, the ideas that happen to make up my mind don't necessarily strive to confirm beliefs that are *in fact* good for my well-being. My mind might be full of ideas or ideologies consolidated by pervasive conventions and strive to confirm those ideas, even if they turn out to be harmful for me. (3) A third point is that, like Mercier, Spinoza would not assume that bias – taken as the way ideas strive – is itself problematic. Spinoza's thesis is rather that ideas just function in virtue of principles that amount to what we call bias. Thus, even countering our adherence to false ideas does not mean to counter the way our minds work, that is, our minds' tendency to believe by inclusion. In other words, there is no non-biased mode of believing. Overcoming false beliefs or a therapy against harmful thoughts would rather lie in gaining an *understanding* of how bias works and what motivates bias in the first place. In this sense, the notion of bias that might be said to be anticipated in Spinoza's theory of ideas is not a negative but, insofar as bias is simply a part of our make-up, rather a naturalist notion.

As should have become clear by now, Spinoza's theory of belief does not only mark an interesting breach with the tradition but is of special interest in the history of the philosophy of mind and psychology in that it provides an intriguing account of the foundations of bias. By contrast, while there is a lot of data generation in the current discussion, even the most recent literature still lacks a proper inquiry of the causes our biases and beliefs.[42] While many metaphysical tenets of Spinoza might seem problematic today, his *Ethics* provides just that: a metaphysical account of why we believe what we believe. This might in fact be a crucial point of departure of the Spinozan theory of ideas from the contemporary discussion of bias and belief.[43]

Notes

1. See Renz (2010, esp. 103–10), where she provides an insightful discussion of this view under the heading of 'epistemic determinism'. See also Curley (1975); Bennett (1984: 162–7); Lloyd (1990); Della Rocca (2003); and more recently Douglas (2015: 119–25). For the psychological discussion see especially Gilbert (1991, 1993) and Mandelbaum (2014).
2. See especially Della Rocca (2003); Steinberg (2005): Lenz (2012); and Schmid (2016).
3. See Nuchelmans (1980, 1983); Ariew (1999: 101–26); and Lenz (2010: 277–89). See Miller (2015: 85–99) for an interesting comparison of Spinoza's and Stoic views.
4. See Lenz (2010: 286–8).
5. AT VII: 52–62.
6. See especially Della Rocca (1996).
7. See Steinberg (2005: 149 and esp. note 6).
8. See Steinberg (2005) in her discussion of Della Rocca (2003), whose paraphrases come close to such an assertion, and also Sharp (2007); and Waller (2012: 71).
9. Le Buffe (2010: 99–108) provides a careful discussion of an egoistic interpretation but resumes by claiming that it is 'not clear how the mind strives insofar as it has inadequate ideas'. This unclarity is resolved once we adopt an interactionist reading, or so I'll argue. In conversation, Andrea Sangiacomo suggests that the striving of the mind simply might be seen as the striving to *think*. This is a good first hunch, but the question remains what it means to do so.
10. As E2p49 suggests we can distinguish the aspects of force and content with regard to

ideas. At the same time it is important to see that this distinction is merely analytical; an idea is never without force or content. See also Lenz (2012) and Della Rocca (2003).
11. This does not mean that all individuals strive consciously. As Renz (2010: 251) argues, only sufficiently complex individuals, such as human minds, strive consciously and have pertinent emotions.
12. See Della Rocca (2003: 208). In Lenz (2012), I have largely followed this interpretation and proposed a strong teleological reading.
13. In the sense that they 'keep the same ratio of motion and rest' (E2p13l5).
14. See Sangiacomo (2015b) on different teleological strands in Spinoza.
15. See Steinberg (2005: 153).
16. See Spinoza's discussion of suicide in E4p20 as the most extreme case.
17. I won't go into the issue of the individuation of ideas. But see Murray (2013) for an affirmation-based account of the identity of ideas.
18. As noted, Steinberg (2005: 149) reads 'exclusion' in the logical sense. Melamed (2012: 194–5) speculates whether Spinoza might wish to ground logical non-contradiction in the contrary nature of things, but calls this move as 'bold' as Hegel's rejection of non-contradiction.
19. See Clark (1999: 43–68) for an overview of discussions of contrariety in ancient, medieval and early modern times.
20. See especially Aristotle, *Physica* V 1; cf. Waterlow (1982) as well as Damerow et al. (1992: 68–125) on the Aristotelian and Cartesian background in general.
21. The foundational role of metaphysical contrariety in the so-called *conatus* argument seems to have been somewhat neglected. Manning (2002) is one of the few exceptions. See Winkler (2016) for a more thorough discussion of contrariety, mainly with regard to the problems it raises for the notion of substance.
22. See Gabbey (1980: 243); cf. Viljanen (2011: 90) for a brief discussion.
23. See Sangiacomo (2015a).
24. See Giglioni (2010: 154).
25. See Knuuttila (2004, esp. 243).
26. See Sangiacomo (2015b) for a detailed discussion of agreement in nature.
27. See also E4ax, where Spinoza explains that, for every singular thing, there is another thing more powerful.
28. In view of Spinoza's monist metaphysics, this problem does of course arise for finite modes *tout court*. This is tackled by Winkler (2016, esp. 106), who shows how contraries are denied on the level of substance but maintained on the level of nature.
29. See Sharp (2011: 16, cf. 2007).
30. See Laerke et al. (2013) for a recent discussion of methodological questions regarding early modern philosophy.
31. See Cottingham (2008: 196–8) for a critical evaluation.
32. See Searle (1983) for a reintroduction of the content–attitude distinction.
33. See Brandom (1994: 79): 'The pre-Kantian tradition took it for granted that the proper order of semantic explanation begins with a doctrine of concepts or terms, divided into singular and general, whose meaningfulness can be grasped independently of and prior to the meaningfulness of judgments.'
34. Although Sellars (2000: 235) lists Spinoza among the people falling prey to the myth, one might argue that Spinoza's notion of idea does not allow the required distinction. See also Brandom (2002) and Lenz (2012). However, one could argue that Spinoza does still use a notion of unmediated content by calling ideas 'inadequate'.

35. See Lenz (2012) and Steinberg (2005: 156).
36. Renz (2010: 106) makes the illuminating remark that 'ideas commit us to certain inferences'.
37. Sharp (2007: 745).
38. See Gilbert (1991, 1993); Mandelbaum (2014, 2015); Huebner (2009); and Kahneman (2011).
39. See Mandelbaum (2014). However, most psychologists presuppose dual process theories that seem to set Spinozan minds for automatic processes of association and Cartesian minds for slower evaluative processes of propositional deliberation.
40. See Sturm (2011) and Anthony (2016) for critical reviews of these discussions.
41. See Mercier and Sperber (2017).
42. As Holroyd and Sweetman (2016) show there is a lot of ambiguity in the philosophical and psychological terminology surrounding the discussion of bias.
43. This paper benefited from discussions with numerous colleagues. I owe special thanks to Karolina Hübner, Michael Della Rocca, Ursula Renz, Doina Rusu and Andrea Sangiacomo. Moreover, I would like to thank Boris Koznjak, Hugo Mercier and Thomas Sturm for providing me with pertinent papers on the contemporary discussion of bias.

Works Cited

Anthony, Louise (2016), 'Bias: Friend or Foe', in Michael Brownstein and Jennifer Saul (eds), *Implicit Bias and Philosophy*, Oxford: Oxford University Press.
Ariew, Roger (1999), *Descartes and the Last Scholastics*, Ithaca and London: Cornell University Press.
Bennett, Jonathan (1984), *A Study of Spinoza's Ethics*, Indianapolis: Hackett Publishing Company.
Brandom, Robert (1994), *Making it Explicit*, Cambridge, MA: Harvard University Press.
Brandom, Robert (2002), *Tales of the Mighty Dead*, Cambridge, MA: Harvard University Press.
Clark, Stuart (1999), *Thinking with Demons: The Idea of Witchcraft in Early Modern Europe*, Oxford: Oxford University Press.
Cottingham, John (2008), *Cartesian Reflections: Essays on Descartes' Philosophy*, Oxford: Oxford University Press.
Curley, Edwin (1975), 'Descartes, Spinoza, and the Ethics of Belief', in Maurice Mandelbaum and E. Freeman (eds), *Spinoza: Essays in Interpretation*, Chicago: Open Court Publishers, pp. 159–89.
Damerow, P., G. Freudenthal, P. McLaughlin and J. Renn (1992), *Exploring the Limits of Preclassical Mechanics*, New York, Berlin and Heidelberg: Springer Verlag.
Della Rocca, Michael (1996), *Representation and the Mind-Body Problem in Spinoza*, Oxford: Oxford University Press.
Della Rocca, Michael (2003), 'The Power of an Idea: Spinoza's Critique of Pure Will', *Noûs*, 37(2): 200–31.
Douglas, Alexander (2015), *Spinoza and Dutch Cartesianism: Philosophy and Theology*, Oxford: Oxford University Press.
Gabbey, Alan (1980), 'Force and Inertia in the 17th Century: Descartes and Newton', in S. Gaukroger (ed.), *Descartes: Philosophy, Mathematics, and Physics*, Brighton: Harvester, pp. 230–320.
Giglioni, Guido (2010), 'Mastering the Appetites of Matter: Francis Bacon's *Sylva*

Sylvarum', in C. T. Wolff and O. Gal (eds), *The Body as Object and Instrument of Knowledge*, Dordrecht and New York: Springer, pp. 149–67.

Gilbert, D. T. (1991), 'How Mental Systems Believe', *American Psychologist*, 46: 107–19.

Gilbert, D. T. (1993), 'The Assent of Man, the Mental Representation and Control of Belief', in D. M. Wegner and J. W. Pennebaker (eds), *Handbook of Mental Control*, Englewood Cliffs, NJ: Prentice-Hall, pp. 57–87.

Holroyd, Jules and Joseph Sweetman (2016), 'The Heterogeneity of Implicit Bias', in Michael Brownstein and Jennifer Saul (eds), *Implicit Bias and Philosophy*, Oxford: Oxford University Press.

Huebner, Bryce (2009), 'Troubles with Stereotypes for Spinozan Minds', *Philosophy of the Social Sciences*, 39(1): 63–92.

Kahneman, Daniel (2011), *Thinking Fast and Slow*, New York: Farrar, Strauss, and Giroux.

Knuuttila, Simo (2004), *Emotions in Ancient and Medieval Philosophy*, Oxford: Oxford University Press.

Laerke, Mogens, Justin E. H. Smith and Eric Schliesser (eds) (2013), *Philosophy and its History: Aims and Methods in the Study of Early Modern Philosophy*, Oxford: Oxford University Press.

Le Buffe, Michael (2010), *From Bondage to Freedom: Spinoza on Human Excellence*, Oxford: Oxford University Press.

Lenz, Martin (2010), *Lockes Sprachkonzeption*, Berlin and New York: De Gruyter.

Lenz, Martin (2012), 'Intentionality without Objectivity: Spinoza's Theory of Intentionality', in Alessandro Salice (ed.), *Intentionality*, Munich: Philosophia Verlag, pp. 29–58.

Lloyd, Genevieve (1990), 'Spinoza on the Distinction between Intellect and Will', in Edwin Curley and Pierre-Francois Moreau (eds), *Spinoza: Issues and Directions. Proceedings of the Chicago Spinoza Conference, 1986*, Leiden: E. J. Brill, pp. 113–23.

Mandelbaum, Eric (2014), 'Thinking is Believing', *Inquiry*, 57(1): 55–96.

Mandelbaum, Eric (2015), 'Attitude, Association, and Inference: On the Propositional Structure of Implicit Bias', *Noûs*, 50(3): 629–58.

Manning, Richard (2002), 'Thoughtful Teleology and the Causal Significance of Content', in Olli Koistenin and Jon Biro (eds), *Spinoza: Metaphysical Themes*, Oxford: Oxford University Press, pp. 182–209.

Melamed Yitzak (2012) '"Omnis determinatio est negatio" – Determination, Negation and Self-Negation in Spinoza, Kant, and Hegel', in Eckart Förster and Yitzhak Melamed (eds), *Spinoza and German Idealism*, Cambridge: Cambridge University Press, pp. 175–96.

Mercier, Hugo and Dan Sperber (2017), *The Enigma of Reason*, Cambridge, MA: Harvard University Press.

Miller, Jon (2015), *Spinoza and the Stoics*, Cambridge: Cambridge University Press.

Murray, Adam (2013), 'Spinoza on Essence and Ideal Individuation', *Canadian Journal of Philosophy*, 43(1): 78–96.

Nuchelmans, Gabriël (1983), *Judgement and Proposition: From Descartes to Kant*, Amsterdam: North Holland Publishing Company.

Nuchelmans, Gabriël (1980), *Late-Scholastic and Humanist Theories of the Proposition*, Amsterdam: North Holland Publishing Company.

Renz, Ursula (2010), *Die Erklärbarkeit von Erfahrung: Subjektivität und Realismus in Spinozas Theorie des menschlichen Geistes*, Frankfurt: Klostermann.

Sangiacomo, Andrea (2015a), 'Teleology and Agreement in Nature', in Andre Santos Campos (ed.), *Spinoza: Basic Concepts*, Exeter: Imprint Academic.

Sangiacomo, Andrea (2015b), 'The Ontology of Determination: From Descartes to Spinoza', *Science in Context*, 28(4): 515–43.
Schmid, Stephan (2016), 'Handlungstheorie der Frühen Neuzeit', in Michael Kuhler und Markus Ruther (eds), *Handbuch Handlungstheorie: Grundlagen, Kontexte, Perspektiven*, Stuttgart and Weimar: Metzler, pp. 34–44.
Searle, John R. (1983), *Intentionality: An Essay in Mind*, Cambridge: Cambridge University Press.
Sellars, Wilfrid [1956] (2000), *Empiricism and the Philosophy of Mind*, reprinted in W. de Vries and T. Triplett, *Knowledge, Mind and the Given: Reading Wilfrid Sellars's 'Empiricism and the Philosophy of Mind'*, Indianapolis and Cambridge: Hackett Publishing Company.
Sharp, Hasana (2007), 'The Force of Ideas in Spinoza', *Political Theory* 3(6): 732–55.
Sharp, Hasana (2011), *Spinoza and the Politics of Renaturalization*, Chicago: The University of Chicago Press.
Steinberg, Diane (2005), 'Belief, Affirmation, and the Doctrine of Conatus in Spinoza', *The Southern Journal of Philosophy*, XLIII: 147–58.
Sturm, Thomas (2011), 'Historical Epistemology or History of Epistemology? The Case of the Relation between Perception and Judgment', *Erkenntnis*, 75(3): 303–24.
Viljanen, Valterri (2011), *Spinoza's Geometry of Power*, Cambridge: Cambridge University Press.
Waller, Jason (2012), 'Spinoza on Conatus and Persistence through Time', *Journal of Philosophical Research*, 37: 51–72.
Waterlow, Sarah (1982), *Nature, Change, and Agency in Aristotle's Physics: A Philosophical Study*, Oxford: Oxford University Press.
Winkler, Sean (2016), 'The Problem of Generation and Destruction in Spinoza's System', *Journal of Early Modern Studies*, 5(1): 89–113.

4

Spinoza on Natures: Aristotelian and Mechanistic Routes to Relational Autonomy

Matthew Kisner

This chapter examines how Spinoza's relational theory of autonomy is grounded in his metaphysics, specifically in his view of natures. Spinoza's view of natures in some ways sides with Descartes' view, most notably, by identifying extension as the nature of substance, which provides some footing for a mechanistic explanation of the physical world.[1] Indeed, Spinoza extends Cartesian mechanism by providing the basis for a mechanistic account of the natures of individual bodies.[2] Yet, in other ways, Spinoza returns to a more Aristotelian view.[3] In particular, Spinoza conceives of individual natures as *conatus*, which sides with Aristotelians in conceiving of individual natures as intrinsic, active powers. Consequently, Spinoza also sides with Aristotelians – at least with many scholastic Aristotelians – in emphasising that individual things are active when their natures determine them to particular changes and effects.[4]

Attending to this view sheds light on two ways that Spinoza provides a metaphysical basis for a relational account of autonomy. First, Spinoza's more Aristotelian conception of natures indicates a relatively unexplored way that he provides such a basis. Spinoza's conception of natures implies that people can be active in the sense that their natures determine them to particular effects, even in cases where the people are also passive, that is, where they are affected by others and where they work cooperatively with others to bring about some effect. Consequently, this account of natures provides Spinoza with the resources to explain how people can be self-determining or autonomous in virtue of their social relationships, where they are affected by others and are cooperative.

Second, the examination sheds light on another way that Spinoza provides a basis for a relational theory of autonomy, one that has been more discussed in the literature. Spinoza offers an unorthodox theory of individuals, according to which individuals are formed whenever things work together to bring about some effect. This entails that any person belongs to multiple individuals formed from any sort of collective action. On this theory, it is impossible to understand individuals atomistically, that is, in isolation from considering their broader social and political context. This is a central commitment of relational theories of autonomy. My examination shows that this unorthodox account of individuals has some basis in Spinoza's theory of natures, more specifically in his effort to extend and shore up Descartes' mechanistic approach to explaining bodies.

The chapter begins by considering the relevant historical background: Aristotelian views of natures (in section 1) and Descartes' views (in section 2). Section 3 explains where Spinoza's view of natures stands with respect to these. The final section considers how this investigation illuminates the ways that Spinoza provides a basis for a relational theory of autonomy.

1. Aristotelian Natures

A primary aim of Aristotle's natural philosophy is to understand the changes that we encounter in the world around us. In taking up this task, Aristotle is guided by a fundamental commitment: things are susceptible to certain kinds of change because of the sorts of things that they are (Waterlow 1982: 32–3; Des Chene 1996: 21). This struck Aristotle, and subsequent philosophers for hundreds of years, as obvious and abundantly confirmed by observation. Wood burns; water doesn't. Acorns grow into oaks; human babies do not. In light of this commitment, understanding change requires understanding the different sorts of things there are, in particular their potentials, capacities or dispositions to certain kinds of changes. Aristotle understands these dispositions to change as constituting the natures of things: 'the nature of a thing is a certain principle and cause of change and stability in the thing' (Ph 192b20).[5]

Aristotle makes a few important claims about these natures. First, natures are the intrinsic powers of a thing (Ph 192b16; Waterlow 1982: 3–6). The presence of such powers distinguishes natural things from artefacts. Aristotle understands powers as potentials or capacities for undergoing certain kinds of changes or being in certain states. For instance, it is the nature of water that it possesses the potential to boil. Second, the nature of a thing is identical to its essence, that is, what it is to be the thing. As such, the natures of things are identified with their form (Ph 193b6), for Aristotle identified forms as the essences of things (Z 1032b1).[6] Third, as forms, the natures of things are general in the sense that they are shared by all things of the same kind. So, the form of cat is the essence and nature of all cats. Individual cats are distinguished from one another in virtue of their matter, more specifically in virtue of their non-essential qualities or accidents.

For my purposes, a key commitment of Aristotle's view is that it allows for the possibility of passive activity; in other words, it does not regard activity and passivity as mutually exclusive. To explain how, I must say more about Aristotle's view of activity. I understand 'activity' to refer, at the most basic level, to causing, in other words, bringing about – or, more broadly, being responsible for – something, usually change or stasis, but possibly a quality, fact or state of affairs.[7] Aristotle employs two notions of activity. First, something can be active in the sense of initiating change, either a change in itself (imminent causation) or in another (transitive causation). For example, when a pot of water is placed over a fire and comes to a boil, the fire is active in the sense of initiating the boiling of the water. This sort of activity is characteristically operative in Aristotle's notion of efficient cause, which he defines as 'the original source of change or rest' (Ph 194b29). This notion of activity also tends to be operative in Aristotle's distinction between agent and patient, which appears repeatedly throughout his corpus. For Aristotle, the agent is generally what initiates change (the fire), whereas the patient is the subject of change, what undergoes change (the water).

However, Aristotle's thinking about natures indicates another kind of activity: the natures of things are responsible for things undergoing certain kinds of changes and for the trajectory of those changes.[8] For instance, the nature of the water is responsible for the fact that the heated water boils, rather than catches fire and, furthermore, for when and how it boils: at what specific temperature, that it produces steam and so forth. Since a thing's nature is its essential potentials or capacities for change, this kind of activity is equivalent to a thing actualising or realising its potential and essence. This kind of activity is operative in cases of formal causation, where a thing's form explains change. It is also operative in cases of final causation, where a thing's ends explain change, since a thing's ends are given by its form (Ph 198a23–6).

The further notion of activity shows how, for Aristotle, a thing can be simultaneously passive and active. A thing can be passive in the sense that it undergoes a change that is initiated by something external, yet still be active in determining the nature and trajectory of its own change. To return to the example, the boiling water is passive in the sense that it is the patient of change initiated by the fire, but it is also active in the sense that its nature and potentials are responsible for its boiling.

Aristotle's notion of natures was developed and refined in a variety of different ways in the scholastic tradition, which provides the more immediate context for considering Descartes' and Spinoza's views on natures. One important development is the introduction of the substantial form, which was arguably invented by Aquinas, though he believed it to be implied by Aristotle (Hattab 2009: 2, 31). Unlike forms generally, the substantial form is the form and essence of a particular substance, rather than of a class (the form of Matt, rather than the form of human beings) (Hattab 2009: 2; Pasnau 2004: 37).[9] Aquinas believed that a particular form was necessary in order to explain the being of particular things in which accidental properties must inhere.[10] A second development can also be traced to Aquinas: he distinguished the substantial form of a human being, which can exist without matter, to the substantial forms of all other things, what he called 'material substantial forms', which cannot (ST I, q. 75, a. 3).[11] Aquinas felt that this distinction was necessary in order to explain the immortality of the human soul.

Aristotle's theory of natures underwent further changes in Suárez, one of Descartes' primary sources for understanding scholasticism (Hattab 2009: 9–13, 189–90).[12] Suárez departed from Aquinas in two main ways. First, Suárez significantly revised the theory of substantial forms, partly in response to anti-Aristotelian criticism of substantial forms, and to refinements to the theory introduced by later scholastics (Hattab 2009: 40).[13] In Suárez, as with other scholastic Aristotelians after Aquinas, the theory of substantial forms was important because it was supposed to explain the relationship between the essence of a substance and its particular accidental properties. It was commonly held that all of a thing's properties, even its non-essential accidents, were supposed to flow from the essence. In Aquinas' words, 'once the proper essence of a singular is cognized, all of its singular accidents are cognized' (Pasnau 2004: 37).[14] Suárez, like other scholastics, conceived of the substantial form as the cause of accidental properties, which is how substantial forms were commonly understood by early moderns (Pasnau 2004: 44). Suárez also departed from Aquinas on substantial forms by avoiding Aquinas' distinction between human substantial forms and material substantial forms. He conceived of all substantial forms as being like the human substantial form, which led him to the view that all substantial forms can exist independently of matter, like the human soul (Suárez 2000: 20–1; Douglas 2015: 15–17).

Second, Suárez rejected Aristotle's basic identification of natures and essences. Suárez distinguished two kinds of forms: the metaphysical and the physical (Suárez 2000: 177). The metaphysical form is the non-accidental form that is the essence of the substance. This form is shared by all things of a kind, for instance the form of human being. Suárez regarded this as the essence of a thing. The physical form, in contrast, is the particular form that combines with matter to create an individual, in which accidents inhere. This physical form is identified with the substantial form. Because this physical form explains the changes that a thing undergoes, Suárez regards it as the nature of a thing. Suárez concludes that physical and metaphysical forms cannot be the same thing – and, thus, that nature and essence cannot be the same thing. Suárez cites, among other reasons for this view, the fact that God and angels possess essences and metaphysical forms, but no physical forms (Suárez 2000: 178).

For my purposes, the important point is that, despite the wide variety of theories about natures in the scholastic tradition, many of the main sources of the tradition for Descartes and Spinoza (Aristotle, Aquinas and Suárez) all agreed on two main claims. First, natures are active in the sense of being responsible for the changes that a thing undergoes; in Aristotelian language, natures are internal active principles. Indeed, Suárez's commitment to this claim is the reason that he identifies the nature of a thing with its physical form, since he regards the physical form as the cause of the thing's changes. In virtue of this claim, they also agree, second, that there may be passive activity. Even when things are patients of exogenous change, like the water boiling, they are active in the sense that their own natures determine them to particular changes and determine the trajectory of these changes.

2. Descartes on Natures: Extension and Thought

Descartes famously breaks with scholastic Aristotelianism on a number of fundamental claims, most notably hylomorphism.[15] Descartes explained the soul foremost as a thinking substance, which can exist independently of a body.

Related to this, Descartes also distanced himself from the scholastic understanding of natures as forms. Rather, Descartes' central innovation was to identify the natures or essences of particular substances with attributes: essential properties in terms of which all of the substance's other properties must be explained.[16] The essence or nature of bodily substances is the attribute of extension and the essence of mental substance is the attribute of thought.[17]

How to interpret these claims is famously unclear. For example, does Descartes understand extension to mean pure extension or is it meant to include something else, such as corporeal nature? Most importantly for my purposes, how does Descartes understand the relationship between the attribute essence and particular essences, such as the essence of an oak tree or a human being? Is the attribute essence meant to supplant these other individual essences or is it meant merely to constrain the way these other individual essences are explained, for instance stipulating that the essences of particular bodily things must ultimately be explainable entirely in terms of extension?[18]

Regardless of how we answer these interpretive questions, it is evident that Descartes departs from the two Aristotelian claims about natures that I highlighted in the previous section. The first of these is the basic claim that natures are internal, active powers of a thing. To begin with, Descartes denied that natures are powers, for he identified natures with extension and thought and neither of these are obviously powers, though these properties may imply certain powers. Furthermore, Descartes departs from the first claim by denying that the natures of things, thought and extension, are active.[19] Descartes endorsed broadly mechanistic explanations of the physical world, which explain change primarily in terms of local motions and it is difficult to see how extension alone can cause local motion.[20] Consequently, it is difficult to see how extension can be active in the sense of being the source of the substance's local motions and changes.[21] It is similarly hard to see how the attribute of thought alone can be responsible for particular thoughts or mental changes.

Descartes' view breaks not only with the Aristotelian notion of natures, but more generally with the Aristotelian notion that bodily states and changes have internal causes. This is largely because of Descartes' commitment to mechanism, which tends to explain changes in the local motions of any body as arising from something external to the body. According to a common view of local motion, any body coming to motion, altering its motion or ceasing in its motion is caused by its contact and collision with some other body.[22] This principle implies that a body's local motions cannot originate from powers or natures internal to the body. Since mechanism endeavours to explain all bodily states and changes in terms of local motions, it seems that mechanism will have a difficult time explaining how the body's states and changes originate from internal powers.[23]

This conception of natures is potentially problematic, particularly by the lights of the Aristotelian tradition.[24] A first possible problem, one that is more worrying to us than to early modern philosophers, is that it makes it difficult to understand how any motion originally comes about. Descartes identifies a supernatural origin of all motions: God (*Principles* II: 36; CSM I: 202).[25] Descartes also allows that motions originate from minds, but he famously fails to explain the nature of mind–body interaction. A second possible problem with this conception of natures is that it makes it difficult to explain apparent cases of change that have an internal source. Concern over this problem is evident in Suárez's defence of substantial forms. Arguing against mechanists and atomists, Suárez argues that substantial forms are required to explain what he regarded as internally caused change, such as heated water naturally returning to a colder temperature (Suárez 2000: 18).[26]

Of course, Descartes and mechanism have resources for responding to these problems, if they even regard them as problems. Most notably, the motions of things are partly caused by the way that they are extended: because of its shape a cylinder rolls down an inclined surface, whereas a cube does not. Consequently, it is possible for a mechanistic account of the natures of bodily things as specific extended configurations to explain their motions and, thus, their changes as arising partly from the natures of the bodies.[27] Nevertheless, Descartes makes no effort to develop a theory of individual natures that would show how they are the active, internal causes of a thing's changes or properties.

This discussion shows how Descartes also breaks with the second Aristotelian claim that I highlighted at the end of the previous section: the possibility of passive activity. The Aristotelian view allows for passive activity because it allows that a thing's nature can still be active in causing and directing the course of externally initiated changes. But Descartes cannot recognise such a possibility without recognising that things are active from their natures. Of course, Descartes' view of natures leaves some conceptual space for particular extended natures that actively determine their changes even when these changes are passively initiated; for instance, even when I tip over the cylinder, it rolls down an incline because of its particular extended nature. But, again Descartes does not take up this possibility.

In fact, Descartes explicitly rules out the possibility of Aristotelian passive activity in his main remarks on activity and passivity, which can be found in the first article of the *Passions of the Soul*:

> I note that whatever takes place or occurs is generally called by philosophers a 'passion' with regard to the subject to which it happens and an 'action' with regard to that which makes it happen. Thus, although an agent and patient are often quite different, an action and passion must always be a single thing which has these two names on account of the two different subjects to which it may be related. (AT XI: 328, CSM I: 328)

There is a lot going on in this very brief passage and it takes a bit of work to draw out the relevant points. The passage asserts two main claims. The first is that passion and action are identical. This is actually a well-known Aristotelian claim: 'the actuality of what is capable of causing change and the actuality of what is capable of being changed are the same' (Ph 202a14). Aristotle's example of a student learning from a teacher illustrates: the action (the teaching) and the passion (the learning) are ultimately different ways of describing the same thing, that is, the change in the student from a state of not knowing to knowing.

However, the passage is clearly supposed to challenge Aristotle, since the article begins by criticising 'the defects of the sciences we have from the ancients' (AT XI: 327, CSM I: 328). The likely target of Descartes' concern is a conclusion that Aristotle draws from the identity of passion and action. Because Aristotle understands change as the transition from potential to actual, he conceives of change as located in the thing that realises its potential, in other words what undergoes change: the patient; 'change takes place in the thing that is capable of being changed' (Ph 202a13). Consequently, if action and passion are identical, then the action must also be in the patient. On this basis, Aristotle is committed to the counterintuitive conclusion that the action of teaching is in the student, rather than in the teacher.

To avoid this Aristotelian conclusion, the passage asserts the second claim: a change is to be described as an action with respect to the agent and as a passion with respect to the patient. In other words, the student's transition to a state of knowing is an action (teaching) with respect to the teacher and a passion (learning) with respect to the student. It follows that the action of teaching belongs only to the teacher, which avoids Aristotle's counterintuitive notion that the teaching occurs in the student.[28] For the present discussion, the important point is that, according to the view stated here, a change can *only* be regarded as an action with regard to the agent that initiates the change. According to this view, the transition to a state of knowing can only be regarded as an action with regard to the teacher; the learning must be passive. This rules out the possibility that a patient of change can be active with regard to the change and, thus, rules out the possibility that a patient can be active in the sense that its nature determines the course of its change.

3. Spinoza's Active Natures

Unlike Descartes, Spinoza is careful to explain the difference between the attribute essence and the essences or natures of individual things. In Spinoza, the attribute essence belongs to the one substance, which possesses an infinite number of attribute essences, including thought and extension. However, Spinoza does not regard the attribute essence as the essence of individual things, that is, individual bodies or minds (see, for example, E2p10). Spinoza understands an essence as what is necessary and sufficient for a thing: 'to the essence of any thing belongs that which, being given, the thing is necessarily posited and which, being taken away, the thing is necessarily taken away' (E2def2).[29] While the attributes of extension and thought are necessary for any particular body and mind respectively, they are not sufficient for them: simply being extended or being a thought is not sufficient to being an acorn or my idea of a shoe.

Rather, Spinoza identifies the essence of individual things with their *conatus* (E3p7).[30] In some ways, this view draws on and even extends Cartesian and mechanistic views of natures. First, Spinoza follows Descartes by accounting for individual natures without any appeal to either a form or substantial form, at least in the Aristotelian sense.[31] Second, Spinoza's view provides the basis for a mechanistic account of the natures of individual bodies, thereby filling an important gap in Descartes' theory.[32] Spinoza holds that all bodies can be conceived through the attribute of extension in a roughly mechanistic way, as extended things in motion. Most (perhaps even all) bodies are composite, that is, bodily aggregates that stand to one another in persisting and fixed spatial relations (see the definition of composite bodies after E2p13ax2").[33] Conceived under the attribute of extension, the *conatus* of these bodies is the power or force whereby they persist in existence and, thus, whereby these parts maintain these fixed relations. This notion of *conatus* draws on the mechanistic theories of Descartes and Hobbes, which conceive of *conatus* as inertial motions and tendencies of motions.[34]

However, in other ways, Spinoza's view of natures departs from Descartes and returns to scholastic Aristotelianism, particularly with regard to the two key commitments discussed above. First, Spinoza understands natures as active.[35] This is evident foremost from Spinoza's well-known criticism of Descartes to Tschirnhaus:

> From extension, as conceived by Descartes, to wit, a mass at rest, it is not only difficult to demonstrate the existence of bodies, as you say, but quite impossible. For matter at rest, insofar as it is in itself, will persevere in its rest, and will not be set in motion unless by a more powerful external cause. For this reason I did not hesitate, previously, to affirm that Descartes's principles of natural things are useless, not to say absurd. (Ep81)

Here Spinoza complains that extension as Descartes conceived it – that is as inert matter or 'mass at rest' – cannot explain the dynamic properties of bodies and, thus, fails as a physical theory. This is because such an account cannot recognise a source of activity in bodies and, thus, must appeal to something other than extension to account for motion and changes in motion. These remarks indicate that Spinoza takes himself to offer a different and better conception of extension. Presumably this is because Spinoza conceives of extension as the essence of the one substance, which is God. This implies that extension is active and causally efficacious, for God's essence is responsible for his own existence and all existing things. More specifically, Spinoza holds that the attribute of extension implies and causes all individual things conceived under that attribute, in other words all modes of extension or individual bodies (E1p16, E2p6). Thus, for Spinoza, the attribute of extension does explain the existence of bodies, just as Spinoza told Tschirnhaus.

There is some, though less direct, evidence that Spinoza holds parallel views about the attribute of thought. Descartes tends to conceive of thought in terms of mental perception (Alanen 2003: Chapter 3). However, in perceiving a thing, one is passively affected by the objects of perception, as in sensory perception, where external objects imprint themselves on the sense organs. Consequently, if the essence of mental substance is thought, understood as mental perception, then it is hard to see how there is an internal source of activity in the natures of mental things. This concern is evident in Spinoza's definition of an idea, which he regards as the basic unit of mental things, the mental parallel of bodies. He defines an idea as a 'concept of the mind' (E2Def3), explaining, 'I say concept rather than perception, because the word perception seems to indicate that the mind is acted on by the object. But concept seems to express an action of the mind' (E2def3 explanation). Furthermore, Spinoza insists that thought is active by conceiving the attribute of thought as God's essence, which implies that it exists from itself and causes all of the modes of thought, all individual ideas and minds (E1p16, E2p6).

In addition to attribute essences, Spinoza also insists that the essences of individual things are active. Just as an attribute essence expresses God's power, so too does the *conatus* of each individual, though 'in a certain and determinate way' (E3p6dem). Spinoza underscores this point by referring to *conatus* as a thing's power. This is a move away from Cartesian essences as special properties or qualities and a return to Aristotelian essences as powers, although Spinoza understands powers in a very different way from Aristotelians.[36] This point is more obvious in the Latin because Spinoza's main term for power – at least, when describing a thing's *conatus* – is *potentia*, which is the standard scholastic Aristotelian term for describing the potentials or capacities that comprise natures.[37]

According to Spinoza, the *conatus* is active foremost because it is responsible for the tendency of things to continue in existence. It is worth pointing out that this view addresses mechanism's potential difficulty in identifying an internal source of change in bodies. When describing the motions of simple bodies Spinoza accepts the common view that all changes in local motion are caused externally: 'a body in motion moves until it is determined to rest by another body, and a body at rest is at rest until it is determined by another to motion' (E2p13l3). However, Spinoza argues that composite bodies consist in a collection of simple bodies that maintain certain fixed spatial relations (see the definition following E2p13ax2"). Spinoza identifies the essence of these composite bodies with the power or force with which the bodies maintain these spatial relations and, thereby, remain in existence. Thus, when it comes to composite bodies, Spinoza is able to claim that some motions originate internal to a thing's nature in a way that is consistent with a broadly mechanistic conception of the physical world.

The *conatus* is active not only in contributing to the continued existence of individual things, but also in directing and determining individuals in ways that promote their power, more specifically in ways that increase their power of activity, that is, the strength of their *conatus*. It is important to recognise here that *conatus* cannot be understood simply as an inertial tendency to maintain some particular proportion of motion and rest. While *conatus* is expressed under the attribute of extension as maintaining bodily integrity, this tendency is expressed under the other attributes in ways that are distinct from motions or extended relations. Furthermore, whereas inertial tendencies merely sustain and maintain motions in a thing, the *conatus* directs a thing to effects that may not yet be present in a thing: effects that increase the thing's power (Viljanen 2011: 109–10).[38] Spinoza asserts this claim in E3p12, where he claims that the *conatus* of the mind works toward imagining whatever increases the power of the body. He then draws on this claim to argue that human beings act from their *conatus* when they act in ways that promote their power. For instance, he claims that one's *conatus* works toward bringing about whatever gives one joy (E3p28), which he defines as an increase in one's power (E3ad3 explanation).[39]

Spinoza also endorses the second Aristotelian commitment: the possibility of passive activity. According to Spinoza's definition, we are passive 'when something takes place within us or something follows from our nature of which we are only a partial cause' (E3def2). This definition implies that a thing is passive when it is acted on by something external, that is, when it undergoes an exogenous effect.[40] This is because such an effect must be brought about at least partly by the external thing, so that the thing undergoing the effect can be no more than a partial cause of the effect. According to Spinoza, when a thing is passively affected in this way, it may simultaneously be active in the sense that its nature or *conatus* is active in bringing about the change (Kisner 2008, forthcoming). For instance, consider taking medicine to treat a health problem: the effect of healing is caused both by the external medicine but also by one's own *conatus*, which plays a role in the healing and which metabolises, uses and processes the medicine. In taking the medicine, then, one is simultaneously passive, because she is affected by the medicine, and active, because her *conatus* is working to bring about the effect.

Spinoza explicitly acknowledges this view in E3p9, where he claims that minds strive insofar as they have both adequate and inadequate ideas.[41] Spinoza understands adequate ideas as ideas following entirely from our nature or striving, expressed under the attribute of thought, whereas inadequate ideas arise partly from the power of external things. Consequently, Spinoza's claim that we strive in conceiving inadequate ideas amounts to the claim that we strive to some extent even when we are exogenously determined to have some idea. According to Spinoza's parallelism doctrine, conceiving ideas is the mental expression of our striving, which is identical to our striving expressed under every other attribute (E2p7s). Consequently, E3p9 implies that anytime we are acted on, for instance when an external body acts on our body, the change is also partly the expression of our striving. Since these claims apply to all things, not just human minds, it follows that no thing is ever purely passive in undergoing change; their natures as striving play some role in bringing about all of their effects.[42]

Before considering relational autonomy, I would like to point out how the foregoing account of Spinozistic natures delivers on two other fundamental Aristotelian views. The first is the view that things are susceptible to certain kinds of changes in virtue of their natures. The reasoning goes as follows. The *conatus*, at the bodily level, is the power by which any thing maintains its particular physical composition. Things are susceptible to certain kinds of change as a result of this composition. For instance, a dog is physically constituted such that being submerged completely in water for a sustained period of time will cause it to drown, unlike a fish. Similarly, a goat is physically constituted such that it is not harmed by consuming poison ivy (apparently goats love it), unlike most human beings. Consequently, the *conatus*, being the power that is primarily responsible for maintaining this composition, makes the dog and the goat susceptible to certain changes or, more broadly, to certain effects. To use an example of a non-living thing, Spinoza holds that the nature of a piece of paper is the power to maintain a particular ratio of motion and rest, which makes the paper susceptible to tearing and burning, unlike a rock.

Spinoza most explicitly recognises this point when he deduces what is beneficial for human beings by considering their distinctive *conatus*. For instance, Spinoza claims that human beings benefit from acting for the good of other people because this leads them to agree in nature (E4p37), whereas they do not receive the same benefit from acting for the good of other animals (E4p37s1), which have an entirely different nature. Thus, because of their *conatus* human beings are susceptible to the effect of benefiting from acting for the good of others, as well as from acting in accordance with reason's commands generally (E4p35), which include many other commands, for instance to avoid compassion (E4p50c; see also E4p18s). By the same reasoning, our *conatus* makes us susceptible to benefiting from eating rice but not poison ivy, to breathing air, but not water, and so forth.

Second, Spinoza's view of natures delivers on the Aristotelian notion that a thing's nature may direct the trajectory of the effects and changes that it undergoes. The reasoning for this claim should be obvious from the previous discussion: when a goat eats poison ivy, it undergoes a natural trajectory of effects and changes: the process of metabolising and nourishing. These processes are determined by the particular physical constitution of the goat, which, in turn, is determined by the goat's *conatus*. Thus, the process is directed or – if that sounds too teleological – determined by the *conatus*. This reading is supported by Spinoza's remarks on the natural growth and development of human beings.

> Anyone who has a body that is capable of very many things, has a mind which, considered solely in itself, is very conscious of itself and of God and of things. In this life therefore we primarily endeavor that the infant body develops into a different body, as far as its nature allows and is conducive to it, a body which is capable of very many things and is related to a mind that is very much conscious of itself and of God and of things, and this in such a way that all that is related to its memory or imagination will be of scarcely any importance in relation to its intellect. (E5p39s)

Thus, the process by which an infant's body develops into an adult body and by which its mind becomes capable of better cognition is determined by its *conatus*. Similar reasoning can be used for non-living things: when a trickle of water runs over limestone, the stone will, because of its *conatus* to maintain a particular bodily composition, undergo a particular process of erosion, different from other kinds of earth and stone.

4. Two Sources of Relational Autonomy

In thinking about autonomy, Spinoza's philosophy is a natural place to look. To begin with, Spinoza's ethics emphasises the value of freedom, which he places alongside virtue and perfection as a central goal of a well lived life. Since Spinoza understands freedom as consisting in self-determination, freedom is broadly connected to the notion of autonomy, that is, self-rule or self-governance.[43] Spinoza holds that human beings become free by conceiving and acting from adequate ideas, for this involves being determined by one's own *conatus* and nature (see E3p1 together with E3p59s and E2p49cs at G ii: 92). Consequently, for Spinoza, human freedom is constituted by the activities of reasoning and acting in accordance with reason's guidance, which are traditionally regarded as central to autonomy (Kisner 2011: Chapter 6).[44]

This section considers how Spinoza's view of natures implies a theory of relational autonomy. First a definition of relational autonomy is in order. Because autonomy involves self-rule it is natural to conceive of autonomy as a kind of independence, that is, as acting from oneself or determining oneself without being directed or influenced by external things. Relational theories of autonomy, however, resist this conception by insisting that an individual's autonomy is importantly assisted and perhaps even partly constituted by her relations with others.

In particular, these theories emphasise two closely related commitments. First, they conceive of 'the self as fundamentally socially embedded' (Armstrong 2009: 44; see also Mackenzie and Stoljar 2000: 4); in other words, they reject an atomistic conception of the self. I take this to mean that individual people are fundamentally shaped by their relations with others so that they can only be properly understood by considering these relations and, consequently, how these relations in turn are shaped and structured by the social and political environment. This implies that we cannot understand what it means for people to be genuinely self-determining – and, thus, that we cannot explain autonomy – without considering their relations to others and the broader environment.

Second, these theories emphasise the value of social relations to our autonomy in a variety of ways. A relational theory may hold that social relations are important to developing the powers and capacities in virtue of which individuals qualify as autonomous (Nedelsky 1989: 12; Meyers 1989). For instance, one may hold that individuals come to be autonomous only through, say, the mentorship and guidance of parents and teachers. More substantively, a relational theory may hold that we express or exercise our autonomy through our social relations, such that social relations are constitutive of our autonomy (Brison 2000: 285; Christman 2004: 147; Oshana 2006: 2). For instance, one may think that being autonomous involves full participation in civic or political life and, thus, that it involves interacting with others in particular ways or standing in certain social relations with them. According to this view, being autonomous requires a community, which is structured and organised in a particular way.[45]

Spinoza's philosophy is friendly to relational theories of autonomy in several ways. I will begin by mentioning two ways that have been discussed in the literature, but that are not directly connected to Spinoza's views of natures. Both of them are based on Spinoza's view of humans as necessarily passive and dependent to some degree. The first way, which I defend in *Spinoza on Human Freedom*, looks to Spinoza's theory of reason to show that he upholds the second commitment above, that is, that he regards social relations as valuable to autonomy (Kisner 2011: 231–4). More specifically, he holds, first, that social relations are necessary for developing our autonomy and, second, that we express and exercise our autonomy through social relations. With regard to the first, Spinoza's conception of humans as necessarily passive and externally determined to some degree entails, at the mental level, that we tend to adopt the ideas of others and to imitate their emotions. Consequently, acquiring and strengthening adequate ideas depends partly on our social relations, for instance on surrounding ourselves with and forming friendships with rational people so that we may acquire and draw strength from their more adequate ideas, while avoiding entanglements with those governed by harmful passions. Since our freedom and autonomy consist partly in the self-determination of conceiving adequate ideas, it follows that developing freedom and autonomy depends partly on these social relations. With regard to the second, Spinoza holds that adequate ideas provide practical direction, as in the dictates or commands of reason (E4p18s). Spinoza understands many of these as social; they command, for instance, acting for the good of others and responding to others with appropriate emotions. It follows that exercising our freedom and autonomy are partly constituted by relating to others in these ways.

The second way looks to a cornerstone of Spinoza's metaphysics, the notion that cognition of a thing requires cognition of its causes (E1ax4).[46] This entails the first commitment of relational autonomy above, that Spinoza conceives of the self as necessarily socially embedded. The reasoning goes as follows. Because Spinoza conceives of human beings as necessarily passive and dependent to some degree, our states and actions are often caused partially by external things. Furthermore, Spinoza holds that all finite modes, including human beings, are ultimately caused by other finite modes. All of this entails that understanding human beings – their existence, states and actions – requires understanding external things. Consequently, properly understanding the self requires attending to its relations with external things, including social relations with other people.

Attending to Spinoza's view of natures enriches our understanding of how his philosophy provides the basis for relational autonomy in two ways. First, it indicates a way that Spinoza provides a basis for relational autonomy that has received little attention in the literature.[47] Theories of relational autonomy oppose the view that autonomy consists in or requires independence (Friedman 1997: 42–4). Conceiving autonomy as independence implies that our relations with others are either an obstacle to our autonomy or fundamentally distinct from our autonomy (Friedman 2000). Rather, theories of relational autonomy reject any dichotomy between autonomy, on the one hand, and, on the other, the dependence and passivity that are necessary features of social interaction and cooperation (Friedman 1997; Armstrong 2009: 44, 49–50). Spinoza's view of natures is helpful for overcoming this dichotomy because it leads him to conceive of passivity and activity as compatible. Spinoza recognises that we can be active in the sense of acting from our nature or *conatus* and, thus, that we can attain a degree of self-determination or autonomy, even in cases where we are passive and dependent, including cases where we are work cooperatively with others. Consequently, Spinoza's view is well situated to recognise how external things – other people, as well as social and political conditions – can contribute positively to our autonomy by working to bring about effects that follow from our natures. My investigation shows, perhaps surprisingly, that this route to a relational conception of autonomy is based in metaphysical commitments that are continuous with the earlier Aristotelian tradition. It would be interesting to look to this tradition, particularly to the notion of *autarkeia*, for the resources to develop relational theories of autonomy.

Second, attending to Spinoza's view of natures sheds light on a fourth way that Spinoza provides the basis for a relational theory of autonomy, a way that figures prominently in work by Armstrong.[48] This way looks to Spinoza's theory of individuals to show that he conceives of the self as socially embedded. Spinoza argues that things form an individual when they act jointly to bring about an effect: 'if a number of individuals so concur in one action that together they are all the cause of one effect, I consider them all, to that extent, as one singular thing' (E2def7).[49] The claim entails that individual people or agents are invariably parts of larger individuals. For instance, in contributing a chapter to this anthology I am part of an individual composed of myself and the other contributors, as well as the publisher and the printer. I am also a part of an individual comprised of anything that contributes to the mission of the university where I work, including other faculty, staff, students, parents and taxpayers, even material things, the buildings, filing cabinets, classrooms and so forth; a similar case can be made for any social organisation, including nations. The fact that individual people belong to multiple nested and overlapping individuals makes it impossible to understand individual people in isolation from their social relations, which is the first commitment of relational theories of autonomy, described above.

My investigation of Spinoza's view of natures sheds light on the historical context and motivation for this relational theory of individuals. Explaining this point requires saying a little bit more about the history. One of the fundamental reasons for the theory of substantial forms was to explain how a thing's different characteristics and qualities are unified in an individual (Pasnau 2004: 34–9). For instance, Suárez argues that the substantial form is necessary to explain the way that accidents come bundled together in a single individual (Suárez 2000: 21). As we have seen, critics of this view worried that it can only explain the unity of an individual by positing something (the substantial form) that is occult or unobservable. Descartes' metaphysics partly addresses this concern by explaining the unity of a thing's essential and accidental properties without appealing to an occult substantial form.[50] Descartes conceives of non-essential properties of things as modes, rather than accidents. Whereas it is not obvious how accidents are unified with a thing's form and essence, Descartes holds that modes are necessarily referred to and conceived through an attribute, which he conceives as the essence of a substance (*Principles* I: 53; CSM I: 210; see also *Principles* I: 56; CSM I: 211).[51] Thus, Descartes' metaphysics implies a tight connection between the essence of a thing and its other non-essential properties, which explains how the different properties of substances are unified in individuals.

However, this Cartesian solution has its own problems. While he may explain the unity of the essence of a substance with its non-essential properties, Descartes' notion of extension as the essence of body famously has a difficult time explaining how to differentiate individual bodily substances.[52] The problems are many. Descartes' conception of extension as the essence of bodies makes it difficult to distinguish bodies from space. Furthermore, this conception implies that there is no vacuum; rather, the whole physical world is a plenum of continuous bodies. How, then, is one supposed to distinguish some regions of the plenum as distinct bodily substances? This problem is compounded by the fact that all bodies, for Descartes, share the same essence in some sense.

Spinoza's view of natures can be read as responding to the difficulties with both the Aristotelian view and Descartes' view. In response to the Aristotelians, Spinoza is able to follow Descartes in explaining the unity of a substance without resorting to occult substantial forms by explaining non-essential properties of substance as modes, which are tightly connected, both conceptually and causally, with the essence attributes. On the other hand, Spinoza's theory of natures offers more resources than Descartes' for explaining how to differentiate particular things. While Spinoza agrees with Descartes that all individual bodies are essentially extended, Spinoza identifies the natures of things with their *conatus*, which allows him to distinguish individuals according to their causal powers: when a body has the effect of contributing to the existence of some thing or increasing that thing's power, then the body belongs to that thing's essential powers and, thus, belongs to that thing.[53] This move to identify individual natures with their causal powers leads him to the view that that multiple things form an individual when they bring about a common effect.[54] In this respect, Spinoza's provocative theory of individuals is importantly connected to his efforts to shore up a problem with the Cartesian project of providing a metaphysical grounding for mechanistic explanation of the physical world. Thus, this fourth route to a relational theory of autonomy is grounded in Spinoza's move away from Aristotelianism and in the direction of Descartes and mechanism.

Indeed, Spinoza's relational conception of individuals can be read as a radicalisation of the modern, more mechanistic view of natures. Scholastic Aristotelianism aims to identify natures with the substantial form and, thus, with a stable and enduring metaphysical unit that houses all of a thing's qualities and characteristics. Mechanism, in contrast, decentres individuals in the sense that it eliminates the substantial form and conceives of individuals rather as collections or organisations of parts. Spinoza's *conatus* provides an alternative metaphysical unit, one drawn from conceptions of inertia in the early mechanism of Descartes and Hobbes. This new unit offers more resources for differentiating things into discrete individuals, but it results in individuals that are in some ways even more radically uncentred than Cartesian bodies. For, as I have shown above, Spinoza's view allows any single thing to belong to a myriad of overlapping and nested individuals. These individuals may be composed of spatially disconnected parts, as in the contributors to this volume, who hail from across the globe. Furthermore, Spinoza's view allows for dynamic individuals: the parts of the individual fluctuate constantly depending on how things contribute to bringing about some effect. Indeed, individuals blink in and out of existence depending on what effects things bring about: once the contributors to the anthology stop their work in bringing about this effect, the individual disappears.[55]

By way of concluding, it is worth pointing out a difference between the Aristotelian and mechanistic routes to a relational theory of autonomy. In one sense, the Aristotelian route is broad. The Aristotelian view holds that any change or effect that a thing undergoes is brought about at least partly by the thing's own nature. Consequently, this view explains how any state of a thing arising from its interactions with external things is also determined partly by the thing itself and, consequently, can involve a degree of freedom and autonomy. Thus, the Aristotelian view is broad in the sense of implying that all exogenous states involve a degree of self-determination. This does not imply that the Aristotelian view is forced to treat all exogenous states as equally self-determining or autonomous. Spinoza offers standards for assessing the extent to which interactions with external things contribute to one's self-determination; while all changes or effects in a thing are partly the result of its own natures, some changes can be much more the result of one's nature than others. One's nature is more active in determining it to some effect – and, thus, one is more self-determining, free and autonomous – when the effect is beneficial, that is, when it contributes to the persistent existence of the thing and increases in its power.

The mechanistic route to relational autonomy is broad in a different sense. Spinoza's effort to shore up difficulties with mechanistic efforts to individuate bodies has the effect of expanding the boundaries of the individual: I am not just this mind and body, but also a part of other collective individuals – my family, my university, the passengers on the bus, my nation and so forth. According to this view, I may be autonomous not just because of how my interactions with other things promote and exercise my own individual striving, but also because of how they promote and exercise the striving of the various group and collective identities to which I belong. For instance, just as the friendship and guidance of a peer can strengthen an individual's striving and, thereby, make her more self-determining and autonomous, the aid of a foreign nation can strengthen the striving of one's nation and, thereby, can increase the self-determination and autonomy of an individual citizen, at least to the extent that her striving is identified with the striving of her nation. Thus, the mechanistic route is broad in the sense that it expands the boundaries of the individual, which provides a greater variety of ways that external things and our relationships with them can promote an individual's autonomy.[56]

Notes

1. I have some reservations about describing Spinoza as a thorough mechanist. See footnote 31.
2. It is helpful to keep in mind here that the term mechanism was not used by historical figures and that it can mean different things. Throughout this chapter I use the term to refer only to the view that natural phenomena should be explained in the way that an early modern philosopher would explain the operation of a machine, such as a clock, that is, in terms of the motions of its material parts.
3. It is important to be sceptical of modern philosophers like Descartes and Hobbes when they present Aristotelians or scholastics as a unified school of thought. There are significant differences not just between Aristotle and his Christian interpretation offered by, say, Aquinas, but also among the many varieties of scholastic Aristotelianism (Ariew 2011: Introduction, chapter 2). Nevertheless, there are general points of agreement among most Aristotelian views – for instance, that there are four causes – and I focus on these shared commitments when I discuss Aristotelian views.
4. Here I emphasise scholastic Aristotelianism because it is somewhat contested whether Aristotle or even Aquinas understood the nature of a thing as a cause (rather than as a principle) of its states and changes (van Ruler 1995: 67–70). After Aquinas, as the theory of substantial forms was developed and became more entrenched, later scholastic Aristotelians tended to become more clearly committed to the notion that a thing's substantial form is the internal cause of its states and changes (Pasnau 2004: 44–5).
5. Quoted translations of Aristotle's *Physics* come from Waterfield (Aristotle 2008).
6. Aristotle (1933). Aristotle's claims here are subject to multiple interpretations, which is evident from the variety of scholastic and medieval views. Pasnau (2004: 33–5) explains some of the issues surrounding essences and their relationship to the form (specifically the substantial form) and to the matter of a thing.
7. One must keep in mind here that Aristotle understands a cause broadly as what explains something. As Vlastos (1969: 294) famously claimed, Aristotle's four causes are really four becauses.
8. A reader has questioned whether Aristotle would have recognised undergoing such changes as a kind of activity. I think he would because undergoing such changes involves a thing realising its potentials and capacities, which is central to Aristotle's understanding of activity. But for my purposes we need not settle this question. Throughout this discussion I use 'activity' and 'active' as I defined it previously to refer to causing or being responsible for some change or effect. I am not using these terms in a distinctly Aristotelian way and, consequently, I am not taking any stand on whether any of these activities would count as activities given Aristotle's theory of activity.
9. Over time it became increasingly important that the substantial form was regarded as individual. In late scholasticism, the principle of individuation had changed from being matter to form, which was connected to the rise of Scotism. In Aquinas, the principle for distinguishing individuals was signate or quantified matter, whereas Scotus insisted that individuals must be distinguished by their essence, which implies that the substantial form must be individual. Some version of the Scotist view was upheld by popular textbooks, such as Eustachius, Raconis and Burgersdijk (Ariew 2011: chapter 4).

10. More specifically, Aquinas holds that accidental properties require a subject in which to inhere. The substantial form provides this subject, though it does not itself require a subject, as it arises from the union of prime matter and form (Aquinas 1961: 435; Aquinas 1950: 80). Aquinas also argues that prime matter, being pure potentiality cannot exist alone. Consequently, the existence of matter requires the union of prime matter and the substantial form. See ST I, q. 75, a. 6 (Aquinas 1981).
11. Aquinas (1981).
12. On Descartes' knowledge of scholasticism generally see Ariew (2011: Introduction, chapter 2) and Schmaltz (2012). In *The Collected Works of Spinoza*, Curley claims that Suárez was likely the most important scholastic influence on Spinoza as well (C1: 223). This is partly because Suárez was important to Dutch scholastics, such as Burgersdijck, Senguerd, Voetius and Deusing (van Ruler 1995: 286; Douglas 2015: 18–20). Consequently, Suárezian views were bound up with the Regius controversy, which is an essential part of the historical context for Descartes' and Spinoza's philosophy. On the controversy, see van Ruler (1995).
13. Some critics charged that substantial forms are obscure (for instance, Sanches 1998: 237–8; see also Hattab 2009: 81). The theory of substantial forms was also refined by a move toward an account of substantial forms that was friendlier to mechanistic explanation (Schmitt 1983; Pasnau 2004: 44–6; Hattab 2009: chapter 5).
14. This is Pasnau's translation of a passage from *De veritate*.
15. By 'hylomorphism' here I just mean the view that substances are composites of form and matter. It is important to note, first, that hylomorphism is an anachronistic term that in its literal sense refers simply to views that make use of form and matter. Understood in this literal way, Descartes did not make a clean break with hylomorphism (Manning 2012). Second, even if we understand hylomorphism in the more restrictive sense as a view of substance, Descartes did not entirely break with hylomorphism because he allowed that the human soul is a substantial form (see letter to Regius of January 1642, AT III 505 (Descartes 1982–91); for a discussion, see Schmaltz 2012).
16. In this respect, the principle attribute takes over the role played by the substantial form (Rozemond 2002: 116–17).
17. Of course, one shouldn't overstate Descartes' originality. The way to Descartes' view was paved by (a) a tendency to more mechanistic explanations by scholastic Aristotelians (Pasnau 2004: 38); (b) the rise of the mixed mathematical Aristotelian science of mechanics (Hattab 2009: chapters 5 and 6) and the revival of atomist physics by Gorlaeus (Hattab 2009: chapters 7 and 8). For instance, Gorlaeus had already proposed replacing the Aristotelian notion of accident with modes.
18. Descartes allows for talk of natures or essences of particular things, without making any effort to reconcile them with his claims about the essence of bodily and thinking substance. Hattab (2009: 56) suggests that Suárez's distinction between essences and natures may explain why Descartes was untroubled by this.
19. I am implying that this is a problem, and many have thought so. But, it is conceivable that Descartes would disagree and that other mechanists would disagree.
20. I use the Aristotelian phrase 'local motion' here to refer to change of place or of spatial position, which is what people nowadays usually refer to as motion. I do so to be clear that I am not referring to other sorts of changes that Aristotelians regard as kinds of motion: substantial change, qualitative change and quantitative change.
21. This is the basis for the common criticism that Descartes' explanation of the essence

of body as extension makes it difficult to explain the dynamic, active properties of bodies. For instance, see Gassendi (LoLordo 2005: 97).
22. The notion that local motion must have an external cause is expressed by Aristotle's 'exteriority principle' in *Physics* VII, 1, 241b24. For a discussion of the principle and how it was interpreted by medieval commentators, see Leijenhorst (2002: 172–9).
23. According to Waterlow (1982: 31–8, esp. paragraph 43), this is one of Aristotle's reasons for rejecting mechanism. More specifically, mechanism would not allow acknowledging that different things have distinctive natures that explain the changes they undergo. According to Waterlow, Aristotle rejects this conclusion in the *Physics* at II, 1, 193a-9. This criticism of mechanism is also evident in Voetius' criticism that Descartes requires external motors to account for all movements, which he regards as absurd (van Ruler 1995: 177–8). Voetius' criticism relied on a scholastic and early modern line of argument showing that natural objects are inherently active, which was used against atomists and early occasionalists (van Ruler 1995: 178–86).
24. There are, of course, other problems. For instance, Descartes' view on the essence of body makes it difficult to explain how forces belong to bodies (see Garber 1992: 293–9). I here focus on problems that would have troubled those who do not accept the mechanistic outlook of the New Philosophy.
25. The question here about the origin of motions is different from the question of occasionalism, that is, of whether Descartes rules out the efficacy of finite causes. For instance, Garber (1992: 305) argues that Descartes is not an occasionalist, but that he locates the beginning of all motion in God. The problem with explaining the origin of motion is also a problem for Hobbes (Leijenhorst 2002: 210–11).
26. This same line of reasoning, with this same example, is also found much earlier in Ockham (*Quodlibet* 3.6). For discussions of Suárez's arguments against substantial forms, see Schmaltz (2012); Des Chene (1996: chapter 3).
27. Along these lines, Pasnau argues that Boyle, Malebranche and Locke all offered mechanistic interpretations of substantial forms (Pasnau 2004: 60–70).
28. It is important to note that Descartes' move here is only effective because he is working with a different understanding of change. If Descartes understood change as the transition from potential to actual, then he would be forced to conclude that the teaching belongs to the student, since the change is the realisation of the student's potential, which would entail that the action, as a way of describing the change, belongs to the subject of the change: the student. Unfortunately, Descartes does not communicate his alternative conception of change. Presumably he is thinking about change in more mechanical terms. Consider the case of the cue ball striking the eight ball, transferring its motion so that the cue ball comes to rest and the eight ball rolls into the corner pocket. In this example, the change is the transfer of motion from one ball to the other, which appears to happen equally in both the agent and the patient. In an example like this, it is less natural to conceive of the change as the transition from potential to actual, since this locates the change in only one party: the patient.
29. There is more to the definition of essence. Spinoza also asserts the converse of the quoted claim: the thing is also necessary and sufficient for the essence. This complication need not concern us here.
30. Here I am skipping over certain complications. Spinoza says that it is the actual essence, but it's not clear how to understand that. These issues do not bear on my view. Also, I am not claiming here that Spinoza equates *conatus* with essence generally, but only that he identifies *conatus* as the essence of individuals, that is, of particular existing things.

31. Spinoza does make some claims about forms (for instance, see E2p10, E2l4dem, E2p21dem), but he does not understand forms in the Aristotelian hylomorphic sense as what is added to matter to create being or substance.
32. Whether Spinoza's philosophy qualifies as thoroughly mechanistic is a difficult question. His conception that bodies are properly understood through the attribute of extension shares much with Cartesian mechanism. However, he also resists mechanism in several ways. First, he tends to think of composite individuals as wholes rather than merely the sum of the interplay between their parts (Jonas 1973: 269). Second, he suggests that our conceptions of bodies as divisible and measurable spatial quantities is a product of the imagination, which is contrary to a proper understanding of extension through reason (E1p15, Ep12). Third, it does not seem that *conatus* can be understood simply as an inertial tendency or force (Viljanen 2011: 109–10). Consequently, since *conatus* is responsible for the dynamic properties of bodies, it seems that Spinoza's physical theory rests on a notion that lies outside the usual mechanistic toolbox of matter and forces. Fourth, it is not clear that Spinoza understands efficient causation in the same way as mechanists (Viljanen 2011: chapter 2).
33. On the nature of simple bodies, see Garrett (1994: 78–82).
34. On the history of the notion of *conatus*, see Viljanen (2011: 84–91). For Descartes' notion of conatus – and for the previous history of the term – see Garau (2014). On Hobbes' notion of *conatus*, see Leijenhorst (2002: 196–203). It is not entirely clear that *conatus* is purely a mechanistic notion. Springborg (2016) argues Hobbes isn't a materialist because his notion of *conatus* is not a material thing.
35. Here I agree with Viljanen (2011: 79–82).
36. Most notably, Aristotelians understand powers as potentials, which they understand in relation to the actual. Spinoza, in contrast, holds that everything possible is actual (E1p33), which prevents him from recognising the same sort of contrast between the potential and actual. For an extended discussion of Spinoza and scholastic Aristotelians on *potentia*, see Viljanen (2011: 59–67, 79).
37. *Potentia* is the Latin rendering of the Greek *dunamis*, Aristotle's term for power.
38. Here I am sidestepping the complicated question as to whether this counts as teleological (though I think it does). For more on whether Spinoza's view is teleological, see Garrett (2003); Carriero (2005); Viljanen (2011: 112–25); Sangiacomo (2016).
39. More specifically, he defines joy as an increase in our perfection, which he describes as an increase in our power of acting (E3ad3 explanation; see also E3p28dem), in other words an increase in the strength of one's *conatus*. He also claims that *conatus* works toward increasing one's power when he claims that our *conatus* is directed to what is good (E3p9s), which he understands as what promotes our power (E4p8dem). Similarly, he claims that our *conatus* is directed to things that we love (E3p13s), which he defines as things that promote – or that we perceive to promote – our power (E3ad6).
40. The definition also implies that a thing is passive when it works jointly with other causes to bring about some effect. For instance, when a team of horses pulls a wagon, each horse is passive.
41. There are many passages where Spinoza claims that the patients of exogenous effects are active in the sense that the effects are caused partly by their natures as *conatus*. Since I have discussed this view at length elsewhere (Kisner forthcoming), I only discuss one here. See also E2l3ax1, E3post1, E4p29dem.
42. Of course, it would be misleading to say that all of a thing's effects are brought about by its nature or *conatus*. For Spinoza, there is an important distinction between

effects brought about by a thing's *conatus*, which necessarily contribute to a thing's preservation or increase its power, and exogenous effects, which may be harmful. Spinoza's point is that the latter sorts of effects are also brought about to some degree by a thing's *conatus*, though not to a sufficient degree that those effects are necessarily beneficial.
43. I disagree here with the view that freedom consists in causal independence rather than self-determination. For a response, see Kisner (forthcoming).
44. It is somewhat surprising that Spinoza's views on autonomy are often overlooked. Presumably this is partly because discussion of autonomy is primarily of interest to ethicists and work on Spinoza has not focused on his ethics. This may be due to the widespread view that Spinoza intends to deflate ethics and reject morality as a kind of illusion (Kisner and Youpa 2014).
45. My distinction here between relational theories of autonomy that regard social relations as conditions for developing autonomy or as necessary to the exercise of one's autonomy is intended to map onto Stoljar's distinction between causal and constitutive theories of relational autonomy respectively (Stoljar 2015: section 3). As Friedman points out (1997: 56–8), the constitutive theory of relational autonomy is the more substantive and controversial commitment. Indeed, merely claiming that relations are necessary for the development of autonomy is perhaps trivially true.
46. This line of argument is present in Armstrong (2009: 51–2, 55), but is not presented explicitly in the way that I formulate it here.
47. Though this way is not unconsidered in the literature. The view is suggested by Balibar, when he writes that, for Spinoza, 'the essence of causality is the unity of activity and passivity . . . within one and the same "subject" (or individual, as Spinoza prefers to say), a unity which defines the individual's singular conatus and relates it to an infinite multiplicity of other individuals' (Balibar 1997: 15, see also 21).
48. Armstrong 2009 focuses on the notion that Spinoza denies an atomistic conception of the individual. For more on this, see Jonas (1973); Sackstedder (1978); Balibar (1997); Ravven (1998).
49. Spinoza offers different explanations for what constitutes individuals of different kinds. For instance, he claims that individual composite bodies are determined by unvarying spatial relations among other bodies (E2p13def). This account clearly cannot explain individual minds, nor can it explain individual simple bodies, which have no parts; rather, he explains individual simple bodies purely in terms of their motions (E2p13sl3). This explanation of individual composite bodies appears – to me, at least – to be different from his explanation of individual singular things, since it is possible that things may contribute jointly to some effect – thereby forming an individual singular thing – even though they do not maintain fixed spatial relations, and, thus, do not form an individual composite body, such as the contributors to this anthology. Nevertheless, Spinoza's explanation of individual composite bodies is continuous with his explanation of individual singular things. This is because individual composite bodies are constituted by aggregates that work to bring about a particular effect: the maintenance of fixed spatial relations among their parts.
50. Descartes' criticism of substantial forms is connected to the common complaint that they are occult (Hattab 2009: 17–24). On his criticisms generally, see Rozemond (2002: chapter 4); Hattab (2009).
51. There is another notable difference between an accident and a mode: a mode depends

for its existence on the substance in which it inheres, unlike accidents, which – at least, on some accounts – can persist through changes in substance (as in the Eucharist).
52. If he even intends to do so. For a discussion of the problems see Garber (1992: 175–80); Des Chene (1996: chapter 8, section 1); Ariew (2011: chapter 4). One should note that mechanism generally has difficulty explaining individuation (Leijenhorst 2002: 166–70).
53. For Spinoza on parts and wholes see Sackstedder (1978).
54. Thus, Spinoza's theory of individuals is continuous with his theory of *conatus*. Claiming that the essence of a singular thing is its *conatus* implies that whether some aggregate of ideas or some aggregate of bodies counts as some individual things (say, me) is determined by whether their powers collectively constitute my *conatus*, in other words whether they work collectively to bring about the effects of maintaining my existence and increasing my power.
55. In this vein, Armstrong (2009: 56) argues that Spinoza's individuals are 'permeable and dynamic'.
56. This is very different from the Aristotelian route, which, by itself, does not problematise the self or expand the boundaries of the individual self.

Works Cited

Alanen, Lili (2003), *Descartes's Concept of Mind*, Cambridge, MA: Harvard University Press.
Aquinas, Saint Thomas (1950), *De principiis naturae*, ed. John J. Pauson, Fribourge: Société Philosophique.
Aquinas, Saint Thomas (1961), *Commentary on Aristotle's Metaphysics*, trans. John P. Rowan, Notre Dame: Dumb Ox Books.
Aquinas, Saint Thomas (1981), *The Summa Theologica of Saint Thomas Aquinas*, Christian Classics, English Dominican Province Translation edition, New York: Glencoe Publishing Company.
Ariew, Roger (2011), *Descartes among the Scholastics*, Leiden: Brill.
Aristotle (1993), *Metaphysics* (Books 1–9), Loeb Classical Library, ed. and trans. Hugh Tredennick, Cambridge, MA: Harvard University Press.
Aristotle (2008), *Physics*, Oxford: Oxford University Press.
Armstrong, Aurelia (2009), 'Autonomy and the Relational Individual: Spinoza and Feminism', in Moira Gatens (ed.), *Feminist Interpretations of Benedict Spinoza*, University Park: Pennsylvania State University Press, pp. 43–64.
Balibar, Etienne (1997), 'Spinoza: From Individuality to Transindividuality', Mededelingen vanwege het Spinozahuis, Delft: Eburon.
Brison, Susan (2000), 'Relational Autonomy and Freedom of Expression', in Catriona Mackenzie and Natalie Stoljar (eds), *Relational Autonomy: Feminist Perspectives on Autonomy, Agency and the Social Self*, Oxford: Oxford University Press, pp. 280–300.
Carriero, John (2005), 'Spinoza on Final Causality', in Daniel Garber and Steven Nadler (eds), *Oxford Studies in Early Modern Philosophy*, 2, Oxford: Oxford University Press, pp. 105–47.
Christman, John (2004), 'Relational Autonomy, Liberal Individualism, and the Social Constitution of Selves', *Philosophical Studies*, 117: 143–64.
Des Chene, Dennis (1996), *Physiologia: Natural Philosophy in Late Aristotelian and Cartesian Thought*, Ithaca: Cornell University Press.

Douglas, Alexander (2015), *Spinoza and Dutch Cartesianism*, Oxford: Oxford University Press.
Friedman, Marilyn (1997), 'Autonomy and Social Relationships: Rethinking the Feminist Critique', in Virginia Held and Alison Jaggar (eds), *Feminists Rethink the Self*, New York: Westview Press, pp. 40–61.
Friedman, Marilyn (2000), 'Autonomy, Social Disruption and Women', in Catriona Mackenzie and Natalie Stoljar (eds), *Relational Autonomy: Feminist Perspectives on Autonomy, Agency and the Social Self*, Oxford: Oxford University Press, pp. 35–71.
Garau, Rodolfo (2014), 'Late-Scholastic and Cartesian Conatus', *Intellectual History Review*, 24: 479–94.
Garber, Daniel (1992), *Descartes' Metaphysical Physics*, Chicago: The University of Chicago Press.
Garrett, Don (1994), 'Spinoza's Theory of Metaphysical Individuation', in Jorge Gracia and Kenneth Barber (eds), *Individuation in Early Modern Philosophy*, Albany: State University of New York Press, pp. 73–101.
Garrett, Don (2003), 'Teleology in Spinoza and Early Modern Rationalism', in Rocco Gennaro and Charles Huenemann (eds), *New Essays on the Rationalists*, Oxford: Oxford University Press, pp. 310–35.
Hattab, Helen (2009), *Descartes on Forms and Mechanisms*, Cambridge: Cambridge University Press.
Jonas, Hans (1973), 'Spinoza and the Theory of Organism', in Marjorie Grene (ed.), *Spinoza: A Collection of Critical Essays*, Garden City: Anchor Books, pp. 259–78.
Kisner, Matthew (2008), 'Spinoza's Virtuous Passions', *Review of Metaphysics*, 61: 759–83.
Kisner, Matthew (2011), *Spinoza on Human Freedom: Reason, Autonomy and the Good Life*, Cambridge: Cambridge University Press.
Kisner, Matthew (forthcoming), 'Spinoza Activities: Freedom without Independence', in Noa Naaman and Tom Vinci (eds), *Spinoza on Freedom and the Passions*, Cambridge: Cambridge University Press.
Kisner, Matthew and Andrew Youpa (2014), 'Introduction', in Matthew Kisner and Andrew Youpa (eds), *Essays on Spinoza's Ethical Theory*, Oxford: Oxford University Press, pp. 1–19.
Leijenhorst, Cees (2002), *The Mechanisation of Aristotelianism*, Leiden: Brill.
LoLordo, Antonia (2005), 'The Activity of Matter in Gassendi's Physics', *Oxford Studies in Early Modern Philosophy*, 2: 75–104.
Mackenzie, Catriona and Natalie Stoljar (2000), 'Autonomy Refigured', in Catriona Mackenzie and Natalie Stoljar (eds), *Relational Autonomy: Feminist Perspectives on Autonomy, Agency and the Social Self*, Oxford: Oxford University Press, pp. 3–34.
Manning, Gideon (2012), 'Three Biased Reminders about Hylomorphism in Early Modern Science and Philosophy', in G. Manning (ed.), *Matter and Form in Early Modern Science and Philosophy*, Leiden: Brill, pp. 1–32.
Meyers, Diana Tietjens (1989), *Self, Society and Personal Choice*, New York: Columbia University Press.
Nedelsky, Jennifer (1989), 'Reconceiving Autonomy: Sources, Thoughts and Possibilities', *Yale Journal of Law and Feminism*, 1: 7–36.
Oshana, Marina (2006), *Personal Autonomy in Society*, Aldershot: Ashgate Publishing.
Pasnau, Robert (2004), 'Form, Substance, and Mechanism', *Philosophical Review*, 113: 31–88.
Ravven, Heidi (1998), 'Spinoza's Individualism Reconsidered: Some Lessons from the

Short Treatise on God, Man, and his Well-Being', *Iyyun, The Jerusalem Philosophical Quarterly*, 47: 265–92.
Rozemond, Marleen (2002), *Descartes's Dualism*, Cambridge, MA: Harvard University Press.
Sackstedder, William (1978), 'Spinoza on Part and Whole: the Worm's Eye View', in Robert Shahan and J. I. Biro (eds), *Spinoza: New Perspectives*, Norman: University of Oklahoma Press, pp. 139–59.
Sanches, Francisco (1998), *That Nothing is Known*, Elaine Limbrick and Douglas Thomson (eds), Cambridge: Cambridge University Press.
Sangiacomo, Andrea (2016), 'Aristotle, Heereboord, and the Polemical Target of Spinoza's Critique of Final Causes', *Journal of the History of Philosophy*, 54: 395–420.
Schmaltz, Tad (2012), 'Substantial Forms as Causes: From Suarez to Descartes', in G. Manning (ed.), *Matter and Form in Early Modern Science and Philosophy*, Leiden: Brill, pp. 125–50.
Schmitt, Charles (1983), *Aristotle and the Renaissance*, Cambridge, MA: Harvard University Press.
Springborg, Patricia (2016), 'Hobbes Materialism and Epicurean Mechanism', *British Journal of the History of Philosophy*, 24: 814–35.
Stoljar, Natalie (2015), 'Feminist Perspectives on Autonomy', in Edward Zalta (ed.), *The Stanford Encyclopedia of Philosophy*, <https://plato.stanford.edu/archives/fall2015/entries/feminism-autonomy/> (last accessed 7 November 2018).
Suárez, Francisco (2000), *On the Formal Cause of Substance: Metaphysical Disputation XV*, trans. John Kronen and Jeremiah Reedy, Milwaukee: Marquette University Press.
Van Ruler, J. A. (1995), *The Crisis of Causality: Voetius and Descartes on God, Nature and Change*, Leiden: Brill.
Viljanen, Valtteri (2011), *Spinoza's Geometry of Power*, Cambridge: Cambridge University Press.
Vlastos, Gregory (1969), 'Reasons and Causes in the *Phaedo*', *Philosophical Review*, 78: 291–325.
Waterlow, Sarah (1982), *Nature, Change, and Agency in Aristotle's Physics*, Oxford: Clarendon Press.

5

Spinoza's Path from Imaginative Transindividuality to Intuitive Relational Autonomy: From Fusion, Confusion and Fragmentation to Moral Integrity

Heidi M. Ravven

In Spinoza's Scheme, 'interaction' (Wechselwirkung) . . . is not derived, it is originary, already involved in the elementary pattern of every causal action. (Balibar 1997)

1. Overview of the Argument

My contribution to the argument that Spinoza anticipated a strong version and specific theory of relational autonomy will be to expand our understanding of the relational character of the cognitive–affective–social life governed by the imagination. I will, first, bring into the discussion several crucial propositions in the *Ethics* about the transindividual relational origin and ongoing constitution of the individual mind and, then, I will turn to the *Theological-Political Treatise* (TTP) to clarify and augment our understanding of the transindividual sociality of the imagination and the political life of the imagination as developed in that text in great detail and depth. Hence, I will call attention to the primitive merger of self and environment that drives the fanaticism and slavery of political tyranny and religious superstition in the life dominated by the imagination. I argue that Spinoza is describing how narrow biographical and cultural and historical experience put together a world, a context, which each of us is born into and born out of. It is that world with which the self is initially and unreflectively, but not smoothly or without conflict, merged. While individual impulsivity and conflict at this stage is a problem, I maintain that it is not the most significant one or the most important one to resolve, in Spinoza's view. At this stage, I argue here as elsewhere, merger, near complete absorption in time and place and group and world, integrates individual desires as the group mind, and too often as group fanaticism, for the dominant structure here is merger into the group while individual impulsivity and conflict and rivalry are secondary and ancillary. My analysis here expands and nuances Balibar's trenchant description of the transindividuality of the person dominated by the imagination:

> [T]his structure [of imagination] is originally relational or transindividual: not only does it confront us with a picture of consciousness in which every

relationship that 'I' can have with 'Myself' is mediated by the Other (more precisely: an image of the Other), but it also shows that the life of imagination is a circular process of successive 'identifications', where I recognize the Other from Myself, and Myself from the Other.[1]

Balibar concludes, '[i]magination is already transindividual because it consists of partial mimetic processes in which both ideas and affects are involved'.[2] I augment this basic theoretical two-person analysis with Spinoza's extension of the model to the social and political group of the TTP. Hence, my paper brings into the discussion the primitive group mind, the social mind as it manifests itself in politics and religion, the two great societal expressions and institutionalisations of the imagination according to the TTP.

Moreover, I argue here that it is the subservience to group and the local world, and the instability of such an imaginative life, that engender the very urge to freedom, and ultimately to individuation. It is precisely the desire for liberation from the initial primitive servitude of often fanatical, and, at the least, emotionally over-intense and unstable passive merger that drives the path to freedom delineated in the *Ethics*, from imagination, through reason, and culminating in intuitive knowledge. For it is largely the urge to emerge from social subservience – which Spinoza's conceptions of passivity and emotional servitude underlie – that drives the entire journey of the psychological and moral transformation of the *Ethics* and without which it cannot be understood or undertaken. It is that merger that initiates the vision of freedom as the desire for freedom from it, because its passivity is felt as constriction, subservience and even enslavement as well as a painful vulnerability to the rollercoaster of fate. Nevertheless, the final accomplishment is not a Freudian-style individualist autonomy but instead reconciles full individuation with full relation; it is a sociality that is not just of utility to the accomplishment of one's basic and higher needs and desires (which I agree with Balibar principally characterises Spinoza's stage of reason based on shared Common Notions[3]), but instead strives for a fuller reconciliation of the two.

For intuitive knowledge, in principle, reconciles one's very singular constitution, one's full independence of mind, with one's infinite causal relations and interactions. It offers the only possibility of an adequate first-person perspective and stance, yet one that is within, and filled in with, the full infinite and shared, universal understanding of the complexity of nature. It is the accomplishment of the view from this very singular point in and by the infinite networks of causes, a network that is at the same time common to all things in the universe as their explanatory constitution. Intuitive knowledge begins with one's singular and social and cultural experiences as they inform the *conatus*, one's emotional patterns, and hence constitute the transindividual self of origin, and reorders them, integrates them into the universe of causal networks from the self out, as explanatory of them. Hence it begins with oneself and moves outward – but that beginning is not isolation but merger. Here we have Spinoza's anticipation, and his own theory and psychology of what we now call relational autonomy. Spinoza has solved one aspect of the problem of the One and the Many. Yet I argue here that there is still another move: in a final move one's own singularity – one's images, that is to say one's emotions, as ordered and constituted by interactions with the external world and by memory, that is, by the imagination – recedes as even a starting point for reflection, and perhaps to some extent the mind can be filled with God as such, manifesting God's knowledge–love and not only the human knowledge–love of God. Only then are all minds one.

2. The Transindividual Origin and Constitution of the Individual

Perception, according to Spinoza, is always of our relations and those relations constitute each of us. All perception, of both internal states and of the external world, originates in the awareness of how the body is affected, and captures precisely that interaction of body and environment by which the body is affected: 'The human Mind does not know the body itself, nor does it know that it exists except through ideas of affections by which the Body is affected'.[4]

We have no privileged access through perception to either the mind or the body, for there is no direct internal access, nor is there direct perceptual access to external objects or events, for 'the ideas that we have of external bodies indicate the condition of our own body more than the nature of external bodies'.[5] Furthermore, peering into our own individual minds can never reveal clear ideas, for Spinoza maintains that 'the idea that constitutes the nature of the human Mind is not, when considered in itself alone, clear and distinct'.[6] That is to say, ideas are not of isolated discrete objects, even of ourselves as a discrete and isolated object. Spinoza writes that (E2p28) 'the ideas of the affections of the human Body, insofar as they are related only to the human Mind, are not clear and distinct, but confused'. For, according to that proposition's Demonstration, 'the ideas of the affections of the human Body involve the nature of external bodies as much as that of the human Body'.

This perceiving and knowing in the human person, and not only in God, is what ideas are (E2def3). For a mind is not a thing that has ideas but is the process of forming ideas, that is, thinking. Thinking, a dynamic process and not a container of ideas, is also what a mind is, what its ideas are:

> [T]o have a true idea means nothing other than knowing a thing perfectly . . . And of course no one can doubt this unless he thinks that an idea is something mute, like a picture on a tablet, and not a mode of thinking, viz. the very [act of] understanding.[7]

Because the essence of our Mind consists only in knowledge, of which God is the beginning and foundation (by 1p15 and 2p47s), it is clear to us how our Mind, with respect both to essence and existence, follows from the divine nature, and continually depends on God[8] and since in God thinking and acting are dynamic (E2p7c), hence so they are also in us. Yet even from the infinite or eternal perspective and not only from the human one, insofar as the nature of this particular human mind can be traced by itself alone to God, it cannot be understood. For

> this idea [of each of our minds] will be in God insofar as he is considered to be affected by the ideas of a great many singular things. Therefore, God has the idea of the human Body, *or* knows the human Body, insofar as he is affected by a great many *other* ideas, and not insofar as he constitutes the nature of the human Mind.[9]

Hence neither minds nor bodies are discrete and have their source and explanation in any singular mind/body considered alone. Even God does not know the human mind as such, as discrete, but only in its interactions, and hence we can come to know our own minds only by taking note of, that is, perceiving our interactions and interrelations in, how those affect us both physically and mentally. To know those interactions by which the body is affected is, however, precisely what it is to know the human mind not only for us but for God:

> But the ideas of the affections of the Body [i.e. its felt and perceived interactions] are in God insofar as he constitutes the nature of human Mind; *or* the human Mind perceives the same affections (by p12), and consequently (by p16) the human Body itself, as actually existing (by p17). Therefore to that extent only, the human Mind perceives the human Body itself, q.e.d.[10]

God knows the human mind only in its interactions, and hence we can know our own minds only by our perceptions that capture our interactions and interrelations and how those affect us both physically and mentally. The clarity comes with the grasp of the causal sources of a given interaction.

Even from the divine perspective there is not an individual, constituted of mind and body, prior to engagement, who then interacts. Just these ongoing interactions and interrelations that our minds perceive (and our bodies enact) are what constitute the nature of the human mind in God, which is to say, as such. We come about in our interactions and interrelations and we can come to know ourselves only in them and as them, for

> [t]he idea of a singular thing which actually exists has God for a cause not insofar as he is infinite, but insofar as he is considered to be affected by another idea of a singular thing which actually exists; and of this [idea] God is also the cause, insofar as he is affected by another third, and so *to infinity*.[11]

It is the network of causes from which we are produced, body and mind, and by which it is knowable, and known as that juncture – and that is what it is because it is that way in God and not just appears that way to ourselves. When Spinoza informs us that '[t]he human Mind perceives the nature of a great many bodies together with the nature of its own body',[12] we can draw the inference that we perceive and come to know ourselves only as embedded in causal contexts and as interactively constituted by them.[13]

3. The Transindividual Nature of Images

We further discover that even images have a transindividual origin and, even or especially, a transindividual nature, for Spinoza says that 'we shall call images' 'the *affections of the human Body* whose ideas present external bodies as present to us'.[14] Hence images are changes in and states of our own body that capture and enact the effects of one's interrelations with the world, and embed them within (and as) the self. Hence it is hardly surprising that 'the ideas we have of external bodies indicate the constitution of our own body more than the nature of external bodies'.[15] Nevertheless, 'the Mind does not know itself, except in so far as it perceives ideas of affections of the Body',[16] that is, through its images – and these images are affectively charged since 'an idea of the affection of the body' is also and precisely Spinoza's definition of emotion (E3def3).

Interactions can be perceived and remembered because they affect one's own body. One can come to know oneself only through the effect upon oneself of these interactions, Spinoza insists, and the interrelational encounters are formed and stored as images-emotions. Hence our minds encounter both self and world not only in but as interactions, as particular interactions affect us (our body–mind) and constitute our idea of the body, which is to say, the self, for the urge of the *conatus* spans mental and physical. Body and mind bring together self and world, imbuing the relation with the urge to persist. The idea of the mind, its structure as well as its content, is rooted in and comes about in our engagements, our embeddedness in our environments. The activity of the mind, which the mind is – and which ideas are, too – relates, brings together, self and world because it captures the body's interactions, the body's reactions, and not the body in isolation prior to, or apart from, its interactions. Individuality emerges from the *conatus* – from the *conatus*'s integration, and ongoing urge toward coherent integration, of these interactions as the individual's particular ratio, its unique homeodynamic stability and identity. And hence the *conatus* – this stable relation of parts and maintenance of coherence amidst the destabilising forces of interaction with the environment – is the essence of each individual (body and mind), its ratio. The mind's *conatus* strives to perpetuate its ideas and stable coherence, as it strives to perpetuate the body's coherence as constituting its ongoing identity as an individual and as this individual made up of the organised and organising ('order') of its interrelationships and interactions. Moreover, 'in just the same way as thoughts and ideas of things are ordered and connected in the Mind, so the affections of the body, or images of things are ordered and connected in the body' (E5p1). It is the ordering energy of the *conatus* as it reflects, brings together, a person's constitutive and unique interactional experiences and engagements that is the source of individuality, which hence is more of a process than a thing. The *conatus* carves out sections of the infinite causal interactions and interrelations as selves, as different bodies–minds, loci of magnetic pull.

4. The Transindividual Constitution of the Body

It has been widely noted[17] that the individual body in its constitution has a relational character according to Spinoza, for he defines individual bodies as, 'distinguished from one another in respect of motion and rest' (E2p13l1). Hence they are not substances (as Descartes held) but instead are defined in terms of their stable internal relations of parts:

> bodies are not distinguished in respect to substance; what constitutes the form of the Individual consists (NS [*Nagelate Schriften*]: only) in the union of bodies ... But this (NS: union) by hypothesis is retained even if a continual change of bodies occurs. Therefore, the individual will retain its nature.[18]

An individual he defines as 'an unvarying relation of movement among themselves' of 'a number of bodies of the same or of different size', so that they 'are united with one another' by contiguity or so 'that they communicate their motions to each other in a certain fixed manner'.[19]

> If the parts composing an Individual thing become greater or less, but in such a proportion that they all keep the same ratio of motion and rest to each other as before, then the Individual will likewise retains its nature as before.[20]

And this obtains to an object in motion as well as at rest. Such composite individuals 'can be affected in many ways, and still preserve [their] nature'.[21]

Moreover such composite individuals are not discrete but can be nested in each other, in larger and larger ones to infinity so that 'we shall easily conceive that the whole of nature is one Individual, whose parts, i.e. all bodies, vary in infinite ways, without any change of the whole individual'.[22] As Yitzhak Melamed points out, 'it may well be the case that Spinoza intentionally designed the building blocks of his finite world as fuzzy units, in order to stress their inferiority to the self-subsisting, self-explaining, and well-defined substance'.[23] Melamed goes on to conjecture that according to Spinoza's definition, an individual could include even these seeming outliers:

> [T]he stipulation that parts of the same individual 'communicate their motions to each other' and preserve the same proportion of motion and rest does not tell us *how long* these parts should preserve the same proportion in order to be counted as genuine individuals. In fact, Spinoza *cannot* name any particular period of time as such a minimum criterion without resorting to the human-centered perspective. If we disregard the human point of view, there is nothing more natural in a temporal scale that measures things by billions of years, or billionths of a second, than the temporal units we are accustomed to.

Hence, even the tiniest period of time in which two bodies communicate their motions in a fixed manner seems to be enough to qualify these two bodies as a genuine individual.[24]

Spinoza mentions several times in his works that the social group can come to be an individual, as we see, for example, in the scholium to Part 4 proposition 18 of the *Ethics*, where he writes:

> [I]f, for example, two individuals of entirely the same nature are joined to one another, they compose an individual twice as powerful as each one. To man, then there is nothing more useful than man. Man, I say, can wish for nothing more helpful to the preservation of his being than that all should so agree in all things that the Minds and Bodies of all would compose, as it were, one Mind and one Body; that all strive together, as far as they can, to preserve their being; and that all, together, should seek for themselves the common advantage of all.

The maintenance of the bodily proportion (ratio) that maintains individuals as such is also manifested in and as their essential desire, their *conatus*. Hence here we find the *conatus* being attributed to the individual, the one mind and one body, that is the social or political group. And that is the main theme of the *Theological-Political Treatise*, both when the group *conatus* strives to persist based on its clear and distinct ideas but also when it endeavours to persist in its own being via its confused ideas (E3p9). The TTP could be thought of as a work in which Spinoza describes in detail what constitutes a deleterious imaginative group mind and how to transform it into a beneficial, yet still imaginative one. For both politics and religion are imaginative phenomena and forms of life, according to him, but can, and ought, to be recruited and shaped to serve the common good rather than disrupt and corrupt it, as is often the case.

5. The Group Mind: The Imaginative Society and Polity

Spinoza presents the imagination as engendering a primitive form of sociality, creating and inducing a subrational conformity, the group mind and body. He writes for example in the *Political Treatise*:

> [T]he whole body of the state is called a Body Politic; . . . the Right of the state, or of the supreme powers . . . is determined . . . by the power of the multitude, which is led as if by one mind . . .
>
> Both in the state of nature and in the civil order man acts according to the laws of his own nature and looks after his own advantage. In each condition, I say, man is guided by hope or fear . . . The principal difference between each condition is that in the civil order everyone fears the same things and that for everyone there is one and the same cause of security and principle of living.[25]

In this characterisation of how an imaginative sociality can be introduced in the masses so as to produce and maintain a polity, a society comes about by the institutionalisation of incentives and disincentives that drive common fears and hopes, punishments and rewards, so that common desires emerge, a social *conatus* of the Social Individual, so to speak. A polity can be organised to become one mind and one body through the political and institutional and ideological conformity and convergence imposed by the state. In this conception of the social and political role and function of the imagination, Spinoza is displaying the influence of Maimonides and the Arabic philosophical tradition of Alfarabi, who characterised imagination as foundational to the political capacity par excellence, and the recruitment and disciplining of the imagination toward a politics of justice and good governance its most important and beneficial use. In its focus on engendering the social and political body, Maimonides' theory of the imagination strongly distinguishes it from modern theories. The Arabic Aristotelian philosophical tradition of political theory invented and developed an account of the imagination as supremely suited, at best, to the service of establishing and governing the virtuous state. Maimonides, following Alfarabi, had interpreted the philosophical commonplace that the focus of the imagination is on the body, as meaning that its focus was upon the political and social body. In the TTP we discover the decisive influence of it upon Spinoza's account of the polity and of the role of religion within it. One of Spinoza's innovations here seems to be that to the imagination is also attributed the great corruptive force in the state of what Spinoza terms superstition, which includes tyranny and fanaticism, as well as mere bodily impulse and perhaps greed, as the Arabic Aristotelians would have it.

Maimonides (1963) had informed the reader of the *Guide of the Perplexed* (in 3: 27) that Jewish 'Law as a whole aims at two things: the welfare of the soul and the welfare of the body.' Yet it is apparent that by 'body' he was referring to the social body as the means to individual well-being.

> As for the welfare of the body, it comes about by the improvement of their ways of living with one another. This is achieved through two things. One of them is the abolition of their wronging each other.... The second thing consists in the acquisition by every human individual of moral qualities that are useful for life in society so that the affairs of the city may be ordered.... Know that as between these two aims, one is indubitably greater in nobility, namely, the welfare of the soul – I mean the procuring of correct opinions – while the second aim, the welfare of the body – is prior in nature and in time. The latter aim consists in the governance of the city and the well-being of the states of all its people according to their capacity.

Spinoza adopts Maimonides' elision of the imagination's concern for the body proper with the concern for the social body, a conflation theoretically supported by Spinoza's account of the transindividual constitution of individuals. For someone versed in the *Guide of the Perplexed*, there is no cause for wonder that Spinoza's treatment of politics and religion centres on an analysis of the social character and political uses of the imagination, that is, that it is the imagination that is charged with engendering common beliefs, practices, laws and mores in the masses. For Spinoza adopts what is a commonplace in Maimonides, namely the social focus and political function of the imagination as both engendering but also regulating the social body.

Moreover, both Maimonides and Spinoza recommend the use of imaginative means to create and maintain the virtuous state. And both recommend the employment of the imagination in the formation and governance of such a polity as a ruse to conduce the masses to an ethical life more practically rational than the means employed. While Spinoza's theory of the imagination is all too often mistakenly interpreted as primarily separating people and engendering conflict while his account of reason is interpreted, in contrast, as that which brings a community into accord, Spinoza clearly insisted that the masses, and hence society as a whole, could never operate according to reason. '[T]hose who are persuaded that the masses ... can be induced to live only according to the prescription of reason are dreaming of the Golden Age of the Poets, or of a myth', he wrote. 'For freedom of mind ... is a private virtue. But the virtue of the state is security', Spinoza informs the reader at the beginning of the *Tractatus Politicus*.[26] The imagination is capable of bringing people together as one mind and body through myth and story and other forms of suasion and symbolic civic practices and legal coercion to produce common belief and obedience. Hence the importance of recruiting a transformed version of religion as social glue and persuasive rhetoric as well as relying on the coercion of law.

Moreover, Spinoza recruited Maimonides' account of 'necessary beliefs' in his *Treatise on Logic* – a concept that Maimonides may have invented – which were beliefs that were not necessarily true but could be induced to engender good behaviour, as foundational to the good society. In the TTP, Spinoza proposed that a civic and ecumenical bare bones religion could be introduced into the state as a set of basic common beliefs underlying and supporting fundamental rules of ethical conduct. They could consist entirely of necessary beliefs, imaginatively inducing obedience to a set of basic tenets even if they were not in fact true. In the *Ethics*, Spinoza comments that people can be induced, 'to live according to the rule of the divine law ... not only by this hope, but also, and especially, by the fear that they may be punished horribly after death'.[27] He came up with an ecumenical – we might call it 'multi-cultural' – code of civil religion in the TTP that every modern society could promulgate which could imaginatively induce in the populace social identification and moral action. Spinoza writes:

> [F]aith does not require tenets which are true as much as it does tenets which are pious, i.e. tenets which move the heart to obedience, even if there are many among them which have not even a shadow of the truth, so long as the person who accepts them does not know them to be false; otherwise, he would necessarily be a rebel.
>
> Only those tenets pertain to the catholic faith, then, which obedience

to God absolutely posits, and which, if they are ignored, make obedience absolutely impossible.[28]

Spinoza thus thinks of religion as a form of collective self-deception, even of wish-fulfilment, which, nevertheless, along with the coercion of laws, is the necessary glue constitutive of and maintaining the Social Body. The theoretical position of the *Ethics* as I have outlined it here, suggests that the references to group mind and social body are not intended by Spinoza as mere metaphors. They cut the world at its joints.

The power of the imaginative passions, especially of fear and hope, to shape belief and hence desire, makes the mind dangerously prone to corruption, for human nature is such that we are prone to believe false hopes rather than face hard truths. 'We are so constituted', Spinoza writes in the *Ethics*, 'that we are ready to believe what we hope and reluctant to believe what we fear, and that we over-estimate and under-estimate in such cases.' The self-deception that resolves cognitive dissonance, as we call it today, that floods the mind with pleasure at the expense of reality, is Spinoza's theme in (E3p13) for he writes that 'when the Mind imagines those things that diminish or restrain the Body's power of acting, it strives, as far as it can, to recollect things that exclude their existence'. Our imaginative beliefs respond to the Pleasure Principle. 'This', Spinoza says, 'is the origin of Superstition to which men are everywhere a prey.'[29] Hence the institutions that mould the group mind and body through the coercion of law and the suasion of common beliefs and desires, create dangerous conditions of political submission and subservience, on the one hand, and intergroup conflict, on the other. Hence the imaginative common life in society, its one mind and one body, induced by fear and hope, religion and politics, is a double-edged sword. For religion's recruitment of the irrational passions of fear and hope as a means of social control creates a group mind that is prone to fanaticism and open to tyrannical abuse. It is a primitive and dangerous kind of merger. Spinoza is concerned with how those in power can manipulate a society, insofar as they control social rewards and punishments and also forms of group belief by suasion, and hence exercise inordinate control over a society's common desires and emotions. Governments in this way all too often gain the compliance of its citizens in their own oppression and complicity in the oppression of others. In a famous passage in the Preface to the TTP Spinoza writes:

> [T]he supreme mystery of despotism, its prop and stay, is to keep men in a state of deception, and with the specious title of religion to cloak the fear by which they must be held in check, so that they will fight for their servitude as if for salvation, and count it no shame, but the highest honor, to spend their blood and their lives for the glorification of one man.

It is the emotional pain and slavery of relational and interactive passivity, what I shall describe as unreflective merger, that primarily set the personal agenda of the *Ethics* (the emotional slavery that Spinoza refers to in Parts 3 and 4 of the *Ethics*), while it is the fanaticism of the group mind that sets the agenda of the TTP. In both cases, the problem to be resolved is how to overcome the deleterious consequences of the local group mind and body. In the *Ethics*, a form of autonomy can be achieved via a path of cognitive-affective transformation: it is toward a Freedom possible for the individual. It is a freedom from passive merger with one's world of origin that, nevertheless, does not eschew relation but instead both globalises it and renders one the initiator of it rather than a mere passive recipient and even the victim of it. It can aptly be designated, relational autonomy.

Yet, according to the TTP, what can be hoped for in a society as a whole is far more limited, namely the employment of the passivity of the imagination toward establishing and maintaining the kind of Group Individual that is an imaginative facsimile of the one mind and one body of individuals who would come to agreement via reason, referred to in the *Ethics* passage quoted above (E4p18s). Yet 'independence of mind', we recall Spinoza telling us, 'is a private virtue'. reason has not the power to achieve such a group mind in the multitude but only in private relationships (such as marriage at its best, E4app20), as Spinoza describes, since the multitude forming a society are necessarily dominated by the operations of the imagination, the passions or passive emotions. In the TTP Spinoza maintains that people in a polity need to be persuaded and induced to political and social conformity but that comes at the price of freedom, for the outward form of the virtuous society is ethical in its principles and actions but the inner state is subordination and subservience – that is, passive obedience. Nevertheless, Spinoza insists in the initial stated purpose and throughout the TTP that such a society must make possible and support the achievement of autonomy for the individual ('the freedom to philosophize'), for those individuals committed to that goal and capable of it.

6. The Transindividuality of Relational Autonomy: Independence of Mind, Moral Integrity and Universal Relation

What the *conatus* strives to maintain, what it strives for as the essence, personality or characteristic desires of a given individual, at first, is the ongoing perpetuation of the given individual's relational images as constituted by her imaginative life, that is, the common (local) order of nature, experience and attitudes. And these, Spinoza tells us, are not only fragmentary and confused but also merge the individual unreflectively into the narrow world of her origin, current environment and often the group. For she is passive, a slave to her environment, to its incentives and meanings, to the imaginative associative order of ideas which is her very self (mind and body), her particular ratio as the *conatus* has been shaped by self-environment encounters and internalised in images and the imaginative environmentally constituted order of images captured in her flesh. Passivity, passive merger with, and reflection of, the arbitrary narrow world of origin turns out often to be slavery, submission and fanaticism, and at best still fraught with narrowness, fear and pain as well as unstable pleasures.

She does not know how to free herself, for she is this imaginatively co-constituted self and nothing more. The project of the *Ethics* is to get out of this closed circle of the merged, and sometimes even fanatical and servile (passive), co-construction of self (desires) and immediate environment. Yet Spinoza envisions liberation from such initial passive imaginative transindividual self-environment merger not in terms of individualist isolation but instead as a cognitive-affective path to active relational autonomy. He outlines a path of cognitive-affective transformation in which the achievement of personal individuation, which is an adequate first-person point of view, and the achievement of independence of mind, on the one hand, and universal transindividual constitution, on the other, come about together and are understood as two sides of one coin. Personal integrity and universal social and natural transindividuality coincide and result in what has now been theorised as relational autonomy, *avant la lettre*.

The self – which is to say, the *conatus* constituted by the given state, scope, directionality and affective charge of its relations – not only engages with life-sustaining exchanges with the environment but, I have argued, is envisioned by Spinoza as the self-reflection into itself of the constitutive relations themselves and also their integration into the patterns of homeodynamic stability (ratio) that maintain individuality and survival. It is this relationally constituted, yet dynamically stable and coherent, individual who comes to aspire to, then develop, and ultimately attain, some degree and form of autonomy. To achieve independence from an initially confused relational merger of origin is the project of the *Ethics*. That autonomy, however, is achieved according to Spinoza not through throwing off and emerging from relationality but instead through a process of globalising or universalising relation, that is, of transindividuality. It is a process that at the same time and in the same way strives to perfect its fundamental relationality as it also makes real and cognitively and affectively available full personal individuation. It is a process of both clarified universal understanding and relation, on the one hand, and fulfilled self-knowledge, enhanced personal agency and relational autonomy, on the other. Let's now turn to how he does this.

It is one of Spinoza's basic principles (E2p7) that '[t]he order and connection of ideas is the same as the order and connection of things'. Hence, the mind in thinking, as the body in (inter)acting, is always co-constituting itself anew in relation to the environment. To achieve independence from an initially confused relational and contextual merger of local origin is the project of the *Ethics*, for Spinoza informs the reader in (E5p29s), that

> [w]e conceive things as actual in two ways: *either insofar as we conceive them to exist in relation to a certain time and place*, or insofar as we conceive them to be contained in God and to follow from the necessity of the divine nature. (emphasis added)

Moreover, Spinoza alludes to the need for independence from the local merger of mind and body as a condition of independence and clarity of mind when he remarks, 'in proportion as the actions of a body depend more on itself alone, and as other bodies concur with it less in acting, so its mind is more capable of understanding distinctly' (E2p13s). It is the mental and affective world constructed by the associative and other passive operations of the imagination delineated in Part 3 (which we can now understand more clearly having reminded ourselves of Spinoza's argument in the TTP) that holds us hostage, as it were, informing our beliefs, desires and even dominating our *conatus* via the incentives and disincentives of the local group mind and social body. (It is not possible to go into the passive operations of the imagination in more detail in this context due to space and time constraints.)

Hence, the form of relational autonomy that Spinoza ultimately envisions rests, first, on a non-individualist conception of the human person at all stages of cognitive-affective development, from imaginative to intuitive. And second, on an account of a path to the achievement of autonomy that entails infinite expansion of constitutive relations as the condition and the very process that, at the same time, produces true and adequate individuation. That vision of asymptotically expansive transpersonal expansion to one's own infinite constitutive relations (i.e. causes in God/Nature) engenders independence of mind from its original passive constitution by the relations of the Common Order of Nature (or experience), namely passive merger in one's local context. Understanding the singular causal interactive constitution of one's own particular emotions (desires as they are passively shaped and aggregated by the interactions of self and environment and integrated into the *conatus*/ratio) gives one a unique first-person point of view from this very point or juncture, yet it reaches out to infinity – an infinity constituted by the universe of causal layers, networks, interactions in every direction and back and forth with mutual effects.

The *conatus*, the desire for self-perpetuation and -determination, is informed expansively and relationally by these causes to infinity, yet at the same time maintains its ratio as it actively searches for and integrates its own causal constitution through self-reflective reconstruction of the causes of one's emotions – which is to say the causes of one's constitution by how one has been affected by one's interactions and interrelations. It is individuated as this point and this singular origin from which to trace the universal order of causes, which at the same time is the universal explanation of all things as well as one's own self-understanding. It is the *conatus* of both self and world and of self-in-world and world-in-self. For each is constituted by all the other points and interactions, which are now within its own internal (universal) order as its own tracing of causes – the intellectual order that is the same in all as it is the divine order, the natural order from the divine perspective.[30] Yet because it acts from itself alone, from its own internal order, it has achieved autonomy (Spinoza's 'activity') (E2p29s).

> The Mind has, not an adequate, but only a confused knowledge, of itself, its own Body, and of external bodies, so long as it perceives things from *the common order of nature*, i.e. so long as it is *determined externally*, from fortuitous encounters with things, to regard this or that, and not so long as it is *determined internally*, from the fact that it regards a number of things at once, to

understand their agreements, differences, and oppositions. For so often as it is *disposed internally*, in this or in another way, then it regards things clearly and distinctly. (emphasis added)

At the same time, the mind acts as (and desires) the universal order of causes (since they 'cannot be privately owned', as Balibar puts it[31]), as internalised – these are its constitutive relations. We can further understand Spinoza's account of relational individuation in this way: because it is one's very own emotions – relational and interactive images and the ideas of them – that are the starting points of coming to intuitive knowledge of them in terms of the universality of infinite Nature, one's causal networks and interactions, one's point of view, is individual or a true first-person perspective. For according to E5p31dem: 'The Mind conceives nothing under a species of eternity except insofar as it conceives its Body's essence under a species of eternity.' This is a first-person point of view. Yet it is also a universal point of view because, by E5p15: 'He who understands himself and his affects [emotions] clearly and distinctly loves God, and does so the more, the more he understands his affects.' And E5p24: 'The more we understand singular things, the more we understand God.'

Nevertheless, there seems to be an implied further stage of ultimate universality achievable by a person when intuitive knowledge comes to dominate the entire mind, if that is indeed possible for some rare individuals. For the state in which 'He who understands himself and his affects clearly and distinctly loves God, and does so the more he understands himself and his affects' (E5p15) does not seem to be Spinoza's final word. When 'the Mind's intellectual Love of God' becomes 'the very Love of God by which God loves himself' (E5p36), the tables seemed to be turned or the tail wags the dog. For while memory, a product of the Imaginative linking of images, constitutes us as rooted to time and place and group and local environment, the Intellect can set us free.

[M]emory . . . is simply a linking of ideas involving the nature of things outside the human body, a linking which occurs in the mind parallel to the order and linking of the affections of the human body. . . . [M]y purpose in saying that this linking occurs in accordance with the order and linking of the affections of the human body is to distinguish it from the linking of ideas in accordance with the order of the intellect whereby the mind perceives things through their first causes, and which is the same in all men. (E2p18s)

Hence, '[w]e strive . . . that whatever is related to [the body's] memory or imagination is of hardly any moment in relation to the intellect' (E5p39s). Insofar as our intuitive universal knowledge has become so distanced from its singular origins in the individual body, and personal memory attenuated to such an extent that it is not even the starting point any longer for the Intuitive tracing of causes to and within God, it would seem that the networks of causes of the universe (rather than of our singular body) have come to fill the mind and the *conatus*. At that point one has transcended a state in which the self, the *conatus*, is emergent principally from the tracing of singular experiences and local relations and social merger back to their infinite order of causal sources and interrelations, and instead one has achieved an ultimate union, a merger as far as possible with God. Yet since 'only while the Body endures is the Mind subject to affects which are related to the Passions' (E5p34), perhaps we may conclude that relational autonomy, the first-person perspective on the universal, is, in Spinoza's estimation, the highest achievement within life. And this is no small thing, for 'Insofar as our Mind knows itself and the Body under a species of eternity, it necessarily has knowledge of God, and knows that it is in God and is conceived through God' (E5p30).

7. Conclusion

Rather than a weak and attenuated version of relational autonomy understood as a theory in which social relationships are merely needed by the individual for her autonomy to play out effectively,[32] Spinoza's philosophical vision suggests a stronger version. Instead, transindividual relations are constitutive of persons at every stage of cognitive-affective development, on the one hand, and, on the other, an infinitely expansive internal self-constitution of the individual by her (causal) relations is a necessary condition of her very fulfilment of the end. Seen from an alternative perspective as the achievement of individuation, the fullest individual causal self-explanation, that state of infinite constitutive relations, is not only necessary but sufficient.

Notes

1. Balibar (1997: 26).
2. Balibar (1997: 28).
3. Balibar (1997: 28–30).
4. E2p19.
5. E2p16c2.
6. E2p28, E2p28s.
7. E2p43s.
8. E5p36s.
9. E2p28dem.
10. E2p19 and E2p19dem.
11. E2p9.
12. E2p16 and E2p16dem.
13. Balibar (1997: 14) wonderfully describes Spinoza's conception of causal networks as follows: '"[T]o cause" is an operation by which something modifies or *modulates the way something else operates* (or produces its effects). But the infinite connexion does not take the form of independent linear series, or genealogies of cause and effect . . .: it typically takes the form of an infinite *network* of singular *modi*, or existences, a dynamic unity of modulating/modulated activities.'

    Nevertheless, I think he overemphasises the discreteness of individuals here, given my analysis and argument (both above and below) for the interactions as constitutive of individuals.

14. E2p17s (emphasis added).
15. E2p16c2.
16. E2p23.
17. For example, Balibar (1997) but also see Melamed (2010: 77–92). Melamed characterises Spinoza's account of individual bodies as dynamically and temporary constructions and nested self-organising units (in E3p13ff.) as 'weak' but I wonder why and whether that denigration is warranted. Melamed points to the difficulty of reconciling Spinoza's functional definition of individuals with his claim of the reality of finite modes. Yet is it obvious that individual bodies are individuated and held together as units in a stronger way and even largely atomically unrelated or loosely related against an environment that serves more as a backdrop. Is it Spinoza's account that is philosophically weak, in Melamed's view, or is he suggesting that it is the discreteness of individuals as such which, in Spinoza's view, has been exaggerated? I think perhaps both, a double entendre. The facts of the case are not merely those of argument and philosophical tradition but also of physics and other natural sciences, especially biology and neurobiology, and regarding these, in this case as in others, Spinoza may be prescient and way ahead of his time. The mainstream philosophical tradition could have gotten it wrong – a point raised by Klein (2000: 41–50.) Yet, Melamed's suggestion is intriguing: that Spinoza's account of individuals and individuation as weak amounts to an 'anti-humanist' tendency – the eradication of the human perspective in terms of scale, temporality and other features – a tendency in his thought that is in keeping with what I have argued is his Maimonidean anti-anthropomorphism, which he has indeed taken to the extreme. We must recall that Maimonides maintained that the world was not created by God for man and to fulfil human needs nor was it 'good' in human terms.
18. E2p13l4dem.
19. E2p13def.
20. E2p13sl5.
21. E2p13sl6 and E2p13sl7.
22. E2p13l7s.
23. Melamed (2010: 91).
24. Melamed (2010: 89).
25. TP3.2–3 (C2: 507–8; Van Vloten and Land (VV&L) (1913) ii: 13–14).
26. TP1.5–6 (C2: 505–6; VV&L ii: 5).
27. E4p41s; VV&L i: 271–2; the Stoic tradition going back at least to Seneca (see e.g. Seneca 1969) mounts a critique of the social servitude and anxiety induced by 'fear and hope', keeping people in a state of both unease and thraldom (see e.g. Letters V & VI: 38, 39).
28. Spinoza writes in TTP14 (C2: 268; VV&L ii: 246).
29. E3p50s; VV&L i: 156.
30. So too, Balibar (1997: 35).
31. Balibar (1997: 36).
32. This account of social utility seems to track with Balibar's account (1997: 28–30) of the Spinozistic stage of ratio, the second kind of knowledge, although a transindividual state of mind is also implied in this stage in Spinoza's notion of the universally held Common Notions that underlie all rational thinking and reasonable cooperative actions and arrangements.

Works Cited

Balibar, Etienne (1997), 'Spinoza: From Individuality to Transindividuality', Mededelingen vanwege het Spinozahuis, Delft: Eburon.

Klein, Julie (2000), 'Etienne Balibar's Marxist Spinoza', *Philosophy Today*, 44: 41–50.

Melamed, Yitzhak (2010), 'Acosmism or Weak Individuals? Hegel, Spinoza, and the Reality of the Finite', *The Journal of the History of Philosophy*, 48(1): 77–92.

Maimonides, Moses (1963), *Guide of the Perplexed*, trans. Shlomo Pines, Chicago and London: University of Chicago Press.

Seneca (1969), *Seneca: Letters from a Stoic (Epistulae Morales ad Lucilium)*, Robin Campbell (ed. and trans.), London; New York; Victoria, Australia; Toronto, Ontario; Auckland, New Zealand: Penguin.

Van Vloten, J. and J. P. N. Land (1913), *Benedict de Spinoza: Opera Quotquot Reperta Sunt, Recognoverunt*, The Hague: Martinus Nijhoff.

6
Revisiting Spinoza's Concept of *Conatus*: Degrees of Autonomy

Caroline Williams

1. Introduction

Reflection upon the conceptual shape and basis of autonomy has captured the attention of philosophers, both ancient and modern. Since the question of autonomy has been tied to the idea of rational self-rule and opposed to a passive state of bondage or heteronomy to either persons or things, it is hardly surprising that the dominant model of autonomy within modern philosophy is intertwined with the dual principles of individuality and free will. To understand how we might will the laws according to which we think and act was the central task of Kant's *Groundwork of the Metaphysic of Morals*, and it is this philosophy that has provided the compass to guide the starting point for many discussions of autonomy within contemporary liberal philosophy. At the same time, this dominant Kantian model has slowly been challenged by the many different voices of modern and contemporary philosophers from republicans and communitarians, to feminists and environmentalists, each sharing a concern for the individualistic roots of autonomy.[1] These diverse voices question whether the ideas of self-governance and rational self-rule grounding modern notions of autonomy might in turn conceal a deeper principle of social or civic relation. Can this principle also be understood to ground the idea of self-rule and shape our individuality? Is it feasible to hold together, perhaps even in tension, the *collective* element at least implied by the broad idea of relationality with the strong notion of *individuality* present in modern concepts of autonomy?

Such a starting point brings many questions and concerns. It might appear paradoxical to unsettle the concept of autonomy in this way by drawing it out of the liberal tradition of Kantian political and moral philosophy where its strongest roots arguably lie. But too much is at stake to abandon this critical work on the concept of autonomy. It is clear that autonomy is not simply a moral or, indeed, solely a philosophical concept; it is deeply political, and inseparable, in practice, from concepts of freedom, agency and power, which cluster around it and give it strong political resonance. Looking closely at the concept of freedom within the history of political philosophy, Hannah Arendt has identified a growing distance between freedom and the realm of politics precisely as the former has become more dominated by the attribute of will and the inner sanctuary of thought (Arendt 2006). For Arendt, the worldly life of politics, that public space where men and women *appear* to each other and act in concert, is synonymous with the concept of freedom. This marriage of freedom, publicity and action has Greek and Republican roots, where being a citizen or a 'free man' required an immersion in public affairs. Here, politics itself is understood as the putting into question of the very terms and presuppositions of its existence. Citizenship is thus conceived as a project of autonomy where self-rule and self-governance demand that the individual be part of the *polis*, and the freedom of one is tied to the freedom of all.[2]

Arendt's attention to the relationship (or gap) between freedom and politics resonates with the focus of the present volume.[3] As Catriona Mackenzie argues in her survey of current research on relational autonomy, autonomy is a multidimensional concept. We need to appraise its proximity to theories of freedom, specifically those conceptions of positive freedom that require complex social goods as well as a democratic infrastructure to support diverse expressions of autonomous individuals. Indeed, once we begin, with both Arendt and Mackenzie, to take seriously ideas of self-rule or self-governance, related ideas of the solitary, detached, self-contained individual, as well as the stability and purity of the inner-domain of the subject, become increasingly unhelpful and strikingly one-dimensional. Feminist theorists have already examined the limits of a model of the liberal political subject and established the importance of relations of interdependency and vulnerability characterising the subject of politics (e.g. Butler 1997, 2005; Armstrong 2009). Mackenzie underscores the need to develop further this kind analysis, not only in terms of autonomy's relation to theories of freedom but also its crucial relation to power and agency. We must consider not only those enabling structures of power that encourage self-determination and non-interference but also those relations that subject, discipline and sometimes dominate. Similarly, a more nuanced theory of agency might help us to think the complex web of interconnections (for example, affective, symbolic, linguistic relations) between and within individuals, which in turn will develop our philosophical and political sense of the concept of relational autonomy.

Whilst Spinoza has not yet played a pivotal role in mainstream debates around the question of autonomy, the proximity of his philosophy to the research agenda set out above is clear, and the diverse contributions composing the present volume aim to explore his place within these discussions. My chapter will therefore draw upon Spinoza's thought in order to enrich our understandings of agency and subjectivity, and to excavate the novel understanding of autonomy to be found there. At first glance, however, Spinoza's abiding allegiance to a principle of necessity, his concern with man's subjection to the passions, and his apparent subordination of human freedom to a schema of natural causality where action is forever determined by some other thing or cause, appear to offer scant resources for thinking how a robust conception of individual autonomy might inform contemporary philosophy and politics. It is largely due to this one-sided (arguably

Hegelian) emphasis upon determinism that Spinoza's philosophy was rendered marginal to discussions of autonomy. But recent scholars of Spinoza have already begun to reposition his philosophy as central to the philosophical and historical development of a concept of relational autonomy (Armstrong 2009; Kisner, 2011). Indeed, both Kisner and Armstrong point out that whilst Spinoza does not directly utilise a concept of autonomy to elucidate his own ethical sense of freedom, his philosophy nonetheless helps to uncover a deeper sense of freedom and presents the discourse of autonomy with a natural yet critical ally.

What, then, might be the conceptual shape and form of a figure of autonomy emerging from a thinker who makes no direct use of the idea, and also suggests that the experience of freedom, being an excellent thing, is as difficult as is it rare (E5p42s)? Recent scholarship (Gatens 2011; Nadler 2015) questions the philosophical status of Spinoza's perplexing discussion of the free man as a being who lives solely in accordance to the dictates of reason and uses these rational powers (as a kind of self-mastery) to garner knowledge of causal relations. Here, the rational or free man is often viewed as acting not according to the passions but from reason alone. This leads some readers to present the ideal image of Spinoza's free man as one without the experience of passions or inadequate ideas, whose *conatus* is strangely unaffected by external things and, ultimately, as a being who appears as outside of nature (see the discussion in Nadler 2015: 111).[4] Such readings make very little sense in the context of Spinoza's broader philosophical naturalism where 'we can never bring it about that we require nothing outside ourselves to preserve our being' (E4p18s) and where 'there is no singular thing that is most useful to man than a man that lives under the guidance of reason' (E4p35c1). Thus, Nadler concludes that, 'external things can be a source of joy (*laetitia*) when they are the cause of an increase in an individual's *conatus*' (Nadler 2015: 114). Freedom, then, does not entail that the subject must withdraw from the world of relationships with beings and things of all kinds, or from the passions and events that give rise to experience:

> The free man will not, *pace* Garber, withdraw from the world. Rather, he will know *how properly to use the world to his own advantage*. He will partake in moderation of those things that aid his *conatus* and bring him joy, but at the same time avoid any excessive pleasures that would debilitate the body and inhibit his mind. (Nadler 2015: 115; emphasis added)

It will be no doubt necessary, based on Nadler's reading here, to return to a set of discussions around the intertwining of action and passion and the relationship of both of these to imagination and the agency of the *conatus*.[5] Reflecting upon Spinoza's observation in E4p4 that 'It is impossible that a man should not be part of nature, and that he should be able to undergo no changes except those which can be understood through his own nature alone, and of which he is the adequate cause' one might prefer to question the bounded quality of the *conatus* and view striving itself as part of an elemental relationality, which happens *between* beings and things and not simply through them. Similarly, one might choose to push an analysis of this dynamic mobility of actions, ideas and affects in the direction of Spinoza's own parsing of their geometric relation '... as if it were a question of lines, planes and bodies' (E3pref). This will entail, as the interpretation below develops, not only an unravelling of the subject and the scene of agency, but also a thinking through of the political – together with the philosophical – effects (the two cannot be separated) of this relational ontology upon the discourse of relational autonomy.[6]

To develop this account of the scene of agency and the unravelling of the subject, I am indebted to some of the continental readings of Spinoza, specifically those of Balibar (1997, 1998); Deleuze (1988, 1992); Macherey (1998, 2013); Morfino (2014) and Negri (1991). A distinctive feature of these studies, particularly those of Balibar, Morfino and Negri, is their refusal to separate Spinoza's philosophical from his political writings. Building upon these inspiring readings, I suggest that Spinoza's relational ontology of individuation permits one to think *together* the collective and individual elements of autonomy where the persistence and power of each depend *wholly* upon the relations composing them. Indeed, I push this analysis further and suggest that when Spinoza's concept of *conatus* is examined as a force or power of *all* things, this engenders in turn a sense of relationality that ties human communicative power and freedom to non-human others and things. Spinoza's dynamic conceptions of imagination and affect are shown to deepen this understanding and help to establish the political stakes of Spinoza's reframing and repositioning of human power as part of nature. My reading of Spinoza will develop two theses of autonomy that I argue help to characterise its relational quality. It will also suggest that his philosophy entails a practical, political formulation of *degrees of autonomy*. Speculating about the natural movement of knowledge of causal relations and practical understanding (common notions), I also offer a wager: as we join powers with more diverse beings and things and increase our shared *potentia* and mutual enhancement, might not increasing degrees of relational autonomy be the natural, practical outcome of Spinoza's philosophy? Whilst this outcome is a real possibility, it is also clear that autonomy is an increasingly fragile project since relations are often governed by conflict as well as reciprocity and mutuality. This practical knowledge of the complexity of relations between beings and things of all kinds is reflected in what I call 'the politics of autonomy' that emerges from my engagement with Spinoza's philosophy, but that we can also identify within the opening up of current research and discussion.

Indeed, if autonomy is a cluster concept, or a multidimensional concept as Mackenzie observes, then it is surely important to appraise its relation to other Spinozist concepts such as affect, power, imagination, democracy and freedom.[7] This will, in turn permit us to trace a path of thinking through Spinoza that has much more in common with republican, communitarian, Marxist and feminist political ideas than with the liberal political tradition, and where autonomy itself is overdetermined by the form of politics that founds it. In the case of the early Marx, for example, freedom or emancipation are inextricably tied to nature, and a truly political society comes into being when human freedom relies no longer on either an estrangement from the world (the alienated liberal subject of modernity), or on the distinctiveness of man from species-life.[8] If one is thus drawn, as Arendt intimated in her essay 'What is Freedom?', to *question* the very shape and form of politics, this is largely because the project, or process, of autonomy is inseparable from the relational ontology to be found in Spinoza's thought. What, then, are the constituent elements of such a project?

2. Spinoza and the Project of Autonomy

Spinoza's philosophy shatters modern Enlightenment conceptions of freedom built upon free will. His resolute commitment to naturalism and his view of the world as substance requires no theory or faculty of free will or subjectivity as a form of interiority, since its starting point precludes the kind of containment or identity that has generally accompanied such a theory. Spinoza's philosophy avoids the lure of anthropocentrism; his concern is with the production of an *individuum* conceived always as a composite of bodies and relations between parts, so that even the human body requires a wider body of organic and inorganic forms to maintain its existence. This premodern concept of *individuum* thus has nothing to do with atomistic, liberal notions that we tend to associate with the bounded individual and possessive individualism. When in Part 2 of the *Ethics* Spinoza constructs an ontology of the production of complex bodies as an *individuum* (E2p13–14), it is apparent that their composition (and decomposition) is a dynamic and continuous process:

> When a number of bodies, whether of the same or different size, are so constrained by other bodies that they lie upon one another, or if they so move, whether with the same degree or different degrees of speed, that they communicate their motions to each other in a certain fixed manner, we shall say that those bodies are united with one another and that they all together compose one body or Individual, which is distinguished from the others by this union of bodies. (E2p13def)[9]

Thus a body or individual is always composed of other bodies that conduct a dynamic relationship with each other whilst simultaneously maintaining a continuous identity. If some of these bodies are removed but the same degree of energy and movement is maintained then the individual can retain its nature or identity (E2p13l5). Indeed, Spinoza further suggests that

> if we should now conceive of another [individual], composed of a number of individuals of a different nature, we shall find that it can be affected in a great many other ways, and still preserve its nature. For since each part of it is composed of a number of bodies, each part will therefore be able, without any change of its nature, to move now more slowly, now more quickly, and consequently communicate its motion more quickly or more slowly to the others. (E2p13l7s)

The more complex a body is, the more relations it will have with other bodies, and the more its identity will be compatible with a great many *different* entities. Each individual thing must be understood as a *singularity*, which has its own causes and conditions, but as a centre of action or *potentia* (or relations of motion and rest) will be connected in various ways with a network of other individuals. It is precisely these relations that give rise to an interdependency and reciprocity between parts, and construct the individual.

Some scholars have argued that Spinoza's ontological physics of bodies offers no obvious path towards his political thought (Rice 1990: 195) Are we to conclude therefore, that a political concept of autonomy has no place in the above analysis? By continuing to dwell in this novel space of individuation, however, we might instead choose to pose the question of its *political* value and think about autonomy's complex field of production: how can the augmentation of 'individual' action and autonomy be compatible with interdependence, exposure, and openness to others and things? How might the individual maintain a ratio between singularity and generality, distinction and unity?

It is in response to this kind of political question that Etienne Balibar analyses the collective composition of the individual by developing the important idea of transindividualism, which he imports from the ontogenetic philosophy of Gilbert Simondon to the fertile context of Spinoza's philosophy, where he argues (contra Rice) that it can be reconciled with the latter's politics.[10] For Simondon, the figure of the transindividual indicates more than the dynamic way in which individuals change over time and, not unlike Spinoza, he is aware of increasingly complex levels of individuation. Metamorphosis becomes possible because of a pre-individual, heterogeneous field of differences, disparities and potentialities that are contemporaneous with the emergence of an individual. In this sense, both the individual and the process of individuation form metastable equilibria whereby a body, or individual, communicates, exchanges, integrates and differentiates its parts from multiple others, and where its conservation also involves openness, and hence a kind of expansion. Thus, 'to say that an individual keeps existing is tantamount to saying that it is regenerated or reproduced. ... what Spinoza implies [here] is that any individual has *a need of other individuals* in order to preserve its form and its existence' (Balibar 1997: 18; E4p18s).

We can identify at this stage a first thesis of relational autonomy: there can be no autonomy without interaction, encounter and connection. In other words, autonomy is an inescapable part of a transindividual process where changes in the autonomy of one individual are connected to changes in the autonomy of others. We might even be able to imagine the possibility of a body composed of several things or parts of different natures which co-exist in a state of relational autonomy (see, for example, E2p16).[11] This important thesis, or element, of autonomy appears at odds with some contemporary views of *autopoiesis*, understood here as a principle of self-organisation. For example, according to the influential studies of Francisco Varela, the living being is a self-organising, self-asserting, sense-making system in constant exchange with its environment, which must have meaning for the metabolic existence of the system itself. Varela suggests, however, that autonomy is represented by the ongoing maintenance of organisational closure and conservation of the system as a unity, while its disintegration signals a loss of identity and its partial or complete disintegration. Varela's work has established important developments within theories of creative evolution and might refine our understanding of the emergence of living systems. Notions of closure and conservation, however, imply that even a rigid system could be considered self-maintaining and, therefore, autonomous. This concern been raised by Cornelius Castoriadis, a contemporary thinker of autonomy, whose regard for the imaginary institution of political forms has an important proximity to the thought of Spinoza.[12] It further suggests the need for a circumspect consideration of the question of power and its place in an account of relational autonomy. Spinoza was well aware that openness to the exterior (which is simultaneously the interior according to the logic of individuation expressed above), will also yield decomposition, degeneration, sometimes death.[13] We need, therefore, to reconcile the competing agencies or activities of self-maintenance, conservation, expansion, disaggregation and decomposition, as well as reflect upon their impact for our consideration of autonomy thus far.

A probing text by Jean-Luc Nancy on the undoing of the subject highlights some of the questions at stake here. In 'The Intruder', Nancy describes a permanent state of mutation of the individual, an experience of estrangement from his own body as his heart gradually became a stranger, slowly refusing, or failing to move, the body in the ways it had done so previously. Even before the heart transplant and the grafting of a foreign organ, Nancy writes, 'I was already no longer inside me', no longer the self-same identity, but besieged by the outside as 'a permanent regime of intrusion'. Nancy describes the unravelling of a subject that begins to *recognise* the powerful effects of other parts upon its organisation and self-maintenance, such that 'the subject's truth is its exteriority and its excessiveness: its infinite expansion' (Nancy 2008: 170), and where the mutating force and power of the impersonal intruder – both *I* and *it* – form 'a disturbing thrust of the strange, the *conatus* of an on-growing infinity' (ibid.:170).[14] This intimate portrait of experience complicates the scene of autonomy since parts of the body now appear to have their own 'relative autonomy', dissolving any sense of an inner-self or agent. It implores us to pause for a moment and consider this extension of the body (to which one might retain only a *degree* of membership), and to consider ourselves as *incarnate* in a wider world (some might call this structure Nature), which extends infinitely beyond the human body. This continuous process of interaction and reciprocal modification also fractures and destabilises relations as it tends towards increasing degrees of autonomy. It thus marks the project of autonomy with a sense of fragility and incompleteness, and poses the thorny question of power as something at once productive and mobile: a field of forces that compose the individual. What, for Spinoza, is the ontological shape of this power, the *conatus*, that pushes beyond the subject and threatens to modify – compose and decompose – the activity of a mode?

3. *Conatus*, Power and Relational Autonomy

We will not consider Spinoza's account of individuation solely as a physical model of the composition of bodies since this also informs his ontology. Balibar suggests that Spinoza's construction of the idea of *conatus* in Part 3 of the *Ethics* expresses his earlier formulation of the movement and rest, or energy and *potentia* of bodies, and identifies each 'as a fraction of Nature's *potentia*' (Balibar 1997: 18). Indeed, for Spinoza, living organisms are distinguished from inorganic bodies only by their degree of complexity and their capacity to establish more or less intensive levels of interaction with other things without sacrificing their composite power. All composite bodies or *individuum* have a tendency to maintain their consistency as a certain ratio or balance of physical integrity. Individuals with higher degrees of complexity, however, have the *potentia* to sustain higher levels of interaction and relational autonomy (see above, the first thesis). Such a body might even accommodate heterogeneous elements, and mutate into another form entirely: 'For indeed, no one has yet determined what the Body can do' (E3p2s).

In the *Principles of Cartesian Philosophy* (PPC), Spinoza defines the active verb *conatur* as a body's natural tendency to move in a certain way (PPC3def3; C1: 297). *Conatus* is the name for the power of *each thing* to 'persevere in its being' (E3p6), to strive for improbable permanence and indefinite existence beyond the present. There is no exclusive relation between the *conatus* and the persistence of the human subject and, as with our examination of individuation above, care must be taken not to anthropologise Spinoza's meaning of it. Indeed, in his early engagement with, and critique of Descartes, Spinoza makes clear that such a striving must be attached not simply to a thought, or a purely human endeavour, but to the boundless form of matter itself (PPC3def3; C1: 297). He is also explicit in his view that one must not distinguish between cause and effect, or the thing and its striving. Of those confused philosophers who continue to labour under such prejudices, Spinoza writes,

> [T]hey distinguish between the thing itself and the striving that is in each thing to preserve its being, although they do not know what they understand by striving. For though the thing and its striving to preserve its being are distinguished by reason, or rather verbally (which deceives these people very greatly), they are not in any way really distinct. (*Metaphysical Thoughts* (CM) 1.6; C1: 314)

To project upon Spinoza's nuanced understanding of the *conatus* a retrospective ontological account of *human* nature as self-movement and self-preservation elides the ontology of encounter described above, and presents the *conatus* as a kind of transcendental a priori category that Spinoza's philosophy always fought rigorously against (see E1app).[15] Whilst it might well be the case that in *Ethics* Parts 2 and 3 Spinoza mostly examines the *conatus* in its *human* situation as a form of desire, when taking into account the *general* claims of his ontology explored above, it becomes clear that the terms of such a debate appear to miss a vital point: the *conatus* principle is an essential characteristic of *all* things and is most usefully conceived *outside* the subject, in the wider context of an ontology of relation.[16] But how might the striving of this non-subjective *conatus* help us to understand the field of production of relational autonomy?

Placed in the context of Spinoza's ontology of relation, conative striving may be described, with Spinoza, as the *essence* of a thing (E3p7), but only if we underscore the way in which the metaphysical notion of a pure essence is challenged, or disrupted. The essence of a thing undergoes mutation and variation; reciprocity of relations enable or produce a transformation of essence and power (E2p10s; Deleuze 1988: 64). It is only in this context that what Deleuze calls the variability or *elasticity* of conative relations can be understood (Deleuze 1992: 222). There are no properties and functions of a body that do not rely on this elemental relationality. In the case of the human being, Spinoza, like Hegel after him, locates *conatus* in desire. But desire should not be read simply as a subjective impulse, or drive. This would be (once again) to humanise and essentialise Spinoza's thought, and to deprive the *conatus* of the relational reciprocities characterising the field of an infinitely variable Nature (see Ep32).[17] We might better understand the *conatus* as a field of forces (relations of motion and rest, speed and slowness) caught up in the *dynamic play of power relations*. It is in and through this deeply political process that individuals and bodies are *mobilised* and *take form*. Indeed, perhaps the *conatus* is this open series of power relations at the heart of every mode of existence: the power (of all things) to persist (and to desist, or resist); a configuration of forces that are *internal* and not prior to the process of individuation itself (for further discussion, see Williams 2017). Such a formulation likewise places the *conatus* at the heart of autonomy and yields a second important thesis: if, as we have argued, there is no ontological distinction between, and discrete autonomy of, human and non-human bodies, it follows that the relational autonomy of bodies of *all* kinds will be constituted by and through *degrees of power*.

The transitive power *between* states or forces of existence, which Spinoza names affect, and a mode or body is defined by a *variable capacity* for being affected.[18] Affect thus describes 'the affections of the body by which the body's power of activity is increased or diminished, assisted or checked, together with the idea of these affections' (E3def3). This 'power of acting' is dependent on external causes and varies in accordance to the degree of agreement with other bodies or parts. Similarly, when Spinoza considers the 'idea of these affections', these too will vary in accordance with the degree of reality or perfection presented by the image (a confused or an adequate idea). This definition of the connection between the activity of bodies and ideas (E2p7) also invests Spinoza's understanding of imagination, which acts in a practical and a virtual sense as a kind of conduit and conductor of ideas.[19] The mind does not simply *have* ideas; these are dynamic activities imbued with affect and, indeed, with memory traces of interactions with other bodies that are *mobilized* by imagination.

Spinoza closely studied the affective density of political life, outlining in Part

3 of the *Ethics* a basis for investigating the earlier physics of bodies with the affective intensities that accompany specifically human actions and affects 'just as if it were a question of lines, planes and bodies' (E3pref). The *Tractatus Theologico-Politicus* had already explored the reality of their vacillation or ambivalence in the imaginary structure of religion; how they might shrink and swell, oscillate endlessly between fear and love, hope and despair, gripping the mass in a condition of superstition and illusion. In *Ethics* Part 3 he returned to consider the power of imagination to harness and move bodies, to strengthen or weaken activity and affect. Objects and images of hope and fear, pity and envy, love and hate, were not viewed simply as relations of recognition or misrecognition whereby individuals project images regarding their similarity and difference from other things. They were also powerful networks of affective relations of agreement and disagreement understood to cohere to varying degrees in imagination.[20]

Imagination thus has a very powerful function, for Spinoza, not as a subjective faculty but as an anonymous structure, an impersonal conductor of affects that works to undo and decompose the subject. Similarly, affects pass *through* and *beyond* subjects (rather than being states of being attributable to them), communicating and unfolding images, ideas, intensities, corporeal traces that become materialised in signs, norms, habits, movements, political beliefs, ethical relations, modes of living, relations to nature and non-human others, social and political practices, and countless other forms, too.[21]

Anchored in the relational ontology described above, the conative power of all things, the impersonal structure of imagination, and the force of affect, each become powerful tools for thinking autonomy. Together, they frame and position human power just as Spinoza intended, as part of nature and not as *imperium in imperio* (E3pref). The argument thus far has developed two important theses that help to characterise relational autonomy. First thesis: there can be no autonomy without interaction and encounter. This permits the speculation that a body might persevere when composed of several things of a *different* nature, but it also recognises fracture and contingency as characteristics of any complex individual, hence making the project of autonomy a fragile affair. This metastable state gives rise to a second thesis that I argue is strongly present and key to the discussion, namely that the relational autonomy of bodies of *all* kinds will be constituted by and through *degrees of power*.

Spinoza's is a practical philosophy where knowledge of the causal powers of relation and interaction require an active understanding that attempts to master a practical problem: 'to capture the power of the body *beyond* the given condition of our knowledge, and to capture the power of the mind *beyond* the given conditions of consciousness' (Deleuze 1988: 18; emphasis added). When body and mind exceed the intimate boundaries and ideological edges of modern conceptions of individualism, when the *conatus* strives to imagine 'those things that increase or aid the Body's power of acting' (E3p12), knowledge of causes is 'globally rather than locally determined' (Ravven 1998: 283) and 'what is common to all things and is equally in the part and the whole, does not constitute the essence of any singular thing' (E2p37). Common notions evolve from an understanding of composition and relation between (and within) combinations, and they constitute ideas about the shape and value of the extended individual (one might think here, for example, of Nancy's (2008) reflection in 'The Intruder', of a contemporary agonistic or fractious model of democracy, or of the human immersion within a complex ecosystem of life) where every general axiom or common notion refers back to the combination of bodies that generate them.[22] Here, reason is a practical reason, charged with strong affective and imaginative dimensions. It is derived principally from the state and complexity of bodies, and linked to the discernment of agreement and common interest between them.[23] Thus we have the makings of a paradoxical formation of overlapping or relational autonomy, permitting us to think together the collective and the individual elements of autonomy, as greater and higher levels of interaction generate greater freedom whilst being mediated by relations of power.

4. The Life of Power and the Politics of Autonomy

Every philosophy involves the taking up of a position of some kind, and in the context of the discussion here, we can call this the 'politics of autonomy'. Autonomy, as many philosophers agree, is an essentially contestable concept, and whilst we might agree upon a basic, theoretically persuasive grammar to articulate a problem or concept, its multilayered or multidimensional aspects generate disagreement that is at once ideological, political and discursive. We now rarely search for the *universal* features of a concept so prevalent is the sense that its truth is drawn, for example, from *local*, empirical configurations, *specific practices* of interaction and relation, understandings of the *scene* of agency, each of which politicise and transform the ground of contestation. Can we nonetheless still search for a common maxim to express this force of conative striving, or life of power?

In the introduction to this chapter I offered a wager: as we join powers with more diverse beings and things, multiplying shared *potentia* and mutual enhancement, increasing degrees of relational autonomy might be a natural, practical outcome of Spinoza's philosophy. Conjoining and collaborating with others, amidst increasingly complex conditions of existence – where we do not always share a like nature – might indeed create conditions for a more diverse individual to flourish or live well. Spinoza gave considerable weight to the relation between human nature, similarity (*affectum imitatio*) and commonality, claiming that the associative bonds of those sharing a common nature, and the common notions that express this, were the basis of a rational politics (E4p31c). We can, however, also reach beyond this human-centred bond, defend the argument developed here, and draw upon Spinoza's reflection on that most complex of individuals, that is, Nature itself: non-teleological and endlessly differentiated, with an infinite power to interact in infinitely varied ways (see E2p13l7). Attentiveness to this world of wider beings and things of a different yet common nature enhances our ability to think, imagine and question the form of these complex combinations: how might our politics enable their flourishing and how is autonomy extended in the process?

There are many places to look within contemporary thought for evidence of this strong Spinozist theme and question. Contemporary philosophers and critical theorists are closely allied with Spinoza when writing about the need to make space in politics for the life and agency of vibrant matter and for 'things-in-assemblage' (Bennett 2010); considering struggle as a question of 'the conditions under which desires for perseverance . . . combine and form enabling or disabling assemblages' (Sharp 2011: 153); examining the composite individual as a 'more than human' form (Ruddick 2016); offering a treatise on existence as a mode of being singular plural (Nancy 2000); and critiquing the subject-centric nature of mainstream discussions of the Anthropocene, where the focus on humanity as the prime mover drowns out and dominates the power of many other forms of life with metabolic mutation and persistence (Bonneil and Fressoz 2016), and symbolises nothing less than the return of the history of the Earth that 'creates a *new human condition* and requires us to reintegrate nature and the Earth system at the heart of our understanding of history, our conception of freedom and our practice of democracy' (Moore 2015: 34; emphasis added).

These creative engagements with life beyond the subject are arguably strengthened by an ethico-political project of relational autonomy that begins not simply with humans or nature but, as Moore writes, 'with the relations that co-produce manifold configurations of humanity-in-nature, organisms and environments, life and land, water and air' (Moore 2015: 5). To respond to the most pressing environmental questions of the present and future requires an approach that thinks the conditions for maximum diversity, strays beyond those of immediate towards virtual encounters, acts with others in mind, and imagines relations that bring together diverse bodies, creating ideas based on an enhanced understanding of the connections between beings and things (E2p16).

5. Conclusion: Degrees of Autonomy

Spinoza's philosophy rescues autonomy from the liberal tradition. In particular, it attends to the risk of detachment and solitude present in liberal theories of freedom without extinguishing individuality or simply *absorbing* it into the whole of Nature. This elementary, first-order relationality involves a reciprocity of interdependent and interconnected processes of individuation that is able to hold in productive tension the collective and individual elements present within modern conceptions of autonomy. The critic might argue that by unravelling the agent of autonomy we have merely reduced freedom and creativity to an all-consuming materialist account that permits no space, no corner, for autonomous action. This criticism echoes one often placed at the door of structuralism. It is perhaps no coincidence that Spinoza has been drawn upon so productively by contemporary thinkers usually associated with structuralism, which famously *displaced* the human subject in favour of a rational, scientific account of structural relations, sacrificing – at least for its critics – freedom and agency to a functional and determinist position.

The argument has drawn upon some of these thinkers associated with the perspective of structuralism to present Spinoza's philosophy as one that has no ontological reliance upon the figure of subjectivity that usually grounds our notions of autonomy. In so doing, it endeavours to establish the manner in which Spinoza's ontology informs a view of relational autonomy. Here, concepts of individuality, *conatus*, affect and imagination challenge the paradigm of subjectivity and the scene of agency, inviting an exploration of the deeply political stakes of Spinoza's argument as it turns towards a wider sense of autonomy. Rather than giving way to determinism or necessity, we might instead consider this practical philosophy in its most active form as the becoming necessary of relational autonomy.[24]

Notes

1. See for example, Castoriadis (1991); Hague (2011); Mackenzie and Stoljar (2000); Pettit (2001).
2. This idea of the one and all, and the relation implied here between freedom, autonomy and power, connects republican and socialist thought, drawing Rousseau (General Will), Spinoza (the multitude), Arendt (*res publica*) and Castoriadis (autonomy) closer to Marx – despite the immanent critique that each might make of Marxian concepts.
3. In *The Experience of Freedom*, Jean-Luc Nancy also echoes Arendt's sentiment here, drawing attention to the modern divorce between the ethico-political realm and philosophy itself. He argues for a thinking of the existential ground of freedom and a removal of the obstacles to a speaking of freedom, namely free will and the *subjectum* of representation: 'Freedom has not been considered as anything other than the fundamental modality of the act of appearing to oneself' (Nancy 1993: 4). For Nancy, Spinoza is a philosopher of existence who calls freedom into question; Spinoza makes freedom a fundamental question of philosophy. Nancy's work is peppered with important reflections and references to Spinoza. A study of the phenomenological elements of Spinoza's philosophy, and specifically its presence and role in Nancy's thought, is much needed.
4. Here I think Nadler includes readers of Spinoza who would, I think, not agree with their inclusion within such a viewpoint.
5. For a survey that raises some of the issues at stake here see Gatens and Lloyd (1999).
6. Here I draw upon the argument developed in Williams (2017).
7. Indeed, Spinoza himself makes this commitment when he thinks at one and the same time God and Nature, Right and Power, Reality and Perfection. The theoretical effects of Latin term *sive* have had an important role in the act of reading Spinoza's concepts.
8. For Marx (1978), the historic conflict between man and nature (also one between existence and essence, freedom and necessity) is overcome only when the human becomes truly naturalised, and politics comes into being, in other words, only with the humanisation of nature and the naturalisation of humanism. We must not read this simply as a form of humanised nature. Thus, in a Spinozist way, Marx writes of society as 'the consummated oneness in substance of man and nature – the true resurrection of nature – the naturalism of man and the humanism of nature both brought to fulfillment' (1978: 85). Autonomy here is inseparable from species-life, as Marx makes clear in his dialogue with Bruno Bauer.
9. As Deleuze points out, 'A body can be anything: It can be an animal, a body of

sounds, a mind or an idea ... a linguistic corpus, a social body, a collectivity' (1988: 127).
10. The philosophy of Simondon has proved to be a very productive interlocutor for Spinoza's thought. See for example, Castelli (2011); Del Lucchese (2009); Read (2016).
11. Relation is not just a link or connection; it is the production of something that did not exist before. It is the enhancement of the body or individual, which now contains/takes hold of something else: the relation itself.
12. Possibly one of the most interesting late twentieth-century thinkers on autonomy is Cornelious Castoriadis, whose later work established a dialogue with this thinker of autopoiesis and autonomous systems. See Adams (2011) for an overview of the themes discussed here. Whilst I would trace these back to Spinoza, Adams focuses on the Romantic roots of some of Castoriadis' concepts.
13. Despite its relevance, I must leave to one side in this discussion of the complex question of how to interpret death within a body of thought emphatically characterised as a philosophy of affirmation, of life. In my view, however, one cannot isolate death from life, or remove from the thoughts of the free man all ideas of death (E4p67). Life-changing metamorphoses that leave no parts of an individual as it was (E4p39s); the unbearable weight of traces of the living-dead in many political bodies (E2p18); and the experiences of grief that mark parts of imagination and intensify the movement of joy (E5p43), each indicate the inevitability of the presence of death in life.
14. Thus, 'The intruder exposes me to excess. It extrudes me, exports me, expropriates me. I am the illness and the medicine, I am the cancerous cell and the grafted organ. I am these immune-depressive agents and their palliatives ... I am these ends of steel wire that brace my sternum ... We are ... the beginnings, in effect, of a mutation: man begins again by infinitely passing beyond man' (Nancy 2008: 170). Whilst the allusions to Nietzsche are strong, we must nonetheless underscore its challenge to a theory of autonomy and the discussion advanced here.
15. Drawing on the terms of this arguably faulty humanist reading, a key discussion among some commentators has centred upon whether the *conatus* can be stretched to incorporate institutions as well as individuals. It seems illogical, they reason, to apply a psychological and individualist concept like the *conatus* to an institutional structure such as the state (Rice 1990). However, to argue on such grounds that the state cannot possess a conative – or for that matter a counter-conative – tendency is to ignore the differential relations of force and power that constitute the state as an institutional body forever in the making. Following the reasoning about the *conatus* developed here, the state may be understood as possessing a complex collective tendency to persevere in its own being.
16. By drawing the force of the *conatus* into proximity with a broader relational ontology, I hope to make clear that I am not seeking to revive early twentieth-century debates about hylozoism, which attribute some form of creativity or consciousness to matter itself. Certainly, there is a kind of materialism being 'practiced' in Spinoza's philosophy, but it is not a crude mechanical type that prioritises some originary principle of matter that in turn becomes a transcendental or a priori 'source' of individuation. The entire direction of Spinoza's thought fights against such an argument, from its formulation in opposition to the view of God as omnipotent creator, to its radical inversion, represented by the delusional idea of individuals as discrete sources of free will. Instead, Spinoza's philosophy gives form to a complex, layered materialism, which must be distinguished from all crudely mechanical or mystical forms that

simply prioritise matter or the body, or which impose a teleological pattern upon the variability and indeterminacy of nature. This is key to understanding both his ontology and his political thought.

17. See E2p16.
18. Spinoza does not attribute affects to the agency of a conscious subject so I will refrain from reading affections as emotional and ideational states of body and mind since they cannot be easily contained there.
19. The reference here to the practical and virtual sense of imagination alludes to imagination's productive function that cannot be considered as either fictive or distortive. We must insist upon this virtual (perhaps invisible) function since it expresses Spinoza's view degrees of reality and perfection, and informs a theory of (practical) knowledge.
20. Many Spinoza scholars have contributed to the elaboration of the concept of imagination, tracing primarily its negative and positive poles, but also emphasising its materialist basis in the body. See Williams (2007, 2010) for interpretations of imagination and affect building upon some of these works and supporting the line of argument developed here.
21. Brian Massumi (2002) writes of the autonomy of affect as an always constructed, mediated and culturalised intensity or force that exceeds the subject.
22. When Spinoza writes that 'the order and connection of ideas is the same as the order and connection between things' (E2p7) he expressed a proposition that also gives shape to the following hypothesis: the more an individual is attuned to affective relations between things, the more that individual can think complex conditions of existence for relational autonomy
23. In this context I prefer the reference to interest rather than utility or advantage since it expresses the sense of openness to life that the reference to more subject-centric notions of utility cannot. See also Collier (2002).
24. Here I paraphrase Balibar's incisive formulation on freedom (1997: 34).

Works Cited

Adams, Suzy (2011), *Castoriadis's Ontology: Being and Creation*, New York: Fordham University Press.

Arendt, Hannah (2006), 'What is Freedom?' in *Between Past and Future: Eight Exercises in Political Thought*, London: Penguin Books.

Armstrong, Aurelia (2009), 'Autonomy and the Relational Individual: Spinoza and Feminism', in Moira Gatens (ed.), *Feminist Interpretations of Benedict Spinoza*, University Park: Pennsylvania State University Press.

Balibar, Etienne (1997), 'Spinoza: From Individuality to Transindividuality', Mededelingen vanwege het Spinozahuis, Delft: Eburon.

Balibar, Etienne (1998), *Spinoza and Politics*, trans. P. Snowdon, London and New York: Verso.

Bennett, Jane (2010), *Vibrant Matter: A Political Ecology of Things*, Durham, NC and London: Duke University Press.

Bonneil, Christophe and Jean-Baptiste Fressoz (2016), *The Shock of the Anthropocene*, trans. David Fernbach, London and New York: Verso.

Butler, Judith (1997), *The Psychic Life of Power*, Stanford: Stanford University Press.

Butler, Judith (2005), *Giving an Account of Onself*, New York: Fordham University Press.

Castelli, Ljuba (2011), 'Politics and Ontology in Barach Spinoza: Individuation, Affectivity

and the Collective Life of the Multitude', PhD thesis, Queen Mary University of London, London.
Castoriadis, Cornelius (1991), *Philosophy, Politics, Autonomy: Essays in Political Philosophy*, New York and Oxford: Oxford University Press.
Collier, Andrew (2002), 'The Materiality of Morals: Mind, Body and Interests in Spinoza's *Ethics*', in Gideon Segal and Yirmiyahau Yovel (eds), *Spinoza*, Burlington, VT: Ashgate.
Del Lucchese, Filippo (2009), 'Monstrous Individuations: Deleuze, Simondon, and Relational Ontology', *Differences*, 20(2–3): 179–93.
Deleuze, Gilles (1988), *Spinoza: Practical Philosophy*, trans. R. Hurley, San Francisco: City Lights.
Deleuze, Gilles (1992), *Expressionism in Philosophy*, trans. Martin Joughin, New York: Zone.
Gatens, Moira (2011), *Spinoza's Hard Path to Freedom*, Amsterdam: Van Gorcum.
Gatens, Moira and Genevieve Lloyd (1999), *Collective Imaginings: Spinoza, Past and Present*, London: Routledge.
Hague, Ros (2011), *Autonomy and Identity: The Politics of Who We Are*, Oxford: Routledge.
Kisner, Martin (2011), *Spinoza on Human Freedom: Reason, Autonomy and the Good Life*, Cambridge: Cambridge University Press.
Macherey, Pierre (1998), *In a Materialist Way*, trans. Ted Stolze, London and New York: Verso.
Macherey, Pierre (2013), *Hegel or Spinoza*, trans. Sue Ruddick, Minneapolis: University of Minnesota Press.
Marx, Karl (1978), 'Economic and Philosophic Manuscripts of 1844', in Robert C. Tucker (ed.), *The Marx-Engels Reader*, 2nd edn, New York and London: W. W. Norton and Company.
Massumi, Brian (2002), *Parables for the Virtual: Movement, Affect, Sense*, Durham, NC and London: Duke University Press.
Mackenzie, Catriona and Natalie Stoljar (2000), *Relational Autonomy: Feminist Essays on Autonomy, Agency and Social Self*, Oxford: Oxford University Press.
Moore, Jason (2015), *Capitalism in the Web of Life: Ecology and the Accumulation of Capital*, New York and London: Verso.
Morfino, Vittorio (2014), *Plural Temporality: Transindividuality and the Aleatory between Spinoza and Althusser*, Leiden: Koninklijke Brill
Nadler, Steven (2015), 'On Spinoza's "Free Man"', *Journal of the American Philosophical Association*, 1: 103–20.
Nancy, Jean Luc (1993), *The Experience of Freedom*, trans. Bridget McDonald, Stanford: Stanford University Press.
Nancy, Jean Luc (2000), *Being, Singular, Plural*, trans. Robert Richardson and Anne O'Bryne, Stanford: Stanford University Press.
Nancy, Jean Luc (2008), 'The Intruder', in *Corpus*, trans. Richard A. Rand, New York: Fordham University Press.
Negri, Antonio (1991), *The Savage Anomaly: The Power of Spinoza's Metaphysics and Politics*, trans. Michael Hardt, Minneapolis: University of Minneapolis Press.
Pettit, Philip (2001), *A Theory of Freedom: From the Psychology to the Politics of Agency*, Cambridge: Cambridge University Press
Ravven, Heidi (1998), 'Spinoza's Individualism Reconsidered: Some Lessons from the *Short Treatise on God, Man and His Well-being*', *Iyyun: The Jerusalem Philosophical Quarterly*, 47: 265–92.
Read, Jason (2016), *The Politics of Transindividuality*, Leiden: Koninklijke Brill.

Rice, Lee (1990), 'Individual and Community in Spinoza's Social Psychology', in E. Curley and P. F. Moreau (eds), *Spinoza: New Directions*, Leiden: Brill.

Ruddick, Sue (2016), '*Governed as It Were by Chance*. Monstrous Infinitude and the Problem of Nature in the Work of Spinoza', *Philosophy Today*, 60(1): 89–105.

Sharp, Hasana (2011), *Spinoza and the Politics of Renaturalization*, Chicago: Chicago University Press.

Williams, Caroline (2007), 'Thinking the Political in the Wake of Spinoza: Power, Affect and Imagination in the *Ethics*', *Contemporary Political Theory*, 6: 349–69.

Williams, Caroline (2010), 'Affective Processes without a Subject: Rethinking the Relation between Subjectivity and Affect with Spinoza', *Subjectivity*, 3: 245–62.

Williams, Caroline (2017), 'Unravelling the Subject with Spinoza: Towards a Morphological Analysis of the Scene of Subjectivity', *Contemporary Political Theory*, 16(3): 342–62.

7

Bodies Politic and Civic Agreement

Justin Steinberg

1. Prelude on Civility

Spinoza's views on natural sociality and civility are complex. On the one hand, he allows in the *Political Treatise* (TP) that humans may be regarded as social animals (TP2.17), only to assert later in the same work that 'men aren't born civil; they become civil' (TP5.2). His position seems to be that while we are naturally, necessarily driven to unite with others, we do not coordinate spontaneously – we must be directed and motivated to act in a coordinated fashion. We are made civil by the imposition of law. As I have argued elsewhere, law-making is also a complex matter for Spinoza.[1] On the one hand, there is a sovereign body that issues the laws, functioning as 'the mind of the state whereby all citizens must be guided' (TP4.1 (G iii: 291)). On the other hand, sovereign authority extends just as far as it is capable of securing reliable compliance, and its issuances constitute genuine laws only insofar as the prescribed behaviours are actually instantiated.[2] Law-making is, thus, a two-way street, depending on a sovereign guide and a complying multitude.

So, while civility is in some sense constructed or imposed, it is also natural, both in the sense that it is, to some degree, a predictable by-product of human activity, and in the sense that it is explicable entirely in terms of the activity of human beings. We see this in the TTP, where Spinoza treats civil law as a species of descriptive law in general, or that according to which things 'act in one and the same fixed and determinate way' (TTP4.1 (G iii: 57)). A civil law is a *ratio vivendi*, or a pattern of living, that one 'prescribes to himself or to others for some end' (*finem*) (TTP4.5 (G iii: 58)). The emphasis on patterned activity is repeated in the TP, where he claims that the chief characteristic of the civil order is that in it individuals share one and the same *ratio vivendi* (TP3.3).

Spinoza's conception of the state as entailing the maintenance of a certain pattern of activity – and, indeed, his insistence on the language of ratio – is very telling in light of the account of individuality in the *Ethics*. Here, in the so-called physical digression between E2p13 and E2p14, Spinoza claims that a collection of bodies constitute a single individual to the extent that they maintain a fixed ratio of motion and rest (*ratio motus et quietis*). This ratio of motion and rest is the 'nature' or 'form' of the individual (see E2p13l4–17), considered under the attribute of extension. Diachronic identity consists in the maintenance of a ratio between component parts, which is realised to varying degrees throughout the universe: from clusters of bonded atoms to ant colonies to solar systems. The scalar account of individuals implies that while social bodies like the commonwealth may be more loosely coordinated than biological bodies, there is no principled ontological distinction between these two classes of composites. And the more tightly members of a social body are bound by a common law or ratio – that is, the more absolute it is[3] – the more fully it is an individual.

Not everyone is convinced, though, that for Spinoza the state can be even a loose or weak individual. Several American commentators – including Steven Barbone, Douglas Den Uyl and Lee Rice – whom I will refer to as Restrictive Individualists, are keen to limit the scope of what counts as a Spinozistic individual. They worry that conceiving of the state as a higher-order individual would undermine the integrity of the human individual. Barbone, for instance, takes it to be a chief virtue of his reading that on its basis 'political institutions take second place in importance to the individuals joined in them' (Barbone 2002: 107). And Rice argues that by restricting what counts as an individual, Spinoza 'evades the twin difficulties of totalitarianism and the metaphysical reification of social aggregates' (Rice 1990: 282).[4] In this paper, I argue that the Restrictive Individualists are wrong both about the ontology of the state and about what state individualism entails. Spinoza not only allows that states can be individuals, he thinks that the more fully they function as individuals, the better they are. And this is perfectly compatible with the normative priority of the human individual.

This, however, raises another problem: if Spinoza is indeed committed to the normative priority of the human individual, why does he insist that civil subjects should always comply with civil law? In the second part of the chapter, I turn to answer this concern, suggesting that the key lies in the account of agreement (*convenientia*) that he advances in his *Political Treatise*, where *convenire* denotes a literal coming together (*con-venire*), or cooperation, and which directly entails being a part of a larger whole or individual. This analysis of agreement reinforces the case for state individualism, while shedding light on Spinoza's commitment to the convergence of individual and state interests.

2. Restrictive Individualism

Spinoza indisputably allows for nested individuals: '[if] two individuals of entirely the same nature are joined to one another, they compose an individual twice as powerful as each one' (E4p18s). This can be scaled all the way up to the 'whole of nature' or the infinite individual (E2p13l7, G ii: 102). Still, a number of scholars think there are conditions for being a higher-order individual that the state fails to meet. One condition is that the laws that govern the activity of higher-order individuals must be more basic than those that govern the activity of lower-order individuals. Rice claims that in the case of nested individuals the 'activity at *lower* levels is *deducible* [from] ... laws at *higher* levels'.[5] And Barbone makes essentially the same point: 'individuals are obliged by the power (*potentia*) of true higher order individuals that contain them'.[6] For evidence that this was, in fact, Spinoza's view, both Barbone and Rice look to Spinoza's letter to Oldenburg from 20 November 1665 (Ep32) – the so-called 'worm in the blood' letter – which suggests that the activity of a micro-organism (the lower-order individual) is constrained by the laws of the higher-order individual, represented here by the vascular activities of the larger organism. Barbone and Rice then argue that if the state were a higher-order individual, it would have to be governed by its own, irreducible (socio-political) laws that in turn explain the functioning of individual humans. We may call this the demand of nomological priority. Since Spinoza's political treatises indicate that socio-political laws are in fact rooted in the more basic laws of human psychology,[7] states fail to meet this demand, and consequently are not individuals.

According to these theorists, the state also fails to meet the demand that individuals have 'intrinsic' conative power, a power that is not reducible to the conative power of its constitutive parts. This is a requirement for all individuals at whatever level: to be an individual is to have intrinsic or non-derivative power.[8] Rice puts this point in the following way: 'a genuine spinozistic individual is greater than the sum of its parts (has more *conatus* than the sum of its conative elements)'.[9] Barbone agrees that conative power cannot be derived, as the *conatus* is 'a force found "inside" each individual'[10] or the 'unifying principle'[11] that separates the individual from the rest of nature. Indeed, he goes so far as to claim that a thing's *conatus* is what makes it what it is: 'the individual *is* this effort to preserve itself'.[12] A mere collection – like the San Diego Chargers football team, to use Barbone's example – may produce unified effects, but it lacks intrinsic power, and so it lacks a *conatus*. On this account, the state is at best a mere collection, its power being wholly derivative, as evidenced by the fact that the power of the commonwealth is conceived of as a *potestas* (*ad aliud* power) that is derived from the *potentia* (*per se* power) of individual subjects. Because the state lacks its own *conatus*, it cannot be an individual.

I must confess that I'm not entirely sure how these two demands are supposed to cohere with respect to lower-order individuals, as the demand of nomological priority implies that lower-order individuals are constrained by the laws of higher-order individuals, while the demand of 'intrinsic power' entails that they act from their own, non-derivative power. I will leave this tension to the side, though, and concentrate on what is common to these two demands: they both entail that the laws and powers that govern the operations of a higher-order individual do not reduce to the laws and powers that govern the operation of its component parts. I think this anti-reductionism stems from a misreading of Spinoza. To see why, let's examine more carefully each of the demands, beginning with the latter.

The demand that there be something 'inside' the thing, as Barbone puts it, that 'gives unity and unicity to an individual'[13] is, as I see it, deeply unspinozistic. Spinoza's view that the 'form' or 'nature' of an individual consists in its structural coherence (ratio of motion and rest) is presented as an alternative to substantival accounts of individuation. Unlike the latter, Spinoza's account does not depend on the existence of some further feature beyond structural coherence that would set an individual apart from the rest of nature. What makes an individual an individual is just the coherence itself. As Alexandre Matheron put it in his review of Den Uyl's *Power, State, and Freedom: An Interpretation of Spinoza's Political Philosophy*

> ... the author in Chapter IV believes that he is able to conclude that the state is not 'an individual, but rather ... an organized set of relations' (p. 80). But what is an individual, according to the definition given after Proposition 13 of Book II of the *Ethics*, if not precisely 'an organized set of relations'?[14]

As structural coherence comes in degrees, so too does individuality.[15] So the Restrictive Individualists' attempt to draw a sharp line between individuals and collections on the basis of the possession or non-possession of 'intrinsic' power is misguided from the start. And the claim that an individual is 'more than the sum of parts' is either trivial true or false. It is trivially true that an individual is more than the sum of its parts, since being an integral whole requires the maintenance of a certain relationship between the parts. But this is not what the Restrictive Individualists are claiming. They demand that there be something more to the power of individual than the power of its parts when arranged in such-and-such a manner. I have no idea what this elusive extra power could be or how it could be made consistent with Spinoza's metaphysics.[16]

The putative distinction between intrinsic and derived power finds no foothold in Spinoza's ontology. The difference between a single human pushing a stone and a collective pushing a boulder consists not in a difference in the kinds of power (*per se* and *ad aliud*) exhibited by these two nominal or logical subjects, but in the extent to which the parts of these subjects exhibit structural coherence over time. So, when we are asking whether or not the state has a *conatus*, we shouldn't seek some power beyond the coordinated power of its component parts; it is sufficient that its parts stand in some sort of patterned relationship to one another. And, as I suggested in the introduction, this is precisely what typifies a state – it is marked by a unified *ratio vivendi* – which explains why Spinoza explicitly claims that the state is a 'natural thing', and consequently is governed by the laws of nature (TP4.4).

But what exactly are the laws that govern the operations of the state? This brings us back to the demand of nomological priority. The Restrictive Individualists' suggestion that there can be more or less basic laws of nature jars with Spinoza's views on the operations of nature (*Natura Naturata*), according to which there is just one set of laws that govern *all things* at *all levels* (E3pref): 'Nature is always the same, and its virtue and power of acting are everywhere one and the same, that is, the laws and rules of Nature, according to which all things happen, and change from one form to another, are always and everywhere the same'. Nothing in Ep32 contradicts this claim, as the suggestion of the analogy of the worm in the bloodstream is not that the activity of micro-organisms is determined by laws of macro-organisms, but rather that micro-organisms and macro-organisms alike are determined by the very same laws, the laws of Nature (or 'of the whole universe', as he puts it in Ep32).[17] So, the fact that there are no distinct, irreducible socio-political laws should not be taken as evidence that states are not individuals.

Animating the Restrictive Individualists' account is the concern that if a state were an individual, the integrity of the human individual would be compromised. The human would be engulfed in the functioning of the state, her striving subordinated to the striving of state.[18] Worries about the relationship between the reification of social bodies and the subordination of the individual are commonplace amongst a certain strand of contemporary liberals. But there is no necessary connection between state individualism and human subordination, and Spinoza shows how state individualism can be reconciled with the ontological and normative priority of the human individual.

Consider the first point: ontological priority. There are reasons for thinking that Spinoza embraces the general principle that parts are prior to wholes;[19] and even if Spinoza does not accept the unrestricted claim about priority of parts, he allows for the composition of novel, higher-order individuals that are posterior their parts (E4p18s).[20] Moreover, contrary to what the Restrictive Individualists claim, larger individuals can in fact be composed out of smaller individuals without the latter losing their independent 'viability'.[21] We need not worry, then, that state individualism implies the disintegration or even the metaphysical subordination of the human individual.

Of course, the primary concern of Restrictive Individualists is that state individualism compromises the *normative*, and not just the ontological, priority of the human individual. Normative priority is taken to depend on ontological priority in something like the following way:

P1: If the state were an individual, then it would be ontologically prior to the human.
P2: If the state were ontologically prior to the human, then it would be normatively prior to human.
C: If the state were an individual, then it would be normatively prior to the human.

Since P1 is false, we may reject the argument as a whole. But we can also offer independent reasons for resisting the conclusion. Normative priority would seem to amount to something like this: X is normatively prior to Y iff the good of X takes priority over the good of Y. On Spinoza's account, however, good and evil are not features of nature itself; rather they are indexed to a particular perspective, or a particular striving. Normative subordination would imply that from Y's (Y = citizen) perspective, the good of X (X = the state) would take priority over Y's own good, which is at odds with Spinoza's striving-relative conception of the good. Consequently, we need not worry that state individualism poses a threat to normative priority.[22] The fears expressed by the Restrictive Individualists that state individualism threatens human individualism are simply unfounded.[23]

3. The Case for Compliance

This last point, however, raises a new worry: if Spinoza is indeed committed to the normative priority of the human individual, we would expect him to claim that citizens should comply with the laws of the state only to the extent that these laws serve the individual's interest, recognising that scenarios are bound to arise in which one's individual welfare would be enhanced by legal non-compliance. However, in both of his political treatises, Spinoza seems to advocate unqualified compliance with the law. For instance, in the *Political Treatise*, he claims that 'Each is subject to the control of the Commonwealth, and bound to carry out all its commands . . . though the subject may think the decrees of the Commonwealth unfair, he's nevertheless bound to carry them out' (TP3.5), and that

> [all citizens] ought to obey all the commands of the King, or the edicts promulgated by the great Council (regarding this condition, see vi, 18 and 19), even if he thinks the commands quite absurd. If he doesn't obey, it will be right to compel him. (TP6.39)

Similarly, in the TTP he maintains that

> Everyone must obey [*parere debere*] [the sovereign] in everything . . . unless we want to be enemies of the state, and act contrary to reason, which urges us to defend the state with all our powers, we're bound [*tenemur*] to carry out absolutely all the commands of the supreme power – even if it commands the greatest absurdities. (TTP16 (G iii: 193–4))

While there is a lot to explicate and disentangle in these passages, this much is clear: Spinoza is committed to some form of the thesis that citizens ought to comply with civic laws, no matter how absurd these laws appear to be. For convenience, I will call this Compliance, which is underwritten by something like the following logic:

P1: Legal non-compliance disempowers the state.
P2: To disempower the state is to disempower the individual citizen.
C: Legal non-compliance disempowers the individual citizen.

One might wonder here whether Spinoza actually embraces an unrestricted version of P1 and, consequently, of the conclusion. In his treatment of treason in the TTP, he allows for forms of non-compliance that 'clearly benefit' the state.[24] The curious suggestion here is that the treasonous subject can act without right, even while doing what is good or empowering for the state.[25] The possibility of a beneficial rebellion not only calls into question the scope of P1, it raises a host of other concerns about Spinoza's conception of right and its relationship to goodness, since he admits that even if one acts in ways that are clearly beneficial, one is 'rightly condemned' (TTP16.48–50 (G iii: 197)).[26] I don't wish to plunge into these muddy waters here. Instead, I want to focus on the reasoning behind P2, to which Spinoza is clearly committed. Given that the citizen and the state are ontologically independent, why does Spinoza think that the power of the citizen is so bound up with the power of the state that it is irrational for the citizen to do anything that would disempower the state? Why does he think that the interests of the human individual and the interests of the state converge (hereafter: Convergence) in the way that Compliance assumes?

4. The Case for Compliance and Convergence

One way of conceiving of Compliance is as a special case of altruism. In E4p37, Spinoza writes: 'the good which everyone who seeks virtue wants for himself, he also desires for other men'. This proposition ultimately depends on E4p31,[27] which reads: 'insofar as a thing agrees with our nature, it is necessarily good'. The demonstration for this requires that one take the *conatus* doctrine (E3p6) as entailing that all things strive 'to aid the preservation of the *nature* of the thing itself', from which it is further inferred that one will strive to aid the preservation of all things that *agree* with this nature: 'insofar as men live according to the guidance of reason, they must do only those things which are good for human nature, *and hence, for each man*' (E4p35dem). It is unclear, however, how the following three claims, which are invoked in these passages, are supposed to fit together.[28]

(A) All things strive to persevere in their being (E3p6).
(B) All things strive to preserve their natures (E4p31dem).
(C) All things strive to preserve other things that agree with them in their nature (E4p35dem).

In E4p31dem, Spinoza asserts (B) on the basis of the *conatus* doctrine (A); but the *conatus* doctrine makes no reference to the natures of things, claiming only that each thing strives to persevere in its *being* (*in suo esse*). The most straightforward way of licensing this inference is to assert that individuals are identical with their natures. And there is some reason to think that Spinoza in fact identified things with their essences or at least took things and essences to stand in a one-to-one relation (E2def2), though the textual evidence is far from conclusive (for evidence of shared essences, see E1p8s). Unfortunately, though, as Michael Della Rocca (2004) aptly pointed out, the inference from (B) to (C) seems to entail that multiple things *can* share a single nature, which directly conflicts with identification of thing and essence that underwrites the inference from (A) to (B). Della Rocca concludes that this argument suffers from an unresolved and seemingly unresolvable tension:

> Thus, in some passages, Spinoza expresses a commitment to the uniqueness of essences and in other places he expresses a commitment to its opposite. The main problem with Spinoza's proof in EIVp35d of the claim that rational

people are advantageous to others is that it expresses both commitments simultaneously. His failure to resolve this tension in his thinking about essences comes to a head in this important demonstration. (Della Rocca 2004: 134)

However, just a few years after the publication of 'Egoism and the Imitation of Affects in Spinoza', Della Rocca appears to have discovered the key to resolving this puzzle. He proposes that Spinoza has a conception of identity that permits him to treat striving to persevere in one's being as directly entailing the striving to aid in the preservation of those who *agree* in nature without equivocating on the possibility of shared natures.[29] He proposes that Spinoza is committed to a scalar conception of the identity of indiscernibles, according to which to the extent that things are similar to me, they *are* (numerically!) identical to me. And to that same extent, their virtue or power is literally mine; consequently, I will strive to enhance this power.

Della Rocca appeals to this argument from identity to justify the case for Compliance:

> ... the rebel has a great deal of similarity not only to the other citizens, but also to the state itself. By virtue of this similarity and to the degree to which the state and its sovereign are rational, the rebel has an obligation to preserve the state and to enhance its power and, in general, to strive for the things the state strives for. In other words, to the extent that the rebel is rational, he strives to enhance the state's power. (Della Rocca 2010: 182)

On this interpretation, doing good for others like me – including my compatriots and, indeed, the state itself – does not merely *instrumentally* redound to my good; rather, to the extent that others agree with me, their good *is* my good, because they literally are me.

This interpretation confirms the fears of the Restrictive Individualists: if the state is an individual, we lose, to some degree, our distinctness and become one with the state.

Della Rocca's interpretation hinges on his understanding of what it means for one thing to 'agree' with another. He takes agreement to mean similarity,[30] which is a function of just two factors: the extent to which things agree in nature (*in abstracto*) and the extent to which they are rational.[31] This is a purely formal conception of agreement or similarity. As far as things agree in nature and are rational, they 'automatically' benefit one another, irrespective of spatio-temporal relationships.[32] Della Rocca acknowledges that this interpretation carries odd and implausible implications (could it really be that a twenty-fifth century [ACE or BCE, it doesn't matter!], highly rational Siberian hermit is more useful than my slightly less rational, but thoughtful and amiable neighbour?),[33] but he is willing to bite this bullet – or, willing to have Spinoza bite this bullet – for the sake of consistency.

While Della Rocca's interpretation is quite ingenious, I think that there are good reasons to resist it. For instance, there is textual evidence that Spinoza does not think that things are identical to the extent that they agree with one another. We find suggestions that he takes agreement to be a relationship that holds between distinct individuals in several passages in E4, the most decisive expression of which comes in E4p18s: 'There are, therefore, many things outside us [extra nos] which are useful to us, and on that account to be sought. Of these, we can think of none more excellent than those which agree entirely with our nature'. Even things that 'agree entirely with our nature' are extrinsic to us. Things don't collapse into one another in virtue of agreeing; they retain their existential distinctness. Indeed, there is reason to think that it is precisely because something is existentially distinct from me that it *can* be *useful* to me, and that powers can compound in the ways that Spinoza indicates (E4p18s).[34] This is to say nothing of the conceptual problems that attend a 'scalar' conception of identity.

But the primary reason that I think we should resist Della Rocca's analysis is that it fails to capture the special utility of civic relations. If similar things were 'automatically' beneficial, as Della Rocca's interpretation entails, border differences would be irrelevant. Geographical proximity and civic ties would not give us any additional reason to aid or empower. We would have reason to empower all states and all people equally, modulating only for degrees of formal similarity. If citizens of another country are more rational, and so more like me, than my compatriots, then – other things being equal – I would have more reason to advance their interests than to advance the interests of my compatriots and my nation. However enlightened this position might be, it is assuredly not Spinoza's. One's power is uniquely bound up with the power of one's *own* state, and thus one has a particular interest in its success.

To his credit, Della Rocca acknowledges that 'political agreement' brings distinct utility. He accounts for this by maintaining that, because of civil arrangements, one is made to share more ends or agree more with one's compatriots than with others (Della Rocca 2010: 181). It is not clear how the suggestion that striving for the same things is a form of similarity is to be squared with the assertion that similarity is the function of just two factors: the extent to which things agree in nature and the extent to which they are rational (Della Rocca 2010: 178). More to the point, though, even if beings become more similar by desiring the same things, the utility of civic relations cannot be explained exclusively in formal terms. Members of other states in other eras – or, to get a bit more fanciful, participants in virtual worlds – may be more rational or may otherwise more formally resemble me than many of my compatriots, but I am uniquely benefited by the latter. The agreement that explains civic utility is not a matter of similarity alone.

But despite my criticisms, I think that Della Rocca is right that the concept of agreement is the key to understanding Convergence. In the next section, I will propose an alternative way of understanding agreement, as a functional, rather than merely formal, relationship.

5. Agreement as Cooperation

In the political works, Spinoza uses two terms that are translated into English as 'agreement': *pactum*, signifying a legal agreement or contract,[35] and the one I want to focus on, *convenientia*. *Convenientia* derives from the verb *convenire* ('to agree'), which is the very same term that Spinoza uses in the *Ethics* to account for the utility of humans to one another: 'the more a thing agrees [*convenit*] with our nature, the more useful, or better, it is for us' (E4p31c). *Convenire* can mean a number of things, and Spinoza takes full advantage of its many valences, using the term in some contexts to mean 'to correspond with' (E2def4) or 'accord with' (TP3.15, TP6.25, TP7.5), in others to mean 'to strike an agreement with', and in yet others to mean to come together, to assemble or even to conspire (TP6.1, TP9.3, TP7.14, TP10.2). It is the last sense of *convenire* as a literal coming together (*con-venire*) – which Lewis and Short (1975) list as its primary meaning ('To come together, meet, assemble, gather, come in a body') – that I want to focus on.

This sense of *convenire* plays an important role in Spinoza's account of state formation in TP2, where he claims to 'deduce' the foundations of the state from human nature, writing that if

> two men come together[36] [*conveniant*] and join forces [*vires iungant*] they can do more together, and hence, together have more right over nature, than either does alone. The more connections they've formed in this way, the more right they'll all have together. (TP2.13)[37]

He repeats this point just two sections later: 'the more they agree as one [*conveniunt in unum*] in this way, the more right they all have together' (TP2.15). On this understanding, what it means for things to agree is for them to combine powers and to act as one. To agree is literally to *co-operate*, to produce common effects, and to constitute a greater singular thing (E2def7). On this reading, things that agree with one another do not collapse into a single entity, rather they retain their distinctness while participating in a new, more powerful entity.

While this account of agreement [*convenientia*] is most perspicuous in the *Political Treatise*, we find glimpses of it in the *Ethics*. Consider, for instance, E3p5, which states 'Things are of a contrary nature, that is, cannot be in the same subject, insofar as one can destroy the other'. The demonstration for this reads: 'For if they agree with one another [*inter se convenire*], or be in the same subject at once, then there could be something in the same subject which could destroy it, which (by P4) is absurd' (E3p5dem). Leaving aside the reasoning here, the salient point for my analysis is that Spinoza infers that if things agree [*convenire*] with one another, then they are *in the same subject*.[38] Two things agree only if they are both in the same (larger) subject.

Now, this passage only demonstrates that things that agree with one another *inhere in* the same subject; it does not establish that they *compose* a larger subject.[39] The latter claim, however, is explicitly made in E4p18, where Spinoza writes:

There are, therefore, many things outside us which are useful to us, and on that account to be sought. Of these, we can think of none more excellent than those which agree entirely with our nature. For if, for example, two individuals of entirely the same nature are joined [*iunguntur*] to one another, they compose an individual twice as powerful as each one. To man, then, there is nothing more useful than man. Man, I say, can wish for nothing more helpful to the preservation of his being than that all should so agree [*conveniant*] in all things that the minds and bodies of all would compose, as it were, one mind and one body; that all should strive together, as far as they can, to preserve their being; and that all, together, should seek for themselves the common advantage of all. (E4p18s)

In order that 'the minds and bodies of all would compose, as it were, one mind and one body', it is not enough for things simply to agree *in nature*; these things must be joined [*iunguntur*] to one another such that they 'compose an individual twice as powerful as each one'. The agreement that Spinoza is extolling here is *agreement in function*, which – as in the passages from the TP – requires the joining of forces and entails the formation of a *larger* individual. To agree in operation is to forge associations, whereby individuals 'bind themselves by those bonds most apt to make one people of them' (E4app12). Once again, agreement entails participating in a larger individual.[40]

This account harmonises with features of Diane Steinberg's interpretation of Spinoza and altruism (or non-egoism). Steinberg attempts to reconcile Spinoza's anti-realism about universals with his appeal to a shared human nature by maintaining that 'the human nature of one person is absolutely indistinguishable as such from that of any other'.[41] Specifically, she conceives of 'mankind or humanity' as a complex individual whose laws bind together and, to some degree, govern the activity of particular human individuals. The point that I want to stress here is that, like me, Steinberg conceives of the 'agreement' in virtue of which human individuals are beneficial to one another as entailing participation in some larger entity, construing this shared nature or agreement in expressly organic terms: 'just as hearts would not be hearts if they did not exist as parts of human bodies, human beings would not be human beings if they were not each a part of mankind' (Steinberg 1984: 319).

Before proceeding, I want to dispel an objection raised by Jonathan Bennett that there is an equivocation lurking in the analogy with the human body. Bennett writes

The picture of men as composing a single individual and together seeking the common advantage of all, suggests a single organism each of whose organs preserves itself through its special contribution to the survival of the whole. But that conflicts with the idea that men should be 'entirely of the same nature' ... the harmony which relates my lungs to my heart and both to my blood etc., and the harmony of a school of fish peacefully swimming in the same direction. He wants us to interrelate like the former, but his arguments all point to the latter. (Bennett 1984: 306–7)[42]

Put somewhat differently, Spinoza seems to slide between agreement in nature – or homology – and agreement in function. As I've indicated, though, I think that in fact Spinoza did intend to distinguish between formal and functional agreement, which is why he is often careful to tag the former as 'agreement in nature' (*natura*). And, while it is true that not all functional unities must be composed of homologous parts, there is nothing incoherent about insisting that certain functional unities – like moral communities or the state – can only be forged out of homologous parts, since only things that agree in nature can be bound by these particular kinds of laws. While we might wish that Spinoza more carefully distinguished between, and expounded on, these conceptions of agreement, we should not take the admission that certain forms of cooperation require similarity as evidence of confusion, as Bennett does.

While I don't intend to defend Diane Steinberg's interpretation wholesale, I do find it instructive insofar as it serves not only as a precedent for this reading of agreement as participation in a larger individual, but also as a model for defending a version of Convergence. She concludes her analysis by indicating how such a view supports Spinoza's non-egoism:

> Why then did Spinoza think it absurd that reason should counsel human beings to have in reality no common laws, that is, to submit to common laws only to the degree that it is in one's own self-interest to do so? I believe it was because he thought it impossible that a person should preserve his own being or promote his own welfare without acting in accordance with a set of laws whose aim is to promote the welfare of mankind. (Steinberg 1984: 322–3)

Individual welfare is so bound up with collective welfare that that 'the egoistic/non-egoistic distinction collapses' (Steinberg 1984: 323). This reasoning applies *a fortiori* to the citizen and the state. As noted in my preliminary observations about civility, individual humans are necessarily driven to come together (*con-venire*), since we are fundamentally powerless in isolation. Coming together with others – forging an agreement and forming a super-individual – provides conditions in which we can each flourish. The better we preserve the laws or *rationes vivendi* that hold together this super-individual, the more effectively we cooperate and more completely we empower or benefit one another.

At this point, we can see how this sense of agreement differs from Della Rocca's. First, it consists in a functional rather than a merely formal relationship: to agree with others is not merely to resemble them in some way; it is to operate as one (*in unum*). It is something achieved or accomplished when the dynamic powers of individuals are united.[43] Second, rather than entailing that we are literally (numerically) identical with others to the extent that we agree with them, my interpretation entails that things that agree with one another maintain existential distinctness, but compound powers by forging a larger individual. And, finally, it accounts for the special utility of civic relations. We benefit from our state and have a special interest in its health not because formally similar things 'automatically' benefit one another, but because we are empowered when we operate in concert with others.

6. Conclusion

The interpretation of civic agreement as cooperation reinforces the case against the Restrictive Individualists by presenting further reasons for supposing that the state, which is constituted by human agreement, is an individual. And the account of Convergence intimated on the basis of this interpretation of agreement in no way undermines the ontological distinctness or the normative priority of the human individual, as the reasons for supporting the state are firmly rooted in the interests of the human constituents.

Still, the preceding analysis leaves unanswered *which* higher-order individuals – which cooperative units – we ought to be most concerned with preserving and strengthening. It is conceivable that the benefits of empowering some non-civil – say, transnational or subnational – association could outweigh the benefits of empowering the state. Think of separatist groups for whom empowering their association requires acts of civil non-compliance, perhaps in the form of revolution or secession.

Spinoza does not directly take up this scenario, but nothing in his account (or its logic) precludes the possibility that the form of agreement that is most beneficial to the individual is transnational or subnational. Rather than attempting to offer a full reconstruction of Spinoza's would-be response, I'll simply note that he was indeed concerned with the possibility that people would prioritise other associations – especially religious associations – above the state. And he thought that the fragmentation or balkanisation of interest groups *within* a state is a sign of civic pathology, for which the sovereign deserves the bulk of the blame (see TP5.2–5.3). Where one's welfare would be advanced – or even would *appear* to be advanced – through counter-civil behaviour, the state has failed, as its function is to coordinate the activity of its members, to induce harmony. If the state is to secure its status as the super-individual nonpareil, it must create the conditions in which citizens see themselves as participants in, and beneficiaries of, the operations of the body politic. So, even if 'men aren't born civil' (TP5.2), in a well-functioning republic, individuals will come to appreciate the extent to which their welfare depends on their cooperation with their compatriots.

Notes

1. Steinberg (2018a, 2018b).
2. Steinberg (2018a). In order for an issuance of law ('law') to be a genuine *ratio vivendi*, a certain threshold of compliance must be met (see TP3.8, G iii: 288).
3. Steinberg (2018a).
4. It is not clear to me why the latter, on its own, is an evil. I can only surmise that Rice's point is that reification brings along its 'twin', totalitarianism. But this is implausible, as Rice himself concedes: 'This is not to say that all of the consequences of such

communalism for the nonautonomy of the individual will follow from the adoption of such a model in Spinoza' (Rice 1990: 274).
5. See also: '[A] complex may be said to be "more than the sum of its parts," and thus an individual from an ontological perspective, if and only if the laws governing those parts are a subset of the implication class of the laws governing the complex whole. If this subset relation does not hold, then the complex is a logical individual' (Rice 1990: 277).
6. Barbone (2002: 107).
7. Rice (1990: 278).
8. Rice draws here on Douglas Den Uyl's distinction between *per se* and *ad aliud* power (Den Uyl 1983). One can exercise *ad aliud* power, or power over another, simply in virtue of derived powers, as when a group of people move a boulder.
9. Rice (1990: 282).
10. Barbone (2002: 100). In fairness, Barbone admits that this is 'to speak grossly'.
11. Barbone (2002: 99).
12. Barbone (2002: 99) Taken strictly, this view is incoherent. If an individual, *I*, is nothing but the striving to preserve *I*, the account is either circular or infinitely regressive, since one is left to answer to what the second '*I*' refers. The upshot here is that the *conatus* should not be taken as the sole basis for metaphysical individuation, even if striving is the essential activity of all individuals. See Garrett (1994: 97).
13. Barbone (2002: 99).
14. Cited in Rice (1990: 27).
15. Others who have argued for degrees of individuality include Michael Della Rocca (1996, 2008) and Yitzhak Melamed (2013).
16. Moreover, by Barbone's own admission, collectives like the state can produce common effects, and to the extent that they do so, they may be regarded as a single thing (E2def7), even if not as an individual ('we cannot properly identify the Chargers as an individual, but only as a single thing' (Barbone 2002: 100)). While there is some debate concerning exactly how the concepts of individuals (*individua*) and singular things (*res singulare*) relate to one another, this much is clear: the *conatus* doctrine applies to *things* (*res*) (see E3p4–7). As singular things are a subset of things – namely they are things that are finite and have a determinate existence (E2def7) – collectives that produce common effects must, like all singular things, *strive to persevere in their being*. So, if Barbone admits that the state is a singular thing, he cannot coherently deny that it strives.
17. I don't wish to claim that, for Spinoza, all laws are reducible to and explicable in terms of a few primary laws. But I am suggesting that whatever laws exist – however many, and however broad in scope they happen to be – are either primary laws themselves or are reducible to the primary laws of nature. Thanks to Andrea Sangiacomo for prompting me to clarify this point.
18. Rice (1990: 274).
19. For instance, Yitzhak Melamed has recently maintained that for Spinoza parts are prior in knowledge and nature to their wholes: 'Parts are prior to their whole both in nature and in our knowledge' (Melamed 2013: 47). He cites three bits of textual evidence: (1) E1p12dem, which claims that it would be absurd to think that 'the whole could both be and be conceived without its parts'; (2) Ep35, where, as in E1p12dem, he denies that God is a complex whole, claiming, that God is 'simple and not composed of parts. For in respect of *their nature* and *our knowledge* of them, component parts would have to be prior to that which they compose'; (3) CM, Part II,

ch. 5 (G i: 258): 'component parts are prior in nature at least to the thing composed' (Melamed 2013: 47, note 145). If this is right, then human individuals, as *parts* of a higher-order whole, would be metaphysically prior to the state. For scepticism about Melamed's reading, see Alison Peterman (2014).
20. Contrast with Den Uyl, who claims that super-individuals would 'also have to be found, at least theoretically, in the state of nature' (Den Uyl 1983: 70).
21. Barbone (2002: 107).
22. Indeed, as we shall see, the power of the individual human is in fact augmented by participating in the functioning of a larger individual.
23. There are two other key claims that Restrictive Individualists make against the possibility of state individualism. One is that Spinoza claims that states are always more vulnerable to internal rebellion than external threats, while singular things can *only* be destroyed by external causes. The other is that Spinoza adopts hedging phrases when describing the mind/body politic, claiming that the state acts 'as if' (*veluti, quasi*) from a single mind, rather than explicitly embracing state individualism. Without attempting to fully rebut these considerations here, I will simply note that I don't think either of them seriously threatens the claim of state individualism. The fact that states can be destroyed by citizens does not mean that they can be destroyed by internal causes. Rather, to the extent that citizens act seditiously, they act from their partially extrinsic nature. Indeed, Spinoza cites the fact that the state is endangered more by its citizens than by its enemies as evidence that the 'transfer' of one's right to the state is incomplete – human individuals always retain their own power (TTP17.1–5 (G iii: 201–2)). This also helps to explain the hedging phrases (*veluti, quasi*), as Spinoza may simply be calling attention to the fact that the decisions of the state are never realised without the consent of disparate constituent minds – the state is never truly guided by a single mind alone. This comports with TP3.2, where Spinoza invokes the hedging phrase *veluti* to describe how the state is guided (as if by one mind), but proceeds unhesitatingly to refer to the 'body and mind of the whole state' (*totius imperii corpus et mens*) (cf. TP3.5).
24. TTP16.48–50 (G iii: 197).
25. So as to leave no doubt, he repeats it a few lines later: 'he's violated the right of the supreme power, has committed treason, and is rightly condemned. As we've said, it doesn't matter how much advantage this would certainly bring to the state' (TTP16.51 (G iii: 198)).
26. One way to make sense of this would be to distinguish between the intention and the outcomes. The treasonous subject might be condemned for acting without authority, even while producing salutary consequences. One complicating factor here is that it is not clear whether the knowledge that it 'would clearly benefit the whole Republic' is part of the aspect under which the treasonous agent acts, or whether this is just apparent from some omniscient perspective. If one could really be quite certain that non-compliance would be empowering, it is hard to see why this would be a condemnable act, unless one thinks that permitting case-by-case determinations of utility is dangerous (see Steinberg 2014).
27. E4p37dem appeals to E4p35c1, which is in turn rooted in E4p31c and, ultimately, E4p31.
28. The following discussion is indebted to Della Rocca (2004). Steinberg (1984) calls attention to similar problems.
29. Della Rocca (2010).
30. This is his gloss in multiple works, including Della Rocca (2004, 2010).

31. Della Rocca (2010: 178).
32. Della Rocca (2010: 179; 2008: 197).
33. Della Rocca (2010: 179).
34. It would be, at the very least, linguistically awkward to suggest that 'I am useful to myself.' To be clear, though, existential distinctness is compatible with agreement in nature.
35. This concept is notably absent from the TP.
36. I've altered Curley's translation here, which reads – infelicitously, in my view – 'If two men make an agreement [*conveniant*]'.
37. I take 'join[ing] forces' here to be just an elaboration of what happens in virtue of coming together.
38. Surprisingly, Spinoza uses *vel* or the 'or' of disjunction, rather than *sive* or the 'or' of apposition. Nevertheless, he is clearly claiming that agreement entails participation in a (larger) subject, and the reasoning is far more intelligible if we take this as an appositive 'or'.
39. In conversation, John Grey rightly cautioned me against conflating the inherence relationship with the composition relationship. I do think, however, that when it comes to things, as opposed to substance, Spinoza's treatment of these two relations is somewhat entangled. For instance, an idea is, at once, *in* the mind and a *part of* the mind.
40. In Ep32 (the worm in the blood letter), Spinoza claims: 'concerning whole and parts, I consider things as parts of some whole to the extent that the nature of the one adapts itself to that of the other so that they [A: all] agree with one another as far as possible', which suggests once again that it is in virtue of agreeing with one another that things constitute parts of some (greater) whole. Sangiacomo (2015) emphasises this point. While this supports my reading, it is worth noting that the Latin verb translated here as 'agree' is *consentire*, not *convenire*.
41. Steinberg (1984: 314; cf. p. 309).
42. Thanks to John Grey for drawing my attention to this passage. If I remember rightly, Hasana Sharp raised a similar concern in response to the analogy with the human body when I presented this paper at a conference at the University of Toronto.
43. Etienne Balibar interprets *convenientia* in a way that draws out the notion of cooperation of unified functioning. He refers to *convenientia* as a kind of 'synergy' (Balibar 1997: 24) that is achieved though 'rational communication' (ibid.: 30). See also Sharp (2011).

Works Cited

Balibar, Etienne (1997), 'Spinoza: From Individuality to Transindividuality', Mededelingen vanwege het Spinozahuis, Delft: Eburon.

Barbone, Steven (2002), 'What Counts as an Individual for Spinoza?', in Olli Koistinen and J. I. Biro (eds), *Spinoza: Metaphysical Themes*, Oxford: Oxford University Press.

Bennett, Jonathan (1984), *A Study of Spinoza's* Ethics, Indianapolis: Hackett Publishing Company.

Della Rocca, Michael (1996), *Representation and the Mind-Body Problem in Spinoza*, Oxford: Oxford University Press.

Della Rocca, Michael (2004), 'Egoism and the Imitation of Affects in Spinoza', in Yirmiyahu Yovel and Gideon Segal (eds), *Spinoza on Reason and the 'Free Man': The Jerusalem Conference*, vol. 4, New York: Little Room Press, pp. 123–47.

Della Rocca, Michael (2008), *Spinoza*, New York: Routledge.
Della Rocca, Michael (2010), 'Getting His Hands Dirty: Spinoza's Criticism of the Rebel', in Yitzhak Y. Melamed and Michael A. Rosenthal (eds), *Spinoza's 'Theological-Political Treatise': A Critical Guide*, Cambridge: Cambridge University Press, pp. 168–91.
Den Uyl, Douglas (1983), *Power, State, and Freedom: An Interpretation of Spinoza's Political Philosophy*, Assen, the Netherlands: Van Gorcum.
Garrett, Don (1994), 'Spinoza's Theory of Metaphysical Individuation', in Kenneth F. Barber and Jorge J. E. Garcia (eds), *Individuation and Identity in Early Modern Philosophy: Descartes to Kant*, Stony Brook, NY: State University of New York Press, pp. 73–101.
Lewis, Charlton T. and Short, Charles [1879] (1975), *A Latin Dictionary: Founded on Andrews' Edition of Freund's Latin Dictionary*, Oxford: Clarendon Press.
Melamed, Yitzhak (2013), *Spinoza's Metaphysics: Substance and Thought*, New York: Oxford University Press.
Peterman, Alison (2014), 'Alison Peterman's comments on Spinoza's Metaphysics: Substance and Thought: Part 2', The Mod Squad: A Group Blog in Modern Philosophy, 22 April, https://philosophymodsquad.wordpress.com/2014/04/22/alison-petermans-comments-on-spinozas-metaphysics-substance-and-thought-part-2/> (last accessed 9 November 2018).
Rice, Lee (1990), 'Individual and Community in Spinoza's Social Psychology', in Edwin Curley and Pierre-Francois Moreau (eds), *Spinoza: New Perspectives*, Leiden: E. J. Brill, pp. 271–85.
Sangiacomo, Andrea (2015), 'The Ontology of Determination: From Descartes to Spinoza', *Science in Context*, 28(4): 515–43.
Sharp, Hasana (2011), *Spinoza and the Politics of Renaturalization*, Chicago: The University of Chicago Press.
Steinberg, Diane (1984), 'Spinoza's Ethical Doctrine and the Unity of Human Nature', *Journal of the History of Philosophy*, 22: 303–24.
Steinberg, Justin (2014), 'Following a *Recta Ratio Vivendi*: The Practical Utility of Spinoza's Dictates of Reason', in Matthew Kisner and Andrew Youpa (eds), *Essays on Spinoza's Ethical Theory*, Oxford: Oxford University Press, pp. 178–96.
Steinberg, Justin (2018a), 'Spinoza and Political Absolutism', in Hasana Sharp and Yitzhak Melamed (eds), *Spinoza's Political Treatise: New Assessments*, Cambridge: Cambridge University Press, pp. 175–89.
Steinberg, Justin (2018b), *Spinoza's Political Psychology: The Taming of Fortune and Fear*, Cambridge: Cambridge University Press.

8

Power, Freedom and Relational Autonomy

Ericka Tucker

In recent years, the notion of relational autonomy has transformed the old debate about the freedom of the individual in society. A simplification of this debate has two poles: on the one side were libertarian individualists who argued that freedom requires complete independence from society, and on the other were those philosophers who argued that without the social there could be no self to be free in the first place. Rather than the old poles of libertarianism versus social constructivism, relational autonomy theorists sought to find ways to understand how we can be free while being fully situated in social lives (Benhabib 1992; Mackenzie and Stoljar 2000; Barclay 2000; Christman 2004; Westlund 2009; Stoljar 2015). While the freedom of an individual is clearly curtailed in some ways by having to follow the law, for example, it is also clear that the society that supports the individual also makes it possible for the individual to do and to be more, that is, in another sense, to be free. In her article 'Autonomy and the Relational Individual', Aurelia Armstrong argues that Spinoza can best be understood as a theorist of relational autonomy (Armstrong 2009). She argues both that Spinozan freedom is relational and, further, that Spinoza's notion of freedom really is one of autonomy. While I agree with Armstrong that we cannot understand Spinoza's notion of freedom without understanding the social and physical relations by which individual power is constituted, I am less sure that Spinoza's theory of freedom is entirely captured by understanding it in terms of autonomy, unless we understand it as a fully naturalised constitutive conception of autonomy (Oshana 1994). By constitutive autonomy, I refer to Marina Oshana's view that external circumstances – social and political conditions – impinge strongly on individual freedom. For Oshana, the external circumstances that foster or limit individual autonomy are both physical and psychological or ideological – all of which are understood naturalistically. Oshana's account recognises that increasing individual autonomy may involve challenging or changing these external circumstances. That is, social change, for example, may be required for individual autonomy. Oshana's account and Spinoza's conception of relational autonomy would be considered 'constitutive' theories of relational autonomy (Barclay 2000; Christman 2004; Oshana 2006; Stoljar 2015). These accounts are constitutive insofar as they not only 'investigate the effects of external "relational" factors on agents' autonomy' (Stoljar 2015) as with causal approaches, but also understand autonomy as both created and limited by external circumstances. For Spinoza, individual humans are embedded in natural, social and political circumstances from which they derive their power and freedom. I take this to mean that Spinoza's is best described as a constitutive theory of relational autonomy.[1]

I will show how by defining freedom in terms of power, Spinoza understands individual freedom as irreducibly relational. I propose that Spinoza develops his theory of power to understand how individual power or freedom is limited and enhanced by the power of those around one. For Spinoza, the power of an individual is a function of that individual's emotions, imaginative conceptions of itself and the world and its appetites. In this paper (1) I will argue that Spinoza reformulates a concept of freedom in terms of power. (2) His mature theory of freedom as power proposes that individual power is determined through social interaction, and is thus best understood as a relational theory of freedom. (3) I will show that as a consequence of Spinoza's theory, individual power and empowerment relies on those around the individual and, thus, to achieve individual liberation we must pursue collective empowerment.

One approach to understanding Spinoza's conception of freedom as an autonomy theory involves appealing to Spinoza's dictum that to be truly free is to be understood to be the sole cause of one's actions (E1def7). Several chapters in this book have investigated this, and rightly so, since it is Spinoza's explicit definition of freedom (Kisner 2011; Kisner, Steinberg, Green and Sangiacomo in this volume). However, while Spinoza set this out as a criterion for freedom, he spends quite a lot of his work investigating what we might think of as 'unfreedom' – the various ways in which humans individually and as a group are impinged upon by external forces, and how we can increase our freedom. Spinoza calls this unfreedom 'bondage' and argues that real freedom consists in understanding how to emerge from this bondage. His answer to how we combat this bondage is articulated in terms of power – Spinoza is concerned with how we, as individuals, can increase our own power. I propose that to understand what Spinoza means by freedom, we need look not just at his explicit definition – which may even be misleading – but rather, we need to look to the theory of power he formulated to offer a path to liberation from bondage (Armstrong 2017).

Despite his explicit definition of freedom as being understood as the cause of one's actions, I propose that Spinoza theorises freedom as increasing power. We are free, or have an increased degree of freedom in Spinoza's thinking, when we have been able to emerge from the bondage of the force of certain affects and false ideas about the world that diminish our power (TP1.1, TP2.3–2.11). Increasing one's power, in Spinozan terms, is increasing one's freedom. There is much to say about this transition from the vocabulary of 'freedom' to that of 'power' in Spinoza's work, and indeed, much more perhaps than can be said here. While I think that Spinoza's notion of power requires more elaboration than is possible here, we can set out a provisional definition: by 'power' Spinoza refers to the power of acting and thinking of an individual. 'Power' in this sense can be understood as an individual human's capabilities or a group's capacity to form and achieve its goals. Although a more extended argument is required for my definition of Spinoza's understanding of power, my contribution to this volume seeks to show that, for Spinoza, freedom is correlated with and defined in terms of power. I take Spinoza's theory and concept of power to be his own attempt to reformulate the concept of freedom. In this chapter, I follow the path of definitions in Spinoza's work that brings us from 'freedom' to 'power'. For my purposes, then, the gloss of 'power' above is less important than the conclusion that whatever Spinoza's means by power, he takes this to also be the definition of freedom.

Exploring the connection between freedom and power is vital for this volume, since Spinoza's theory of power is explicitly relational. Individual power, and therefore individual freedom, is determined through social interaction. This does not mean that, for Spinoza, individual 'freedom' is impossible. Rather, he proposes that in order to achieve individual liberation we must pursue collective empowerment.

In section 1, I will offer textual arguments for the correlation between freedom and power and will argue that Spinoza replaces the notion of freedom with his new theoretical term 'power'.

1. From Freedom to Power

Spinoza is possibly best known for his rejection of the notion of free will (E1p32, E2p48–9). In Part 1 of the *Ethics* he infamously denies freedom of the will even to God, who, he argues, acts only through his power, that is, his essence (E1p34). In the appendix to Part 1, Spinoza shores up this rejection of God as one acting through freedom of the will. Although he still refers to God as 'free' he rejects the notion that God's will is free. Instead, he writes that, 'All things have been predetermined by God, not from his free or absolute pleasure, but from the absolute nature of God, his infinite power' (E1app). In the place of 'freedom of the will' of God, a doctrine that is almost universally approved, Spinoza argues that it is not God's freedom or will that cause his actions, but his power (E2p13sl5, TTP16, TP2.1). This makes more sense if we substitute Spinoza's term 'Nature', which he uses interchangeably with 'God', to yield the idea that Nature does not act through freedom of the will, but rather through its power. Since human individuals are part of Nature, modes of God, to understand individual power we need to understand the power of God, or Nature. Spinoza argues that individual human power is derived from, or expresses the eternal essence of God, that is, God's power (E1p25, E2p45). Spinoza writes, 'Individuals, insofar as they are part of the power of Nature, constitute a part of the power of Nature' (TTP4). Human individuals, then, have part of the power of Nature.

When Spinoza later formulates his rejection of free will for human individuals, he similarly rejects the idea that human beings have free will, while defining human essence in terms of power. We humans have what Spinoza calls a '*conatus*', or particular individual essence, which Spinoza defines that individual's power:

Therefore, the power of any individual thing, or the conatus with which it acts or endeavours to act, alone or in conjunction with other things, that is, the power or conatus by which it endeavours to persist in its own being, is nothing but the given or actual essence of the thing. (E3p7def)

While perhaps unnecessarily wordy, the conclusion is clear: human individuals have as their essence their power.

Yet even as Spinoza rejects the notion of free will, he reintroduces the notion of freedom. He explains in the final lines of Part 2 of the *Ethics* that understanding of the human mind offers us insight into politics. In particular, he says, 'it teaches the manner in which citizens should be governed and led; namely, not so as to be slaves, but so as to do freely what is best' (E2p49s). We may well ask what the meaning of this second use of 'freely' is.

One answer, at least for the human case, is that individuals acting according to the dictates of reason are said, by Spinoza, to be acting freely (E4p52, TTP20, TP3.7). We may take reason to be a certain threshold of human power, particularly the power of the mind to overcome passive affects (*Short Treatise* [KV] 21, 22). However, Spinoza's definition of reason suggests that it is closer to *conatus* itself. He writes, 'To act from reason is nothing else but to do what follows from the necessity of our own nature considered solely in itself' (E4p59def). This last proposal requires that the necessity of our own nature and our essence can be understood as one and the same.

There is another sense in which Spinoza uses reason – and that is perhaps the one closest to what he means by free action – one can 'live by the guidance of reason'. This might at first seem to be a normative conception of reason, but Spinoza avoids this by defining reason in terms of power: 'Man's true power of activity, or his virtue, is reason itself' (E4p52). Here, Spinoza explicitly defines reason in terms of power, allowing us to say that insofar as an individual's power is active, one is living or acting according to reason, and thus is free. However, here it would appear that reason is defined as a high degree of power, or power as active rather than passive. As Spinoza explains in E3p11, the mind can undergo many changes, and indeed 'can pass now to a state of greater perfection now to one of less perfection'. Acting through reason is surely a perfection of the mind. But 'perfection' is defined by Spinoza in terms of power (E1app). Indeed, the two are treated interchangeably. This should come as no real surprise given that Spinoza, in the appendix to Part 1 of the *Ethics*, has rejected the usual notion of perfection as being anything other than individual preference. He argues there that 'The perfection of things should be measured solely from their own nature and power' (E1app). By dropping the notion of perfection as mistaken, Spinoza retrieves it by defining it in terms of power. This manoeuvre of using the accepted vocabulary of philosophers but with a new and often tendentious definition is one Spinoza employs regularly. He also does this with the notion of 'virtue' in definition 8 of Part 4 of the *Ethics*, where he writes, 'By virtue and power I mean the same thing' (E4def8) and with the notion of blessedness in Part 5, Proposition 42 where he writes, 'Blessedness is not the reward of virtue, but virtue itself.' From this we can say that if the transitive property holds of Spinozan definitions, then blessedness is power, or a degree of power. Finally, Spinoza defines blessedness as 'freedom of the mind' (E5pref). The careful reader will note a pattern emerging. Essence, virtue, reason, blessedness and perfection are all defined in terms of power. Freedom is defined in terms of blessedness and reason, and, thus, we can conclude that freedom can be understood in terms of power. To increase one's freedom, for Spinoza, is to have increased one's power.

Why would Spinoza define freedom in terms of power? The reason for this move is hinted at in the appendix to Part 1 of the *Ethics* – Spinoza seeks to reclaim a genuine notion of freedom apart from the false notion of free will. To do so, he employs a term that could not be mistaken for free will, and one which he can use to explain that whatever power individuals have, it is through being part of God or Nature. Freedom, in Spinoza's sense, does not transcend nature. Rather, God or Nature is that through which we have the power to act in the world at all.

In this section, I have shown that Spinoza's notion of power was meant to replace the notion of free will. I proposed that freedom is not alone in being redefined in terms of power. In the *Ethics*, virtue, blessedness, perfection and right are redefined as power. We may ask, what does this really accomplish? Once we understand the interconnection between the power of the individual and the power of the collective, we can see how individual freedom is constituted by, and relationally affected by, the power of those around one. Understanding the upshot of the connection between freedom and power requires delving into Spinoza's theory of power. This discussion will be unavoidably technical. However, if we can bear with the technical, we can see what Spinoza offers us – a rich conception of the ways in which social, political and psychological forces shape individual and collective freedom.

2. Individual Power as Relational

As human power derives from Nature, of which each individual is a part, human power is relational from the very start. Each individual derives his or her power from their parthood relation (or mode relation) with Nature (or God). (TTP4 (C2: 126; G iii: 58)) Thus, human power is derived power, and hence relational in at least this first way. What I hope to show is that, for Spinoza, there is another way in which human power is relational, although this second relational dimension of power derives from the first. As each individual, human or otherwise, derives its power from God, so the individuals together are affected by this first relation, their relation to God as parts. This gives rise to the second dimension of their relationality, in that since they are each parts of God, together they are all parts of God, and thus are related to one another. Each individual, as part of Nature, is related to each and every other part of Nature. As all are parts of God or Nature, their interactions impact one another, and these impacts can affect their power. For Spinoza, the more we increase our power, the more we increase our freedom. In this section, I will set out Spinoza's proposals for how individual power works, how it can be increased and decreased, and how our relations with others affect our power.

For Spinoza, each individual has a degree of power (E3p9, E3p9s, E3p7def). This power is derived from the power of Nature of which each individual is a part. Spinoza calls this power *'conatus'* (E3p7def). As the individual is part of nature, so he or she is also made of parts. The forces of the natural world can impinge upon these parts differentially, requiring the individual to coordinate their power by coordinating these parts (E2p13s). One coordinates one's affects through constructing a 'self', that is, an idea of oneself that one uses to interpret and corral one's affects. Spinoza insists that human individuals are made up of parts that can be differentially affected by external forces. Our ideas of ourselves our concept of our 'self' prioritises appetites, interprets emotions and develops strategies for moving about in the world. These ideas of our 'selves', what a self is and ought to be, are then shaped socially. Through social interaction, first in the family and then in the larger community, we shape how we coordinate our ideas, our emotions and our appetites.

An individual's power can increase or decrease depending on the individual's ideas about itself and the world, its affects or emotions, and its appetites – or what it seeks (E3p11s). Power can increase or decrease in each of these dimensions, that is, one can become more powerful by having more adequate ideas, more active affects or more self-preservatory appetites, or less powerful by having less adequate ideas, more passive affects or less self-preservatory appetites.

Each of these dimensions requires some clarification. I will begin with the affects. We may think of affect as an emotion. There are some complications with this, but what Spinoza identifies as affects – hate, love, fear, envy and so on – are what we would broadly call emotions.[2] Spinoza distinguishes between active and passive affects. Affects like joy express an increase in an individual's power. When one understands the causes of this joy, one becomes more powerful still. Passive affects, like fear, hatred or sadness, express a decrease in an individual's power (E3p11s). The quality of one's idea of oneself and the world can further increase or decrease one's power (E3p1, E3p9). If one understands oneself as part of Nature, and affected by external causes, then one has a more adequate idea of oneself than someone who believes their body to be, for example, impenetrable.[3] As an individual gains greater knowledge of themselves and the world, their knowledge is said to be more adequate and their power increased. If one understands the causes of one's affections, one's power increases. If one is ignorant of the causes of one's affections, one's power diminishes.

Desires and appetites are in a sense determined by one's ideas of the world around one and one's affects – however inadequate or passive. These desires can lead one to further knowledge of the world, which increases one's power, or to seek out dangerous or foolhardy things, which diminish one's power. More adequate ideas of oneself and the world have the potential to redirect one's desires, but, for Spinoza, ultimately, desires are more powerful than reason and we humans have a particular gift for seeing the better and doing the worse. What this power amounts to is something rather straightforward, despite it being defined in terms of perfection, virtue, blessedness and freedom: it is the power to act and think (E3p9s). The greater one's power, the greater one's ability to act and think in the world. Since, as I've argued above, freedom is defined as power, we can see what this freedom really amounts to; namely, for Spinoza, freedom amounts to the capabilities one has to think and act in the natural world of which one is a part. In the next section, I will delve into how Spinoza's notion of power or capability to act and think in the world is relational – that is, determined by forces which are themselves relations.

3. Social Power: The Imitation of the Affects

In Part 3 of the *Ethics*, Spinoza sets out his conception of individual power, or *conatus*. Power is scalar, and can both increase and decrease. More positive affects, more adequate ideas and more self-preservatory desires increase one's power, while affects based on pain, less adequate ideas and less self-preservatory desires decrease individual power. These are the bare bones of the theory, taking for a moment the individual human alone and separate from others, with his or her power determined somehow internally. However, Spinoza does not think that human affects, ideas or desires are created in a vacuum – they are shaped in societies among other individuals to which we closely attend. In the third part of the *Ethics*, from Propositions 27 to 57, Spinoza sets out how individual affects, desires and ideas are shaped by those around us. He begins with a developmental story.

Spinoza notes that individual humans are born among other humans: those who raise us and to whom we look for the most basic cues about what to desire and avoid, what to love and hate, and how to interact with others. While it is hardly revolutionary to note that humans have parents, families, and that they are not indifferent to these other human beings, it sets the stage for Spinoza's psychology and theory of mind. Spinoza writes,

> For we find from experience that children, because their bodies are continually, as it were, in a state of equilibrium, laugh or cry simply because they see others laugh or cry. Moreover, whatever they see others do, they immediately desire to imitate it. And finally, they desire for themselves all those things by which they imagine others are pleased. (E3p32s)

As individual humans develop, each shapes his or her goals, affects and ideas in relation to other humans and within a society that shapes that individual in turn. Through the mechanism of joy that increases our power, and our own joy at being esteemed by others, and sadness at being rejected or rebuked by others, our 'selves' are shaped – our actions, our desires, our affects and our ideas about ourselves and the world, in reciprocal relation with other human beings. In Spinoza studies this is referred to as the 'imitation of the affects' (E2p27s, E3p27–57) and is a well-known aspect of Spinoza's psychology (James 1997; Gatens and Lloyd 1999; LeBuffe 2015; Della Rocca 2004; Steinberg 2016). We have the strongest desire to emulate those we love; however, Spinoza contends that 'We endeavour to do whatever we imagine men [men for whom we have felt no emotion] to regard with pleasure, and on the other hand we shun doing whatever we imagine men to regard with aversion' (E3p31). We seek esteem from others who we perceive to be like us, and shape our actions to conform to what we believe they esteem.

Our relations with others are mediated by our own ideas about them. Our desires, ideas and affects are affected by what we imagine others love, hate, desire and believe. Spinoza holds that if we imagine that someone loves, desires or hates something that we love, desire or hate, this very fact will cause us to love, desire or hate the thing more steadfastly. But, if we imagine he dislikes what we love, or vice versa, then our feelings will fluctuate (E3p27s). Spinoza describes this process as involving 'the imitation of the affects'. He explains how this works in great detail in part 3 of the *Ethics*. I have argued elsewhere that Spinoza's elaboration of this imaginative process (E3p27s, E3p29, E3p31c, E3p32s, E3p33–4) is the foundation of his social theory. What I hope to establish here is the less ambitious thesis that, for Spinoza, our individual human power is relational. As affects, ideas and desires determine individual power, and as individual affects, ideas and desires are shaped by others in society, so we can conclude that individual power is shaped – increased or decreased – by interactions with other individuals. Through his explanation of the imitation of the affects, Spinoza shows us that since human affects, imagination and ideas are shaped socially, so is our power. For Spinoza, each individual human derives their power from coordinating their affects, ideas and desires into a stable and recognisable pattern of motion and rest (E3p17s, E2p13s). This power can increase and decrease. As individual power increases, the individual is able to do more within Nature. Power is the power to think and to act in the world. The sources of this power – emotions, ideas and appetites – are shaped relationally, within and among other human individuals, and in the context of particular environments.[4]

Spinoza's recognition that individual power is shaped socially has been a worry for those in the twentieth century who hoped to bring Spinoza's political philosophy into the Western canon of political thought. For entry, Spinoza had to be seen as a philosopher who did not violate principles of liberal autonomy. In her article 'Spinoza's Ethics and Politics of Freedom', Aurelia Armstrong takes up this worry directly. In order to allow Spinoza's ideas to be taken seriously, commentators like Steven Smith and Douglas Den Uyl had to argue that Spinoza's notion of freedom was not one that was strongly socially embedded in order to avoid his work being understood as 'perfectionist' and 'authoritarian' in the categorisation of Isaiah Berlin. In order to argue that Spinoza does not propose to engineer the social, Armstrong argues, Smith and Den Uyl misrepresent the social nature of Spinoza's conception of individual empowerment, and indeed the essential idea of Spinoza's political works – that the emotions of the citizenry ought to be understood in order to yield political order through affective coordination of the multitude. This places interpreters of Spinoza's political philosophy in a difficult position. Either Spinoza says nothing about the social and is acceptable in contemporary debates about politics, or he is a philosopher of the social, and therefore of no use to liberal political theory. Those philosophers who have taken this aspect of Spinoza's social philosophy seriously have each had to wrestle with this problem (Wetlesen 1969; Rice 1990; Den Uyl 1985; Balibar 1998; Gatens and Lloyd 1999; d'Allones 1999; Mercon 2007; Armstrong 2009; Sharp 2011; Ravven 2013; Tucker 2013b).

In many ways, this debate within Spinoza studies is a historical relic of pre-behavioural economics and pre-affective neuroscience. Indeed, it is a relic of the Cold War era, when talking about how to coordinate or understand human emotion could only be understood as social engineering, emotional manipulation or even brainwashing. What is interesting about Spinoza is not that he thinks we ought to coerce the public's emotions, but rather that he recognises how powerful emotions are. Not only are emotions powerful, but they are always already shaped within social and political institutions. As such, we have no choice but to take them into consideration when considering these same institutions. Engaging in the work of political philosophy, as Spinoza sees it, requires understanding how emotions are shaped – whether or not we intervene in this process. Any interventions that do not understand the effect on human emotions are liable to harm or to fail. For Spinoza, individual power is indeed reciprocally affected by the power of those around us. How our societies function, what roles they offer individuals and how individuals are recognised affects what kind of power we are able to have (Gatens and Lloyd 1999; Sharp 2007; Gatens 2012; Tucker 2013b). Insofar as there are institutions that repress or limit human power, for Spinoza, we must intervene. If we wish to increase human power, we must change institutions that diminish it and build institutions that enhance it (Sharp 2011; Tucker 2013a; Field 2015).

Spinoza is ambivalent about the way in which affects, ideas and desires are transmitted socially. Bad ideas are as catching as good ones, and he is far from sanguine about the 'best' ideas winning out. Nevertheless, it is clear that those things which yield individual power – affects, ideas and desires – are developed among other humans and are highly susceptible to the influence of the social world. What Spinoza has shown us additionally is that the self, itself, is socially coordinated. For Spinoza, individual humans are complex. The self is that way in which the parts of the complex human body and mind are coordinated. This coordination is a process that happens within societies, within families and within the natural world. As such, one learns how to shape a self in the process of developing one's emotions, desires and ideas about the world situated within a specific cultural, historical, societal moment. Our selves are social. Moreover, how we organise these selves yields our power as individuals. Thus, for Spinoza, our power and our freedom are increased and decreased among others, relationally. Spinoza's account of power is, thus, a relational account. Human power is a function of the affects, ideas and desires which are developed and sustained through social interaction. This means that the power of an individual human is constrained by the affects, ideas and desires of those around that individual. Even Spinoza's free man – an individual with the highest degree of individual power one could have – needs society to survive (E4p37s2, E4p73def, TP2.15). In a society which denigrates reason or learning, the free man's power may be weakened, thereby weakening the society itself. A society which includes, engages and supports investigation of the natural world empowers its members, with their additional power accruing to the power of the society as a whole. This dimension of Spinoza's work is one that has been a regular theme in an often-overlooked area of Spinoza scholarship (Gatens and Lloyd 1999; Lloyd and Gatens 2000; Gatens 2000; Ravven 2009; Sharp 2007; Gatens 2009; Ravven 2009; Armstrong 2009; Lord 2011; Tucker 2013b; Grosz 2017).

Feminist Spinoza scholars have shown how Spinoza's understanding of individual power as social explains how individual liberation requires reforming social customs, norms, ideas and attitudes, or more specifically, how women's emancipation requires revision of misogynistic norms and practices within communities. Spinoza's theory of the emulation of the affects (ideas and desires) and its effects on the power of individuals has provided the theoretical basis for a critique of theories of freedom as independence or self-sufficiency (Armstrong 2009). For Spinoza, individual freedom can only be achieved socially (E4p37def; Tucker 2015). Feminist theories of relational autonomy emerged out of a similar project to show the way in which freedom can be both constrained and enhanced through relations with others. Whether to call this freedom 'autonomy' is another question, but my aim here has been to show that, for Spinoza, power and freedom are relational.

4. Paradox of Individual (Citizen) and Individual (State) Power

In *Spinoza and Politics*, Etienne Balibar notes what he identifies as a paradox of democracy in Spinoza's work – that is, Spinoza argues for absolute democracy but seems to worry about its power and about the power of those who participate in it. Balibar interprets this as Spinoza worrying about the people, the vulgus, or the multitude (Balibar 1998: 19). However, I think the conflict is something slightly different, and one to which Balibar himself alludes elsewhere (Balibar 1997: 34–5; Balibar 1989: 187).

Spinoza was worried about the power that individuals gain from the state, and about the power of the state itself. While individuals can join their power together, when this power is joined in a state, it can be used against them. For Spinoza, then, it is joining political society that is fraught for the individual, although it is never really a choice. Individuals are already socialised beings who are part of one or more communities. The crucial issue is this: without the state, one is weak. With the state, one is strong, gaining power from the power of those organised together into a state. However, should one differ from those in the state, and find the collective power of the state stacked against one, one's power is again just one's own physical and mental strength, that is, weak.

Against the power of the many we are weak; with the power of the many we are strong. The many, however, can be and probably are often wrong. This is where the worry of Balibar and indeed Spinoza re-emerges – the danger of the multitude. Agreement with them yields power and thus freedom. In moments of disagreement one loses both one's power and, because they are identical, one's freedom at precisely the moment where both matter most. Staying with the collective, even if it disempowers us individually to a certain extent, is always going to be, for Spinoza, better in terms of our overall power. We are always weaker alone, even if our companions are organised fools. Should we make ourselves their enemy, we will learn soon enough that the collective power of fools is strong enough to destroy a single human. Spinoza is quite clear about this: our power alone cannot yield meaningful freedom. We need others – even if they in some sense limit what we are able to be and do – because alone we are weak. Our weakness and dependence on the power of others becomes particularly clear when the power of the state is considered against the individual or for the individual.

Although the challenge of remaining free when part of a state is indeed a challenge, it is not a problem just for Spinoza or his account of power. It is not a weakness in his argument, but a genuine problem with human social and political life. Spinoza's theory *tracks* a real problem. Instead of magically giving individual humans power against the multitude of which they are a part, Spinoza recognises and theorises how individual power is developed from the social. This is not a weakness or incomplete moment in Spinoza's thought. Rather, it is what makes it a useful theory of power and freedom, as it tracks real places where individuals struggle to gain freedom and power through negotiation with others in the social and political world in which they find themselves. The multitude, in Spinoza, is neither good nor bad necessarily. The power of those around us can either empower us or diminish our power (TP2.13–15, TP3.2, E4p18s). Depending on how our state is organised, and our place within it, other humans can either help us to flourish or if we find ourselves in conflict with the state, those around us may diminish our power (Balibar 1997; Den Uyl 1983). However, without other humans, alone we have very little power (E4app32, TTP16). So even in a diminished form, we are more powerful among other humans than we are alone (TTP4, TTP20, E4p18s, E4p73, E4app9, E4p37s, and in *Treatise on the Emendation of the Intellect* (TIE) 14–15). There is no outside to the social – one can escape of course, but not with one's power (freedom) intact. It is almost perverse, at the moment that one is most weak, to call an individual free. Hobbes allowed that there was one moment where resistance to the state is possible, that is, when the state condemned one to jail or death, which may have been nearly synonymous in Hobbes' time (Hobbes 1994: XXI). At this moment one becomes, in Hobbes' view, free from the obligation to the state. This freedom of the state of nature, for Hobbes, is not what we might value as freedom. On a Spinozan view, to call this individual liberated is absurd. Without power, one cannot be free.

Through identifying power and freedom Spinoza shows us a rather stranger aspect of freedom, that through negotiation with those around us we gain our freedom and power at the same time. This moment, where the individual and the state clash is often theorised as a conflict between state power and individual freedom. For Spinoza, it is always a conflict of individual power and state power, and, at the same time, of individual freedom and state freedom – since, for Spinoza, freedom and power are one in the same.

5. Power, Freedom and Collective Liberation

Human beings might have been constructed such that we were utterly indifferent to the emotions, ideas and desires of others.[5] We might have had a stock of true ideas about the world that meant we did not need embodied experience of the world to flourish. We might have been able to ignore entirely the scolding look of a parent, and the conceptions of the world taught to us in school. We might have been immune to the desire-shaping effects of advertising or peer pressure. This, however, is not the case. We are wired such that we are able to recognise – and indeed often unable to ignore – what we perceive to be the emotions and judgments of other individual humans. We are social beings with constitutively social selves (Barclay 2000: 61–5). Our experiences of the world are shaped by our ideas, emotions and desires, which are in turn shaped by our perceptions of the emotions, desires and ideas of others. We are shaped in ways that are difficult, later, either to recognise or to change. The emotions, ideas and desires of other humans, or at least our interpretations of them, shape who we are, affecting our power and, thus, for Spinoza, our freedom.

I have argued above that Spinoza defines freedom in terms of power. If I have been successful, then we can understand Spinoza's theory of power to be his theory of freedom. Power plays the functional role of freedom – explaining what we are able to do and be. For Spinoza, the power of individuals within a group is mediated by the affects, ideas and desires of that group. If freedom and power are coextensive, then we can conclude that, for Spinoza, the freedom of an individual is ineluctably related to the power of the community of which that individual is a part. Further, we can begin to see the practical dimension of Spinoza's theory of freedom or power – once we know how our freedom is impacted by and impacts the freedom of others, we may revise our strategies for liberation.

Spinoza recognised that our freedom was intertwined with that of others – this intertwining could be empowering or enervating, depending on the degree of freedom of the individuals around us. The final moment in Spinoza's blueprint for individual freedom, power and perfection is not in the *Ethics*, but in the political works. In the *Theological-Political Treatise* and in the *Political Treatise*, Spinoza argues that democracy is both the best, freest and most powerful form of state – the only context in which we could hope for individual empowerment, that is, freedom (TTP5, TTP16, TP7.2, TP11.1). Thus, for Spinoza, the path to individual freedom is through the social and political.

Notes

1. I believe there is also evidence for categorising Spinoza's view as strongly substantive; however, arguing for that would require a different sort of investigation into how specific preferences or goals can diminish the power of an individual and thus be contrary to autonomy however chosen by the individual. Such an argument is compatible with the present account, but outside the scope of the current argument. I am overall in agreement with Keith Green's proposal in this volume.
2. I'm hedging here on two accounts: strictly speaking, Spinoza distinguishes between

conscious and unconscious affects, which some have called a distinction between affects and emotions. This follows a distinction Spinoza makes in Part 3. Further, in the evolving literature in the philosophy and cognitive science of emotion there are competing definitions of emotion. For clarity, I've omitted a discussion of these issues here.
3. There is a much more detailed and technical discussion one could have about the notion of adequacy of ideas in Spinoza, but I hope, for the present, this brief discussion will stand.
4. One might wonder how it is possible for individual humans to increase their power, since this power derives from God. Is it possible to have a greater share of God's or Nature's power? Does one become a greater part of God or Nature? This seems to be entailed, and indeed seems not to be a problem unless we consider God or Nature to be finite. More discussion of this would be useful, but might take us further from the focus of the present chapter.
5. There are those who are able to inure themselves to the emotions of others – at least in part. I refer the reader to a Spinozist account of psychopathologies in Moira Gatens and Genevieve Lloyd's (1999) *Collective Imaginings*.

Works Cited

Armstrong, Aurelia (2009), 'Autonomy and the Relational Individual: Spinoza and Feminism', in Moira Gatens (ed.), *Feminist Interpretations of Benedict Spinoza*, University Park: Pennsylvania State University Press.

Armstrong, Aurelia (2017), 'Spinoza's Ethics and Politics of Freedom: Active and Passive Power', in Kiarina Kordela and Dimitris Vardoulakis (eds), *Spinoza's Authority: Resistance and Power*, London and New York: Bloomsbury.

Balibar, Etienne (1989), 'Jus-pactum-Lex', *Studia Spinozana: An International and Interdisciplinary Series*, 1: 105.

Balibar, Etienne (1997), 'Spinoza: From Individuality to Transindividuality', Mededelingen vanwege het Spinozahuis, Delft: Eburon.

Balibar, Etienne (1998), *Spinoza and Politics*, London and New York: Verso.

Barclay, Linda (2000), 'Autonomy and the Social Self', in Catriona Mackenzie and Natalie Stoljar (eds), *Relational Autonomy: Feminist Perspectives on Autonomy, Agency, and the Social Self*, New York: Oxford University Press.

Benhabib, Seyla (1992), *Situating the Self: Gender, Community, and Postmodernism in Contemporary Ethics*, New York: Routledge.

Christman, John (2004), 'Relational Autonomy, Liberal Individualism, and the Social Constitution of Selves', *Philosophical Studies*, 117(1–2): 143–64.

d'Allones, M. (1999), 'Affect of the Body and Socialization', in Y. Yovel (ed.), *Desire and Affect: Spinoza as Psychologist*, New York: Little Room Press.

Della Rocca, Michael (2004), 'Egoism and the Imitation of Affects in Spinoza', in Yirmiahu Yovel (ed.), *Spinoza on Reason and the Free Man*, New York: Little Room Press.

Den Uyl, Douglas (1983), *Power, State, and Freedom: An Interpretation of Spinoza's Political Philosophy*, Assen, Netherlands: Van Gorcum.

Den Uyl, Douglas (1985), 'Sociality and Social Contract: A Spinozistic Perspective', *Studia Spinozana*, Vol. 1: Spinoza's Philosophy of Society. Alling: Walther & Walther Verlag.

Field, Sandra (2015), 'The State: Spinoza's Institutional Turn', in Andre Santos Campos (ed.), *Spinoza: Basic Concepts*, New York: Imprint Academic, pp. 142–54.

Gatens, Moira (2000), 'Feminism as Password: Rethinking the Possible with Spinoza and Deleuze', *Hypatia*, 15(2): 59–75.

Gatens, Moira (2009), *Feminist Interpretations of Benedict Spinoza*, University Park: Pennsylvania State University Press.

Gatens, Moira (2012), 'Compelling Fictions: Spinoza and George Eliot on Imagination and Belief: Compelling Fictions', *European Journal of Philosophy*, 20(1): 74–90.

Gatens, Moira and Lloyd, Genevieve (1999), *Collective Imaginings: Spinoza, Past and Present*, New York: Routledge.

Grosz, Elizabeth A. (2017), *The Incorporeal: Ontology, Ethics, and the Limits of Materialism*, New York: Columbia University Press.

James, Susan (1997), *Passion and Action: The Emotions in Seventeenth-Century Philosophy*, Oxford and New York: Clarendon Press and Oxford University Press.

Hobbes, Thomas (1994), *Leviathan: With Selected Variants from the Latin Edition of 1668*, Indianapolis: Hackett Publishing Company.

Kisner, Matthew J. (2011), *Spinoza on Human Freedom: Reason, Autonomy and the Good Life*. Cambridge and New York: Cambridge University Press.

LeBuffe, Michael (2015), 'Spinoza's Psychological Theory', in Edward N. Zalta (ed.), *The Stanford Encyclopedia of Philosophy*, <https://plato.stanford.edu/archives/spr2015/entries/spinoza-psychological/> (last accessed 7 December 2018).

Lloyd, Genevieve and M. Gatens (2000), 'The Power of Spinoza: Feminist Conjunctions: Susan James Interviews', *Hypatia*, 15(2): 40–58.

Lord, Beth (2011), '"Disempowered by Nature": Spinoza on the Political Capabilities of Women', *British Journal for the History of Philosophy*, 19(6): 1085–1106.

Mackenzie, Catriona and Natalie Stoljar (eds) (2000), *Relational Autonomy: Feminist Perspectives on Autonomy, Agency, and the Social Self*, New York: Oxford University Press.

Mercon, J. (2007), 'Individuality and Relationality in Spinoza', *Revista Conatus*, 1(2), December.

Oshana, Marina A. L. (1994), 'Autonomy Naturalized', *Midwest Studies in Philosophy*, 19(1): 76–94.

Oshana, Marina A. L. (2006), *Personal Autonomy in Society*, Aldershot: Ashgate Publishing.

Ravven, Heidi (2009), 'What Spinoza Can Teach Us about Embodying and Naturalizing Ethics', in M. Gatens (ed.), *Feminist Interpretations of Benedict Spinoza*, University Park: Pennsylvania State University Press.

Ravven, Heidi M. (2013), *The Self beyond Itself: An Alternative History of Ethics, the New Brain Sciences, and the Myth of Free Will*, New York: New Press.

Rice, Lee (1990), 'Individual and Community in Spinoza's Social Psychology', in Edwin Curley and Pierre-Francois Moreau (eds), *Spinoza. Issues and Directions. Proceedings of the Chicago Spinoza Conference*, Leiden: Brill.

Sharp Hasana (2007), 'The Force of Ideas in Spinoza', *Political Theory*, 35(6): 732–55.

Sharp, Hasana (2011), *Spinoza and the Politics of Renaturalization*, Chicago: The University of Chicago Press.

Steinberg, Justin (2016), 'Affect, Desire, and Judgement in Spinoza's Account of Motivation', *British Journal for the History of Philosophy*, 24(1): 67–87.

Stoljar, Natalie (2015), 'Feminist Perspectives on Autonomy', *The Stanford Encyclopaedia of Philosophy*, <https://plato.stanford.edu/archives/fall2015/entries/feminism-autonomy> (last accessed 9 November 2018).

Tucker, Ericka (2013a), 'The Affective Disorders of the State', Special Issue: Crimes against Humanity and Cosmopolitanism, *Journal of East-West Thought*, 3(2): 97–120.

Tucker, Ericka (2013b), 'Spinoza's Hobbesian Naturalism and its Promise for a Feminist Theory of Power', *Revista Conatus*, 7(13): 11–22.
Tucker, Ericka (2015), 'Spinoza's Social Sage: Emotion and the Power of Reason in Spinoza's Social Theory', *Revista Conatus*, 9(17): 23–41.
Westlund, Andrea C. (2009), 'Rethinking Relational Autonomy', *Hypatia*, 24(4): 26–49.
Wetlesen, Jon (1969), 'Basic Concepts in Spinoza's Social Psychology', *Inquiry*, 12: 105–32.

9

Spinoza on Affirmation, *Anima* and Autonomy: 'Shattered Spirits'

Keith Green

The claim that Spinoza regards autonomy as a fundamental feature of human good or flourishing is likely to strike many readers as paradoxical. And the reason is that our intuitions likely lead us to suppose that being 'free' in some sense of having 'free will' is a necessary condition for having autonomy. Spinoza insists that being '*sui iuris*', or 'a law unto oneself', is a primary aim of ethical reflection.[1] Yet he famously denies that our wills are 'free' in an 'absolute' way that causally sets them apart from anything else in nature. I begin, in section 1, by making the case that it does no interpretive violence to read some of Spinoza's texts as anticipating a notion of autonomy. But I point out that, to the degree that he does so, he grounds autonomy in a very different, and perhaps paradoxical seeming, notion of freedom. To use Spinoza's own choice of words, one is 'free' to the degree that one acts 'from the necessity of her own nature'. The rest of this essay will make the case that this conception of freedom yields what Catriona Mackenzie (among others) calls a substantive relational view of autonomy where there are ethically and politically significant degrees of autonomy. What passes for autonomy, when it is conceived as grounded in a notion of 'free will', is at best merely phenomenal autonomy; but it is the autonomy of 'shattered spirits'. Having a genuine capacity to be *sui iuris*, however – literally to be a law unto oneself – represents a more perfect, yet still intrinsically relational, autonomy. It is this autonomy that marks the fullest possible emergence of individual agency, and constitutes the freedom of the 'free man'. Achieving this freedom is, for this reason, a guiding aim of ethical reflection, according to Spinoza's ethical theory.

In section 2, I begin by noting that Spinoza grounds having power to be *sui iuris* in 'power of mind/spirit', and he locates the source of this power in affirmation, distinguishing indifferent or passive (unthoughtful) affirmation from active (or thoughtful) affirmation. In section 3, I begin with Spinoza's thought that causes whose effects empower or *animate* one's nature already 'agree' with it (in at least some critical sense of *convenientia*). I then argue that Spinoza's critical contribution to understanding autonomy rests in the idea that one's affirming the *animating* effects of other natures can be unthoughtful or thoughtful. Unthoughtful agreement, under the condition of *animi impotentia*, can animate, but without having adequate ideas of the causes and natures that do so, it yields up only phenomenal 'free will' and, thus, only limited and phenomenal autonomy. In section 4, I show that under the condition of *animi impotentia* individual agents who are merely phenomenally autonomous are exposed, nonetheless, to the risk of domination and oppression, a condition Spinoza calls 'servitude'. This is a condition under which one is not actually 'a law unto oneself' and is not able to orient one's choices and action toward one's 'genuine advantage' or 'good'. Under the illusion of phenomenal autonomy, moreover, one's exposure to domination and forms of oppression to which domination makes one vulnerable, can even be engendered by one's own phenomenally 'free', 'internal' but passive affects, desires and voluntary (uncompelled) choices, and the actions that they motivate. In section 5, I argue that 'strength of mind' *animates* one's nature by empowering thoughtful (or active) affirmation of motivationally salient affects that are effects of natures that 'agree' with one's own, but does not extricate one from their animating power. 'Strength of mind' yields, furthermore, desires and actions that further the 'end' of one's own persevering and flourishing, but also that of the other natures that 'agree' with one's own. It is for this reason that one who is genuinely autonomous does no harm to others, and is thus 'a law unto oneself'. It is critically important to see, however, that on Spinoza's view, having the power of mind that engenders autonomy does not extricate an individual from causal dependence upon natures that are literally *animating*, or that affectively motivate actions that engender one's own end, nor from dependence upon others' more adequate ideas of oneself. In conclusion, I point out that Spinoza anticipates a substantively relational conception of autonomy, at both the phenomenal and self-animating levels.²

1. Autonomy without Free Will?

That Spinoza anticipates a notion of autonomy is evident in texts like *Ethics* (E4p37s2), where he claims: 'Now if men lived according to the guidance of reason, everyone would possess this right of his [sovereign natural right] (E4p35c1) without any injury to anyone else' (C2: 562; G ii: 237). Three ideas converge in this claim that, together, are broadly constitutive of a notion of autonomy, and they are necessarily connected in Spinoza's thought: (1) having 'sovereign natural right', (2) living by the guidance (*ex ductu*) of reason, and (3) the idea that in doing so, one declines to harm others. One is *sui iuris* – a 'law unto oneself'. Without requiring any motive power beyond the power of one's own mind, one restrains oneself from harming others.³ It is because these three things necessarily come together in Spinoza's ethics and political thought, that it does not do interpretive violence to employ the notion of autonomy to describe the 'freedom' that Spinoza regards as constitutive of human 'good' or flourishing.

That exercising the capacity to be *sui iuris* amounts to autonomy becomes clearer with brief but telling comparisons to Hobbes and Kant. For Hobbes, one who voluntarily and reasonably declines to harm another is, in doing so, surrendering just as much of his original natural liberty as he can count on the other to surrender. He is, therefore, already implicitly surrendering 'sovereign natural right'. For Spinoza, by contrast, (1) an individual's 'right' is commensurate with her 'power'. And (2) even if one already lives under a 'system of laws', if one is motivated to obey laws by the strength and activity of one's mind or 'nature', one conforms one's actions to the law through one's own power, so one *retains* one's 'sovereign natural right'. One surrenders one's sovereign natural right only to the degree that one is moved to obey law through the power of external causes moving one to act by way of one's 'internal' actions. In Spinoza's view, this occurs when one is moved to obey by way of unthoughtful affects and desires caused by natures 'external' to one's own body and power of mind. To the degree that one is moved to obey by fear or hope, or by passively affirming others' painful ideas of oneself as blameworthy or weak, and imitating their affects, one is moved to obey, or to restrain oneself, by the power of another. So it is hardly surprising that Spinoza argues (in E4p63), that one motivated to obey law by fear does not act from the guidance of reason. He does not, therefore, act from the power of his own mind, so he does not retain 'sovereign natural right'.

Spinoza's remarks in *Theologico-Political Treatise* (TTP) 17 also makes it clear that he thinks that to the degree that one is so moved to act by passive love or fear, even 'from one's own decision' or 'judgment' (*tamen ex proprio suo consiliat deliberat*) one fails to act from one's own power. So one fails, *ipso facto*, to act 'from one's own right' if one is moved to act by affects that can only have an 'external' cause:

> For whatever reason a man resolves to carry out the command of the supreme power, whether because he fears punishment, or because he hopes for something from it, or because he loves his Country, *or because he has been impelled by any other affect whatever*, he still forms his resolution according to his own judgment, notwithstanding that he acts in accordance with the command of the supreme power.
>
> So we must not infer simply from the fact that a man does something by his own judgment that he does it by his own right, and not the right of the state. For since he always acts by his own judgment and decision – both when he is bound by love and when he is compelled by fear to avoid some evil – if there is to be a state and a right over subjects, political authority must extend to everything that can bring men to decide to yield to it. So whatever a subject does which answers to the commands of the supreme power – whether he's been bound by love or compelled by fear, or (as indeed is more frequent) by hope and fear together, whether he acts from reverence (a passion composed of fear and wonder) or is led by any reason whatever – he acts by the right of the state, not his own right. (Curley 2, 297; G ii: 202; emphasis added)

The contrast to Hobbes marks Spinoza's decisive conceptual step toward a notion of autonomy. And it comes in the idea that insofar as one is motivated not to harm others, and so to obey civil law, 'from the power or strength of one's own mind', one is *sui iuris*, and so *retains* 'sovereignty' over one's own actions. For Spinoza, but not for Hobbes, if one obeys whatever law one has a civil obligation to obey, and thus refrains from harming others, from the strength of one's own mind, then one retains power over one's actions. So one is autonomous in retaining 'sovereignty' over oneself.

Spinoza's connecting acting 'from one's own power' or 'right' with 'strength of mind' (*potentia agendi*) and so 'acting from the dictates of reason' to being *sui iuris* certainly anticipates Kant's notion of autonomy. Spinoza, however, prefaces his summary of the origins of political power, and law, in E4p37s2 with the claim that 'Everyone exists by the highest right of nature, and consequently everyone, by the highest right of nature, does those things that follow from the necessity of his nature' (C1: 566; G ii: 237). In the late *Political Treatise* (TP) 2.9, Spinoza even more explicitly connects 'acting from one's own power' to a very un-Kantian, and perhaps paradoxical sounding, conception of 'freedom' – a conception of 'freedom' that remains contested to this day.

> A person's faculty of judging can also be subject to someone else's control insofar as the other person can deceive him. From this it follows that a Mind is completely its own master (*Mentem eatenus sui juris omnio esse*) just to the extent that it can use reason rightly. Indeed, because we ought to reckon human power not so much by the strength of the Body as by the strength of the mind (*Mentis fortitudine*), it follows that people are most their own masters (*illos maxime sui iuris esse*) when they can exert the most power with their reason, and are most guided by reason. So I call a man completely free (*liberum omnio*) just insofar as he is guided by reason, because to that extent he is determined to action by causes which can be understood adequately through his own nature alone, *even though they determine him to act necessarily*. For (as shown in §7), freedom does not take away the necessity of action, it assumes it. (C2: 512; G iii: 280; emphasis added)

For Spinoza, genuinely free actions are not uncaused by causes unfolding exceptionlessly according to the same laws of nature that bring about all motion of all bodies 'in nature'. Indeed, Spinoza, echoing earlier scholastic views in a way, regards this inexorable law as 'Divine Law'. The causes that move an individual's actions are 'imposed' by one's nature *in se ipso*, or to use the language that Spinoza uses in the text just quoted (and in E4p37s2), to the degree that it is one's nature that 'imposes' the 'necessity of action', then one's action is 'free'.

According to Spinoza – and in contrast to Kant – human beings, as individual modes, are never the uncaused cause of any of their actions. Even where an individual can, alone, be cited as a sufficient causal explanation of a change or motion, an individual is always only a proximate cause of her action. In every case, she, like every other individual in nature, acts 'from necessity' of causes that stretch indefinitely back in time, and of which only God can have an adequate idea. Matthew Kisner makes starkly clear the implications of this point for any notion of autonomy.

> [H]uman beings, understood at the most basic level, are finite modes, which are determined by other finite modes. More specifically, our minds are collections

of ideas, representing a particular body, which is determined by its interactions with other bodies. It follows that our minds, and consequently our beliefs, ideas and character, are shaped by external forces acting upon us. This way of thinking irretrievably problematizes the notion of an autonomous person as a discrete, self-defining, independent individual. (Kisner 2011: 232)

Humans do not constitute a 'kingdom within a kingdom'. The distinction that is critical for autonomy, on Spinoza's conception of an individual, must, instead, be found in the distinction between acting from the necessity of one's own nature *in se ipso* as opposed to being moved to act through the necessity, or causal effects, of other stronger or more powerful natures. These natures would include *any* that can move or produce agents' actions by way of a causal sequence that involves their 'internal' action, or 'judgment and decision'.

Spinoza claims (in E4app1, among other places) that *all* our strivings and desires follow from the necessity of our nature in such a way that *either* they can be understood through it alone as their *proximate* cause, *or* they are a part that cannot be adequately conceived through itself independently of the other parts. Whether or not one's strivings and desires follow from the necessity of one's nature *in se ipso*, one acts if movement is produced through a sequence of causes involving judgment and decision; and one must be cited as the proximate cause of any change or motion brought about by means of this sequence of causes. Lee Rice has already made this critical point well and helpfully: 'The affects themselves are modifications in an individual; and it is not the affects that are causes, but rather the individual so modified who is connected to subsequent behavioral episodes as their causal antecedent.'[4] He might well have said 'connected to subsequent behavioral episodes as their proximate or immediate cause'. The critical question is whether the effects that take place through one's action represents the power and character (or ratio) of one's own nature, as opposed to the power and natures of causes that causally produce one's 'strivings and desires' or affects.

Spinoza clearly incorporates a conception of an individual's 'power of acting' into a picture of its being affected by causes whose 'nature' and power are represented in their effects, *per se*. He claims, for example, in E3post1: 'The human body can be affected in many ways in which its power of acting is *increased* or diminished; and also in others which render its power of acting neither greater nor less' (C1: 493; G ii: 139; emphasis added). And, in the following proposition from *Ethics* Part 2, an individual's 'power' is the power of one's 'body' to be 'disposed' or affected, not excepted or extricated from the effects of other efficient causes (E2p14s): 'The human body is capable of perceiving a great many things, and is the more capable, the more its body can be disposed (*disponunt*) in a great many ways' (C1: 462; G ii: 103).[5]

Acting from the power of one's nature and, thus, from one's right, is engendered by relationships of causal dependence that 'animate' or empower one's body/mind (and thus, one's 'nature') as opposed to relations of causal dependence that limit or diminish one's power to act self-consciously toward the end of one's own persevering and flourishing. It is not (in contrast to Kant) engendered by extirpating relationships of causal dependence *per se*.

It is to just this distinction that Aurelia Armstrong points when she comments that 'Spinoza does not contrast dependence with causal independence or isolation, but rather, contrasts cases of causal dependence that disempower to relations which are mutually empowering-relations of agreement or *convenientia*.'[6] The critical contrast to both Hobbes and Kant should be clear. 'Negative liberty' alone, conceived as 'free will' where individual agent's actions are conceived as not caused by efficient causes at work (as it were) in all of nature, is simply impossible, and can never constitute a necessary, let alone sufficient condition for autonomy. In E2p35s, Spinoza famously comments that the idea of 'uncaused' choice or will as 'free' is merely a matter of being aware of purposes that one has adopted in acting, but ignorant of the causes that yield one's action, and so acting under an illusion of 'freedom'. And for Spinoza, this turns out to be a dangerous illusion, a failure of self-knowledge, that intensifies one's penchant for hatred and exposes one to the risk of servility and oppression, where one will just as likely 'fight for slavery as for (one's) survival'.

Spinoza invests the power to be *sui iuris* in having the power to act 'from the necessity of one's own nature'. Having this power must consist in affirming affects caused by natures whose effects *animate* (or empower) an individual's nature to persevere optimally over time. An individual, individuated by its 'nature' or essence – a ratio of motion defining the relationship between its constituent parts over time – is in 'agreement' (in Spinoza's sense of *convenientia*, as in E4p31, for example) with the natures of causes that engender and sustain its power of activity over time. It follows, broadly, that giving an account of the power that makes it possible for an individual to be *sui iuris* must consist in giving some account of both the relationships of causal dependence that, quite literally, *animate* an individual, and of an individual's 'affirmation' of affects produced by these causes

2. Affirmation, and 'Strength of *Anima*'

Spinoza claims that a human's 'true power of activity', or his/her virtue, is her/his 'power of reason' (E4p52dem) or the power of her mind. And the power and activity of reason enables one, first of all, to 'affirm' or to decline to affirm *actively* (as opposed to passively) images and affects caused ('in' one's consciousness) by other natures. And to the degree that one has power of mind, other natures do not have the power simply to 'dispose' one causally to act. To the degree that one affirms images 'passively', other natures 'dispose' one to be affected and to act in ways that represent the natures and power of the causes that produce the images and affects moving one to act. It is important to recall that, for Spinoza, if an image or idea is 'present to mind' it is, *pace* Descartes, already being affirmed 'passively' (according to E2p49s), or is already a belief, *unless* it is 'denied' or 'endorsed' through the activity of an individual's mind, reasoning logically from adequate ideas to more adequate ideas[7] (see Martin Lenz's chapter in this volume). It is interesting to note, here, how Spinoza connects this 'power' to 'affirm' with 'freedom' in a letter to Blijenbergh: 'our Freedom is placed neither in contingency nor in a certain indifference, but in a manner of affirming and denying, so that the less indifferently we affirm or deny a thing, the more free we are' (Ep21 to Blijenbergh, C1: 378). Notice that Spinoza is relocating 'indifference' here. Read alongside Spinoza's remark about the sources of error in E2p17s, he should be read as claiming that an individual is a sufficient cause of one's 'mode of affirmation or denial' just when one is 'active' (as opposed to 'indifferent') in affirming, or declining to affirm, images, desires and affects that are present to mind. One's mind is 'less indifferent' when affirming is the product of the activity of one's own mind, 'reasoning' its way to more adequate ideas of the causes producing its affects, such that ideas 'contrary' to images and ideas are present. Otherwise, through one's 'indifference', one 'suffers oneself to be led' by external and 'contrary' causes, by means of the images and affects that are 'present to mind' through their causal effects. In the face of 'indifferent' or passive affirmation, they causally yield one's desires and actions.

Spinoza famously illustrates the distinction between 'active' versus 'passive' affirmation with respect to the imagination ('images' in the mind that include all of one's perceptions) by reference to one of two examples (in E2p35s) which he takes to exemplify how 'error' consists in 'privation'. He draws an analogy to our perception of the sun as close, or (in E4p1s) as sinking into the sea, but being able to have more adequate ideas of it as far away and not actually sinking into the sea. 'Error' consists not simply in the presence in one's mind of the images of the sun as close, or as sinking into the sea, but in passively affirming these images. The images are, after all, the causal effects of the sun upon the bodies of those who perceive it, and Spinoza claims (in E2p17s and E2p49s) that one cannot be mistaken, as such, regarding the contents of the images that are 'present to mind'. The content of the images simply 'represent' the natures of the external body, together with the way that the nature of an individual's body (one's own strength, weakness and relative position) *disposes* it to be effected. An image just 'is what it is', so to speak.

Minds have the power not to affirm ideas/images, however, through their own activity. They exercise this power through actively acquiring adequate ideas and intuitive knowledge about the sun and its causal effects upon other bodies, located at a certain distance from the sun and having attributes that 'dispose' it to being affected in certain ways by the sun. It is this active capacity to generate, through reasoning, more adequate ideas about the causes producing the image contents within one's mind, and thus one's affects (and so, of one's ideas of oneself), that 'frees' the mind. It enables one's belief formation to be 'autonomous', as opposed to being determined passively, simply by images 'present to mind' when bodies bear causally upon one's body. One's mind's 'active' affirmings, are not simply determined by the images that are caused to be 'in' or 'present to' (in E2p17: *veluti praesentia contemplemur*) one's mind through the effects of other bodies upon her body, even though the 'images' are 'there'.

The natures of the causes are represented in the *de re* contents of the images and affects they produce in any given body/mind.[8] Spinoza claims that the power or strength of an individual's mind is reflected in the 'strength' of every affect/emotion; and claims it is a ratio or proportion of the power of an external cause compared with our own power of mind (E5p20s).

> For (by E4p5) the force of each affect is defined by the power of the external cause as compared with our own (power). But the power of the Mind is defined by knowledge alone, whereas lack of power *or* passion, is judged solely by the privation of knowledge; i.e. by that through which ideas are called inadequate. (C1: 605–6; G ii: 293)

In the same text, Spinoza describes these affects of pain/sorrow (*tristitia*), of which these ideas are constituent, as 'emotions contrary to our nature'. And if they are 'contrary to our nature' they must be the ideas/affects that he describes in E3p11s as ideas/affects that are 'contrary to' the idea that constitutes the essence of our mind. To the degree that these affects are 'contrary' to one's nature, they are one's affective cognisance or awareness of the weakening of one's nature by external causes (so they are experienced as pain or sorrow), but without adequate *de dicto* ideas of the causes of one's being weakened, and of one's own nature as the bearer of effects of other causes, or as vulnerable to being effected in specific determinant ways (E5p38s).

If we keep in mind that Spinoza essentially equates 'virtue' and 'strength of mind' (E4p56dem, at least by implication), we should note a critical parallel between the sun analogy and the following claim about 'suffering oneself to be led' by one's affects, which Spinoza at least comes close to making himself in E4p37s1:

> Furthermore, from what has been said above, one can easily perceive the difference between true virtue and lack of power [*impotentiam*]; true virtue is nothing but living according to the guidance of reason, and so lack of power consists only in this, that a man allows himself to be guided by things outside him [*quòd homo à rebus, quæ extra ipsum sunt, duci se patiatur*], and to be determined by them to do what the common constitution of external things demands, not what his own nature, considered in itself [*quæ ipsa ipsius natura*], demands. (C1: 566; G ii: 536)

If we also keep in mind Spinoza's spectacular collapsing of 'affirmation', 'desire' and 'willing' in E2p49s, in the context of his claiming that there is no such thing as 'a will', then action *per se* expresses the natures that have the power to determine what one affirms. Unless one's mind has the power to actively affirm (or dis-affirm) painful or pleasurable images and ideas, one will 'suffer oneself to be led' by the natures and power of which the affects are an inadequate cognisance, and thus be moved 'internally' to act, but from the power of another.[9] And an adequate or sufficient causal explanation of one's action, especially actions done under the illusion of 'free will', must cite as causes the stronger and potentially 'contrary' natures that causally produce the images and affects 'in' one's mind.

Where one has the 'power of mind' to affirm actively, however, though the images or affects remain present, they do not alone 'dispose' one to 'affirm' and, thus, to act. The activity of one's mind yields 'contrary' and more adequate ideas, enabling one to actively affirm (or to decline to affirm) the images and ideas to which motivationally salient affects are conjoined. This activity of the mind alone can 'free' one from motivational salience of images and affects that are caused by external causes. And only then can one (be said to) act from the power of one's mind – that is, only then is the power of one's mind reflected or represented in one's actions.

3. *Impotentia Animi,* and the 'Autonomy' of 'Shattered Spirits'

Taking stock, we must see that on Spinoza's terms, many actions that pass for being '*sui iuris*' to the degree that they appear or feel 'free' are anything but autonomous. Desires, choices and actions are 'phenomenally' voluntary to the individual agent, are anything but autonomous in the sense that matters on Spinoza's view. They cannot be cases where an individual is genuinely *sui iuris*. These are actions where an individual is (in the language of TTP17 and TP2) 'acting from the power of another' and so, acting from another's 'right'. This includes actions that are motivated by affects such as hatred and pity. It is, however, especially reflexive affects that imitate painful or pleasurable ideas or images of oneself imputed to others, and thus other's affects of love or hatred for oneself, by which means an individual 'suffers' himself to be 'led by the power of another'. These are the affects for which Spinoza accounts in E3p30s (love of esteem (*gloria*), shame (*pudor*), self-esteem (*acquiescentia in se ipso*) and penitence (*pœnitentia*)), and after E3p53, and which he defines after E3def.em.24: (pride (*superbia*), shame (*pudor*), penitence (*pœnitentia*), humility (*humilitas*), and abjection or self-abasement (*abjectio*)). And we should note that it is *abjectio* which, he claims, is actually the opposite of pride (pointedly, not of genuine self-love–self-esteem (*acquiescentia in se ipso*), which presumably has no 'opposite').[10] In E4p54, Spinoza also describes the person who repents an action as 'doubly weak', and *suffering* from 'weakness of spirit'. These painful reflexive affects, that (according to E3p30s) imitate others' love and hatred of oneself, more often than not move agents to act under the illusion of freedom. But since all individuals act 'from the necessity of their nature', Spinoza claims (in TTP17) that any power by means of which the state produces obedience to law, even where it moves individuals to use their judgment and decide in determinate ways, extends 'right' over individuals. Even if obedience is (again, as in TTP17) an 'internal action of the soul' (*quod animi internam actionam respiciat*), it amounts to acting from the power of another, and not being *sui iuris*. So an individual's apparently autonomous moral self-restraint, even if it is not produced through overt *coactio* (compulsion or force), and even if an individual takes herself to be acting freely, are anything but autonomous.

If we examine the ideas that are necessary constituents of the painful reflexive affects that Spinoza defines following E3p53, and in light of E3p27 and E3p30, and following the explication of E3def.em.24, we see that being liable to imitating others' hatred or love of oneself amounts to being liable to passively affirming two sorts of reflexive ideas.[11] Spinoza asserts (in E3p30 and in the explication of E3def.em.28) that simply having an idea of oneself as a source or cause of pain or sorrow to another is (all by itself) to have a painful idea of oneself. And he claims in E3p30s that these affects are 'species of love and hatred'. One may also, however, impute to others (and passively affirm) even erroneous ideas in virtue of which one believes others love, hate or deride oneself. One who feels shame, for example, passively affirms an idea of another having a painful or sorrowful idea of oneself, *and also* the idea that one is dishonourable; and in passively affirming both ideas, one imitates another's hatred of oneself. One who feels humility imputes to others (and passively affirms) an idea of another having a sorrowful or painful idea of oneself, *and also* an idea of oneself as weak or incapable. One who is penitent passively affirms an idea of another having a painful or sorrowful idea of oneself, *and also* an idea of oneself as having acted freely but wrongfully or viciously. And regarding one's action under the illusion of freedom, the sorrow or pain is intensified by the fact that one forms no *de dicto* idea of its actual 'external' cause, in one's vulnerability to passively affirming others' ideas of oneself and imitating their affects.[12]

An individual, lacking 'strength of mind', is moved causally to affirm others' ideas passively or with indifference, and in doing so, to imitate others' affects (E3p27 and E3p30s). Indeed, in reprising his account of painful reflexive ideas and affects in the exposition of E3def.em.28, Spinoza emphasises that in order to understand how one can think ill of oneself, we need only to 'direct our attention to the way that others see him'. In no fewer than three places (E3p55s, E3p27 and especially E4app13), Spinoza hypothesises that one is made liable to passively affirm painful ideas of oneself as a cause of sorrow or pain to others by one's parents (whom one loves more intensely, and so whose disapproval is especially painful), unfavourably comparing one to others in order to motivate one to please them. Being vulnerable to passively affirming others' ideas of oneself, as such, however, renders one more liable to affirming any image or idea of oneself as a source of joy to others, however inadequate or unwarranted, and to imitating the affects of those to whom one imputes such ideas. In E3def.em.29, Spinoza argues, for this reason, that humility and pride are not 'opposites'. He also goes on to claim that a penitent individual's mind is rendered doubly 'weak'. It is hardly surprising, then, that Spinoza claims in E3p55s that the self-abasing *suffer* from 'extreme weakness of spirit' and that these affects indicate 'extreme ignorance of self'. In all these cases, Spinoza claims that it is being 'ignorant of oneself' that leaves one vulnerable to passively affirming others' painful, and so hateful, ideas of oneself, and so imitating their love or hatred for oneself.

Affects, unthoughtfully imitated under the condition of *impotentia animi*, have motivational salience for individuals even when an individual is not overtly compelled by what Spinoza calls (in Ep56) 'force' (*coactio*). Agents, therefore, experience themselves as 'judging' and 'deciding' or 'willing', and acting voluntarily (from their own judgment and decision) or freely (without an awareness of one's desires or actions being caused). This is, once again, only because they do not have the 'strength of mind' to reason their way to adequate *de dicto* ideas of the causes that bring about their affects and desires, the power of their own nature or mind and, thus, their actions.

Acting, however, without any *de dicto* idea, or without adequate ideas of the causes that yield one's strivings and desires, or without adequate ideas of one's own nature (or body/mind) as the bearer of effects that represent the natures of 'external' causes, is – according to Spinoza (in E2p35) – acting under a phenomenal illusion of 'free will'. And we should keep in mind that in this text, he adduces this notion of freedom as one of two examples of error, each consisting in privation, or lacking more adequate 'contrary' ideas which would enable one not to passively affirm others' ideas or the images caused in one's own body by other bodies, and thus imitate their affects:

> [M]en are deceived in that they think themselves free (NS: they think that of their own free will, they can either do a thing, or forebear doing it), an opinion which consists only in this, that they are conscious of their actions, and ignorant of the causes by which they are determined. This, then, is their idea of freedom – that they do not know any cause of their actions [*quòd suarum actionum nullam cognoscant causam*]. They say, of course, that human actions depend upon the will, but these are only words for which they have no idea. (C1: 453; G ii: 117)

It is noteworthy that Spinoza's other example of 'error' consisting in privation, in this proposition, is none other than the sun analogy. As we noted in our discussion of it above, one passively or unthoughtfully affirms the idea that the sun is close to the degree that one's mind lacks 'contrary' but more adequate ideas that empower one's mind not to affirm the images caused in it by the sun effecting one's body.

'Acting' under the illusion of having 'free will' and under the condition of 'weakness of soul or mind' can actually further diminish one's power to persevere and flourish by means of the activity of one's mind. If one has no idea of the causes that produce and move one's 'desires and strivings', then even if those causes happen to move an individual to act in ways that engenders her perseverance and flourishing over time, only the 'weakness' of that individual's nature is causally represented in actions yielded by those motivations. In the mind's incapacity to actively affirm more adequate ideas of the natures of causes yielding her actions, the causes themselves yield desires or other affects, and it is their nature and power that is expressed through the action. Any furthering of the perseverance of the agent is fortuitous.

Actively, as opposed to passively, affirming ideas and affects, however, entails that the actions they yield reflect the power of the individual's mind, and not merely its weakness or vulnerability to being moved by causes, of which it literally has no idea. Passively being moved to act by means of unthoughtful ideas and affects may well empower an individual to persevere or even to flourish – to undergo the strengthening of their own mind's power of activity. This is, indeed, the case when one is motivated to obey otherwise reasonable laws by means of liability to blame or penitence, or a desire for honour or reputation, or even by fear. The power that moves one to obey secure for one, beyond or even in spite of one's self-conscious intentions or aims, the benefits of security and cooperative human activity.[13] But with no more adequate ideas of the sources of one's power to live securely and flourish, that one's flourishing is yielded is merely fortuitous, and the empowering itself does not reflect the power of one's own mind upon one's real well-being.

Spinoza recognises fully well that where agents act under the illusion of 'free will' (and thus, under the condition of *impotentia animi*), the 'animating' effects of imitated reflexive affects upon one's power to persevere and flourish may be fortuitous or not fortuitous. But lacking more adequate ideas of the natures that produce, and are represented *de re*, in the images and affects that move one to judge, decide and act, an individual has no adequate *de dicto* idea of the causes or effects. It follows that such an individual has no power to resist affects causally effected by 'contrary natures' that motivate actions that are not fortuitous.

It is important to note that this recognition extends beyond reflexive affects, but includes them. Hatred may move one to defeat an attacker, and thus to succeed in persevering (E4p59). Pity, which Spinoza describes (in E4p50s) as 'evil, in itself' may, nonetheless, motivate one to act with humanity.[14] It is, however, reflexive affects that pose the greatest danger of motivating infortuitous actions, precisely because they likely do so under the illusion of free will. Shame opens one to being affectively motivated to live honourably (E4p58s), yet as a form of humility; it makes one more vulnerable to pleasures of flattery and pride. Spinoza regards penitence as a weakening effect of blame, which he consistently regards as abuse and injury, from the *Short Treatise* all the way through the *Ethics*. But he ultimately admits (in E4p56s) that in being vulnerable to being moved to act by it, agents may be motivated to obey otherwise rational laws to the end that their *securitas* and perseverance is extended. Hence he refers to prophets' inclination to 'massage' it in order to enjoin obedience as the 'sin' of the prophets. Blame (*vituperium*) is, after all, a form of hatred; yet it is in being caught up in the tendency to blame and in being motivationally liable to exposure to blame which gives moral ideas like wrongfulness or evil their normative force or motivational purchase upon those who cannot act well from strength of mind.[15] And (in the explication of E3def.em.28) Spinoza claims that in all cases where an individual has an idea of herself as having acted in a way that is 'customarily' regarded as wrong, it is the fact that such an idea of oneself is painful that gives it its motivational salience.

Though individuals who are moved to act by painful reflexive affects have an idea or 'opinion' of themselves as 'free', they in fact obey and live 'under the law', specifically a law that can only originate in being enjoined by a sovereign power. So their obedience, however thoroughgoing, never instantiates being *sui iuris*. One does not act and obey through one's own power: so one does not enjoy whatever fortuitous benefits their obedience secures as a causal effect of one's own power. One can do so only through the power of another, and so through another's 'right'. And Spinoza ultimately describes such agents (in E4app13) as 'shattered' or 'broken' spirits.

The trouble for autonomy is that it is when agents are moved to act under the illusion of 'free will', under the condition of *impotentia animi*, agents are also liable to be exposed to domination, and thus lack any power to resist being oppressed by means of their own 'internal actions'. It is critical to keep in mind that when Spinoza describes the person who repents an action as 'doubly weak' (in E4p54), it is because (a) she is unaware that in hating herself for an action she takes herself as having done freely, especially because it is something 'customarily' regarded as wrong or evil, she is being weakened, and moved at the level of her motivations by the power of another. And (b) her mind lacks the power to form adequate ideas of the causes of her weakening and pain. She, thus, blames herself. She cannot, then, actively resist, or decline to affirm the ideas and affects in virtue of which she is moved to act when the effects of her own actions on her persevering are anything but fortuitous. So the trouble with merely 'phenomenal' autonomy is that the causes that move one's obedience, but of which one has 'no idea', can subordinate one's power of activity and perseverance to the ends of other natures' power – that is, they can 'use one up' for the ends of another.

We should note that otherwise 'free' or 'wilful' actions to which agents are moved under the condition of *impotentia animi* are contested cases in contemporary arguments about autonomy. In Paul Benson's words, they are 'situations in which agents act willfully but are unable to govern the content of their wills'. Benson notes: 'In these cases, agents are prevented from regulating or authorizing their effective motives on the basis of what matters most to them, or of what they most care about or value.'[16] It is not enough merely for an agent's action to be wilful or voluntary (where one conceives her action as yielded by her own judgment and decision) and uncompelled (without what Spinoza calls 'force' or *coactio* in, for example, Ep56 to Boxel, C2: 421). Without some control over the formation of one's will itself, an agent's own 'good' can be subordinated to the power of stronger 'contrary' natures *through* their power to 'animate' an agent's 'will'. Since Spinoza collapses 'will' into affirmation, it follows that an agent's own nature has power over her 'will', or the motivations which move her to 'judge', decide and act, just to the degree that she can affirm those motivations actively rather than passively or 'indifferently'. But this requires, as a necessary condition, having the power of mind to reason one's way to having more adequate ideas of (1) the natures of other causes acting upon her body, and (2) of the ways in which the nature of her body/mind predispose her to be affected by them. If her own nature has the power to affirm actively, she can authorise empowering affects caused by natures that 'agree' with her own, and which register in her consciousness or experience as motivationally salient joyful affects.[17] And she will not be 'indifferent' to the power of 'contrary natures' whose weakening causal effects register as painful affects, such as reflexive hatred, shame or penitence. She can actively decline to affirm the inadequate ideas inherent in them, and thus not imitate them, nor be moved to act by them. One who is aware of the causes of desires and other affects that move her to act is analogous to a scientifically informed person with more adequate ideas of the sun and its effects upon her body. The scientifically informed person has 'in mind' ideas that make it possible for her to actively decline to affirm images of the sun as close, or as sinking into the sea as it sets.

4. Oppression and the 'Autonomy' of 'Shattered Spirits'

Interpreters aiming to rehabilitate Spinoza as a moral theorist have not seen with sufficient clarity that moral motivation, in the most basic and straightforward sense, can (on his view) lay subjects open to domination and oppression. Being motivated to act well or justly by means of one's ideas of one's own actions as wrongful or unjust, or by ideas of one's character as evil, weak or vicious, cannot but have motivational salience without, at the very same time, laying subjects open to domination and oppression.[18] One of the challenges of Spinoza's ethical theory is that (1) simply obeying conventional moral rules, under the illusion of free will, and so under the condition of *impotentia animi*, is not necessarily ordered to the end of optimising any specific obedient individual's perseverance or flourishing. (2) Moral rules really only originate as the commands or 'constructions' of a real sovereign power and so can subordinate the ends and activity of those who in fact exercise sovereign power. (3) Sovereign power, through its law-making, however, ultimately yields what comes to be 'customarily' regarded as wrong or vicious (E3def.em.27). So (4) having ideas of one's actions or their motivational sources in character as wrongful, evil, weak, vicious, or morally good or virtuous, is to have only an inadequate idea of the actual causal sources of motivations (see E4p64). One may also lack a grasp of the effects of acting in ways that these ideas/affects motivate one to act upon one's own striving, or the *conatus* of specific individuals. So the subordination of individuals' basic ends, or what Spinoza calls their 'genuine advantage' to persevere and act to others' 'ends' may well be concealed. And so (5), Spinoza argues that a genuinely 'free' individual would form no idea of their own or others' actions as 'evil' or 'good' (E4p68). More forcefully, under the condition of *animi impotentia*, it is by means of an individual's 'internal actions' or one's own motivationally salient affects (including desires), that a 'whole' or 'multitude' can subordinate constituent individuals' ends of perseverance and flourishing to those of the 'whole' of which they are a 'part'. Or to put the point in terms of power, those who have the power to enforce obedience to anything that they legislate for others by way of fear or other affects, makes others vulnerable to domination and oppression, even if laws or legislation are, incidentally, ordered to the end of their persevering and flourishing. Finally, those whose ends are subordinated may have no idea (*de dicto*) of the actual causes of sorrow or pain that they suffer, when (for example) one views one's own desires, choices or actions under the illusion of freedom, and under the description of evil, weak or shameful.

We can see this point most clearly, and appreciate its far-reaching implications, by noting the critical overlap between Spinoza's notion of 'servitude', especially within the context of the contrast that he makes, in TTP16 (C2: 289; G iii: 195), between slaves, subjects and citizens, and Philip Pettit's notion of domination.[19] Like Spinoza, Pettit notes that subjects' or citizens' 'liberty' or power to act can be secured or extended in a 'positive' as opposed to 'negative' sense even by compulsion, by threat of punishment, to obey laws which, as a matter of fact, extend or optimise their perseverance and flourishing. Laws or rules that one is compelled to obey by causes beyond one's own power of mind to grasp nonetheless enable one to benefit from cooperation, just as Hobbes argued. For both Pettit and Spinoza, however, it is making the perseverance and flourishing of individuals (as 'subjects,' and for Spinoza, constitutive 'parts' of a 'whole') *the end* that guides the making of laws, which secures individuals' 'liberty' or 'freedom' from servitude or domination.[20]

Spinoza, however, clearly and famously claims that to the degree that an individual acts from the guidance of reason, that individual is *necessarily* seeking the 'end' of their own perseverance and flourishing, and from the power of their own mind, or the necessity of their own nature.

> Now it remains for me to show what reason prescribes for us, *which affects agree with the rules of human reason*, and which, on the other hand, are contrary to those rules. . . . Since reason demands nothing contrary to nature, it demands that everyone love himself, seek his own advantage, what is really useful to him, want what will really lead a man to a greater perfection, and absolutely, that everyone should strive to preserve his own being as far as he can. (C1: 555; G ii: 222, emphasis added)

It follows, on Spinoza's terms, that having the power of mind to make the self-conscious end of one's own perseverance and flourishing the aim of one's obedience and other actions is a necessary condition of autonomy, or of being *sui iuris*. But as we have already seen, it is most emphatically not the case, for Spinoza (and in contrast to Hobbes), that one is acting toward one's own 'real advantage' simply in choosing without compulsion (what Spinoza calls *coactio*) to satisfy whatever preferences one happens to have. One can, nonetheless, obey laws from one's own power (the power of one's own mind) and, thus, one's own right. We have seen already that the painful reflexive affects that are caused by imitating others' hatred of oneself are 'contrary' to one's nature insofar as they register in consciousness, albeit with only inadequate ideas of their actual cause, one's being weakened by contrary natures. One's idea of oneself (one's mind) is necessarily made painful, only by another 'contrary idea' (E3p11s). One moved to act by means of painful reflexive affects is vulnerable to domination because she lacks the power of mind to direct her own judgment, desire and decision, and thus her actions, to her own 'genuine advantage', however fortuitous her obedience to law, or however 'willful' and 'uncaused' her obedience 'feels' to her.

Spinoza most clearly links *impotentia animi* to being vulnerable to domination in two places. The first is in his remarks that *impotentia animi* causally exposes one to the power of 'contrary natures' that yield up uncompelled suicide (in E4p18s and E4p20s, taken together) and the second in remarks about failures of courage (*animositas*), especially in E3p54dem and in the explications of definitions of pride and despondency (*abjectio*) (E3def.em.28 and E3def.em.29).

Spinoza claims that 'that those who commit suicide are of weak spirit, and completely overcome by external causes opposed to their own nature' (*que se interficiunt, animo esse impotentes, eosque a causis externae naturae repugnantibus, prosus vinci*). In E4p20s he claims that uncompelled suicides are cases where: 'unobservable external causes conditioning (*disponunt*) a person's imagination and affecting his body' cause 'his body (to assume) a different and contrary nature', but 'a nature of which there can be no idea in mind'. These 'contrary natures' can motivate actions that, even if they satisfy the desires and preferences an agent happens to have at a given moment, or that happen to assuage the agent's painful reflexive affects, quite literally destroy or 'use' an agent by means of the causal sequences that yield her own 'internal' actions.[21]

Another claim about affirmation and the mind (in E3p54dem) leads Spinoza to identify a critical second sense in which *animi impotentia* diminishes capacities that are constitutive of the power to act from the necessity of one's own nature, or from 'strength of mind'. He remarks (E3p54dem): 'the essence of mind affirms only what the mind is and can do, and not what the mind is not, and cannot do'. Where one has a painful idea of oneself as unable to do something or as weak (which affectively constitutes humility), the activity of one's own mind cannot, by itself, explain the contents of the image or idea of oneself that one forms, or the pain inhering in the idea. And one's declining to act in ways that (other things being equal) one otherwise has the power to act, that is, failures of courage (*animositas*), the contents of the painful image or idea of oneself that one forms reflects the nature and power of a 'contrary' nature. In the exposition of E3def.em.28 (of pride), Spinoza makes a claim that is bound to strike many of his readers as counterintuitive: that nobody actually thinks ill of oneself because he imagines that he cannot do something. And the argument that he gives hearkens back to E3p55s:

> For whatever a man imagines he cannot do, he necessarily imagines, and he is so disposed by this imagination [*hâc imaginatione ita disponitur*] that he really cannot do what he imagines he cannot do. For as long as he imagines that he cannot do this or that, he is not determined to do it, and consequently it is impossible for him to do it. (C1: 537; G ii: 198)

And so, it follows, 'from the necessity of his nature' that he is unable to do it.

The commonalities of language that Spinoza employs in adducing the causes of uncompelled suicide and failures of courage is noteworthy, and anything but accidental. In both cases, one's imagination is 'disposed', by causes of which one has 'no idea'. This is essentially the condition of acting under the phenomenal illusion of having free will as Spinoza describes it in the appendix to Part 1 of the *Ethics*:

that men think themselves free because they are conscious of their volitions and their appetite, and do not think, even in their dreams, of the causes by which they are *disposed* to wanting and willing, because they are ignorant of [those causes].

When Spinoza turns to examine reflexive affects in E3p53dem, he refers back to his argument in E2p19 and E2p23 that one knows (or is cognisant) of oneself only through affections of the body and 'their' ideas; and these affections register changes in one's essential natural striving (*conatus*) that are caused by 'external' causes, and to which the nature (and relative strength or weakness) of one's mind/body 'disposes' one. We should recall that perceptions and all images caused to be present to mind by causes external to one's body are, for Spinoza, 'imagination' (E2p26dem, E2p17s). And as Ursula Renz has argued, to the degree that one is 'disposed' to being affected, one's individual nature, in its relative strength or weakness, sets one up (as it were) to be affected in determinate ways by causes acting upon one's body. And in both the case of uncompelled suicide and failures of courage, it is in lacking *de dicto* 'ideas' of the causes – both of one's own nature, and the natures of causes bearing upon one's body – that lay one's actions open to being yielded causally through one's 'internal' acts, such as (in TTP17) one's phenomenally voluntary obedience to law, but to the 'ends' of another 'contrary' nature.

Even if, as Spinoza claims (in E4p73s, among other places), a 'liberated' individual is only optimally free when he is living under a 'system of laws' that otherwise exposes him to domination, he can conform his actions to the law from the power of one's own mind, and from judgment and decision reflecting more adequate ideas of conditions that conduce to one's perseverance and flourishing. Even if one cannot extricate oneself from subjection to laws that subject one to domination, and the best one can do (as Spinoza claims is always the case) is to obey the laws under which one happens to live, one's obedience can be motivated by desires arising from one's reason, and not from affects caused by one's nature being weakened by a 'contrary' nature.[22] And as we noted in our earlier contrast with Hobbes, obedience through rational concurrence, even under such circumstances, is obedience from one's own power of mind, and so, from one's own right. Even under conditions where obedience makes one vulnerable to oppression, one obeys, but one can do so without 'transferring' power or right to another.

Under any condition, however oppressive, an individual with 'power of mind', and adequate ideas of her own nature, has some knowledge of the conditions conducing to her own perseverance and flourishing. The reason is that having adequate ideas of one's own nature entails having a capacity to distinguish the effects of natures 'animating' or 'contrary to' her own from affects registering the power of one's nature. It follows that with sufficient power of mind, she would be able to form adequate ideas of forms of oppression to which laws subjecting her to domination continue to subject her.[23] And though she might otherwise be unable to extricate herself from the effects of past domination (i.e. oppression), she optimises her own good as far as practically possible from her own power and right even if the best she can do is to obey what laws she must from strength of mind. Even under these conditions, she is *sui iuris*.[24] To *whatever* degree her obedience secures her perseverance and flourishing, however limited, if she obeys from strength of mind, she is not subjected to oppression by means of her own 'internal acts'. She secures whatever degree of security is practically possible through her own power and, thus, her own right.

It is here where Spinoza clearly anticipates critics of purely proceduralist, as well as individualist, conceptions of autonomy. In John Christman's words, these critics claim that '(we) wrongly attribute autonomy to those whose restricted socialization and oppressive life conditions pressure them into internalizing oppressive values and norms'[25] Spinoza argues that one is not really *sui iuris* where one's motivations even to act well are the effects of his having a weak spirit, even when his actions are 'phenomenally' free. Such an individual acts 'from the power of another, and so 'from another's right'. And being motivated 'internally' to act by means of this causal sequence also lays one open to being unthoughtfully moved to 'fight for one's servitude'. The implicitly necessary condition for autonomy, or for being *sui iuris*, is not 'authenticity' – 'owning' the preferences and interests one happens to have as one's own, or 'identifying' with them in a Frankfurtian sense – but a certain kind of *introspective* competence. One must have knowledge of the way in which those motivations mediate the causal power of other natures upon one's own essential striving, and how they effect it. And one must also have some grasp of the way in which the condition or relative strength and position of one's own nature (within a causal nexus) 'disposes' one to be effected. An individual must have, in other words, what contemporary theorists of autonomy call a substantive conception of one's 'good' and of the specific causal conditions within which one is being moved affectively to desire and act. Only with these introspective elements of self-consciousness or self-knowledge can one know whether one's own affective motivations to act subordinates one's power of activity to that of another at the expense of one's own perseverance and flourishing.

It is finally important to keep in mind Spinoza's claim that to the degree that an individual acts from the guidance of reason, that individual not only advances the end of their own perseverance and flourishing but, *ipso facto*, that of other 'natures' that 'agree' with one's one.[26] The more adequate ideas an individual must have in order to direct their action to the end of their own 'good' are also ideas of the natures of causes that presumably effect other individuals with similar natures in similar ways. It follows that in seeking the end of one's own perseverance and flourishing – seeking one's own 'good' – one actively or thoughtfully declines to affirm hateful or acquisitive affects that would also motivate harm to another.[27] To the degree, however, that this knowledge is necessarily introspective, one affirms affects, especially love and the enjoyment of friendship, that 'track' (as it were) the empowering or animating of one's nature even where one lacks adequate ideas of the cause of one's affects.

5. The Upshot: 'Strength of Mind', Agreement and Autonomy

We see, so far, that Spinoza accounts for 'phenomenal' autonomy – the 'autonomy' of 'shattered spirits' – in terms of relations of causal dependence that can sustain an individual's 'real advantage' or 'good' *or* subordinate it to that of others. But if these causes engender one's genuine advantage, they do so fortuitously, and for the subject, unselfconsciously. Under conditions of domination, merely phenomenally autonomous individuals nonetheless remain vulnerable to unrecognised sources of oppression. More troubling, however, is the implication that merely phenomenally autonomous 'shattered spirits' may act in ways that are 'phenomenally' free, but engender their own oppression (or 'servitude') through their uncoerced choices and actions. We have also seen that Spinoza does not envisage overcoming this exposure to oppression by extricating oneself (*per impossibile*) from the sources of causal dependence that *animate* one *per se*. It is critically important to see that, on Spinoza's view, a genuinely 'free' individual is no less dependent upon others' empowering ideas and actions, both in acquiring and in securing the power of mind that engenders autonomy over time. A genuinely 'free' person is still 'animated' through relationships of causal dependence, including those whose effects are expressed through a causal sequence yielding motivationally salient affects. One's autonomy, or capacity to be *sui iuris*, is yielded by coming to have adequate ideas of natures which 'agree' with one's own, and of one's own nature as the bearer of the effects of external causes, where the 'natures' of those causes are represented (*de re*) in the ideas an individual has of the causes. These are natures whose empowering or 'animating' effects upon one's own nature is represented in consciousness (however inadequate) as one's idea of the causes of joy or love (in E3def.em.6: 'joy accompanied by the idea of a cause'), including self-love.

Spinoza recognises, however, that not all occasions of joy, loves or desire 'track' the animation of one's 'nature' as such. Titillation, for example, 'tracks' the empowering of a part in consciousness, effecting a change in its ratio of motion with other 'parts' (E3p11s, E4p60).[28] But love or joy that registers in consciousness the animating of one's *nature* to persevere and to extend one's power of mind, can be recognised as the effect of natures that 'agree' with one's own, and that are 'animating' it (quite literally 'ensouling' it). So once again, it is not at all by cultivating a Stoic posture of *apatheia*, or by extricating oneself from being causally effected (*per impossibile*), which liberates an individual from hatred, self-hatred, and even from enjoyments that open one to domination and oppression. One is 'liberated' or becomes *sui iuris*, in being moved to act through self-consciously affirming the loves and other joyful affects that register, in conscious awareness, the effects of natures that actually animate. They motivate one to act in ways that engender one's 'genuine advantage' or power.[29]

Spinoza is confident, moreover, that being moved to act by love that registers one's nature being animated, never moves one either to subordinate one's own power to persevere and act to the end of another, nor does it, or need it, subordinate the end of others' power to persevere and flourish to one's own genuine advantage. It is for just this reason that Spinoza argues that there is a necessary connection between love, including genuine self-love (in texts like E4p18s and E4p35c2), and never being moved to harm another. And it follows that being moved by love is commensurate with being a 'law to oneself'. It is under just these circumstances where an individual's affective motivations make them genuinely *sui iuris*.

We do well to recall, once again, that Spinoza appeals to the sun analogy (in E2p35s) to illustrate epistemic 'autonomy'. This autonomy of mind is a function of one's mind having power to affirm more adequate ideas, than the ideas one forms of the bodies that cause the images that happen to be 'present to mind'. And this 'autonomy' secures one from 'error' to which one is inherently liable in unthoughtful, passive affirmation. We must notice that the sun analogy is also closely paralleled by Spinoza's description (in E5p10s) of how a person, under the 'guidance of reason' is 'freed' from being moved to act by affects such as hatred, humility, shame, mere pity or a sense that one has acted blameworthily. All of these affects are conjoined to inadequate ideas of actions 'as 'wrong', 'sinful' or 'evil' that we are liable to affirm in our condition of 'unfreedom'.

> If we have ready also the principle of our own true advantage, and also of the good that follows from mutual friendship and common society, and keep in mind, moreover, that the highest satisfaction of mind stems from the right principle of living (by IVp52), and that men, like other things, act from the necessity of their own nature, then the wrong, *or* the Hate usually arising from it, will occupy a very small part of the imagination, and will easily be overcome. (C1: 602; G ii: 222)

Spinoza claims that it is acquiring the ability to rightly 'arrange and associate' the affections of the body, and not to extirpate or 'transcend' them, that enables one to resist being moved to desire and act by affects that register and perpetuate one's being weakened or 'morphed'. Recall that in E2p35s and E4app1, he argues that even though perceptions or images caused by the sun remain 'present' in imagination, simply as the causal effects of other bodies upon one's own body, their presence-to-mind no longer has the power to effect what one affirms or believes about the sun. It is through the mind's power to 'arrange and associate' ideas, reasoning to more adequate ideas, that engenders its activity, determining what it affirms. Likewise, though hatred is 'wont to arise' from wrongful or hateful actions of others, if one can (1) remember that human beings always only act 'from the necessity of their nature', and (2) keep in mind one's 'real advantages', (then) the hatred will 'occupy just a small part of one's imagination, and be easily overcome'. It is not that an individual's body and ideas will not register the weakening effects of 'contrary' causes, but that it need not passively affirm, and so be moved by, these affects to participate unthoughtfully (as it were) in one's own weakening, morphing or 'use' by another.

Just as the activity of a mind informed by more adequate ideas that are 'contrary' to the images/ideas/beliefs caused by the sun can avert error, the activity of one's own mind informed by adequate ideas of the natures yielding one's affects can avert being moved to act by affects that engender one's subordination and oppression. And Spinoza evidently embraces the idea that this remains true even when one's activity of mind motivates one to obey *any* laws one has a civic obligation to obey. Another necessary condition for actively affirming animating affects is that one must keep in mind one's real advantages; and it is clearly no accident that Spinoza retrieves this language from E4p18s. He contrasts an individual whose power is 'checked' by 'uncertain and random emotions' to one who is 'led' or by a '*recta ratio vivendi*' or 'right rule of life'.[30] It is an individual's possessing the power of mind to form more adequate ideas of one's 'real advantage' (*suum utile, quod reverâ utile est*) that enables her to be 'led' by a 'right rule of life' to further her own ends, but without any harm to another.

It is critical to note, at this point, that Spinoza's language in E4p18s (quoted above) clearly implies a contrast between what is genuinely 'useful' to an individual, and what is only apparently useful.[31] Recall that in Spinoza's language, another nature 'agrees' (in the sense of *convenientia*) with one's own to the degree that it is genuinely useful (*utile*), or genuinely empowers (animates) one's nature or mind to persevere and optimise its power through its own activity.[32]

It is also critical to keep in mind that one's enjoyment and loves are not guaranteed to be consciousness of one's nature *per se* being empowered or animated, especially under the condition of mere phenomenal freedom. One's ideas of the causes of one's affects must be adequate enough for an individual to identify the loves that register in consciousness the empowering of one's nature as such (genuine self-love) as opposed to the empowering of a part at the possible expense of the whole (titillation). Affects that register in consciousness the animating of one's nature as such, also motivate actions that engender the power of all other natures that are similar enough to be animated or empowered by the same causes – natures that 'agree' with one's own.[33] And because Spinoza hews to the earlier scholastic idea that love necessarily has more motivational salience than hatred, one who is self-consciously moved to act by loves that track the animating of one's nature will avert being moved to act by hatreds that register in consciousness the weakening effects of 'contrary' natures.[34] Nor will one be moved by loves that do not register the empowering of one's nature as such, but only that of a part of one's body.

We noted at the outset that Spinoza associates one's power *as such* (as an individual) with power of mind. We may not see, however, that Spinoza's conception of a 'singularly powerful spirit' or 'mind' is also an individual whose power is necessarily engendered and sustained by animating relationships of causal dependence throughout the duration of its existence. Spinoza claims (in E4app13) that love and nobility (*generositas*), which serve to unite persons in friendship, is the work of a 'singularly powerful spirit: (*singularis animi potentiæ opus est*) which is able to forbear with each according to his disposition (*ingenium*) and *to restrain oneself from imitating their emotions*'. It is not only that genuine friendship and cooperative associations secure social conditions under which one's perseverance and well-being may be extended and optimised. Spinoza infers that it is the contents of reflexive ideas formed within the context of love-animated relationships that are necessary to 'animate' individuals to act from 'strength of mind' and according to a *recta ratio vivendi*, rather than by unthoughtful forms of hatred, including self-hatred.

Spinoza claims, after all, that one's idea of one's body (i.e. one's mind) is a complex idea 'composed of many other ideas' (per E2p11s) that simply *is* an individual's mind, insofar as one's body actually exists. So it is hardly surprising that Spinoza claims (in E3p9dem):

> The essence of mind is constituted by adequate and inadequate ideas (as we showed in E3p3) and so (by E3p7) it endeavors to persist in its own being insofar as it has both of these kinds of ideas, and does so (by E3p8) over an indefinite period of time. (C1: 499; G ii: 147)

If the 'essence' of mind *consists in* adequate and inadequate ideas alike, it is a description of 'mind' that encompasses the minds of the 'strong minded' as well as those who 'suffer' from *animi impotentia*. Spinoza also implies that we cannot but affirm some ideas of ourselves that cannot arise from the activity of our own minds (per E4p39s) but that can only originate as images of our body in the perceptions (or imagination) and, thus, in the minds of others (per the Peter/Paul example in E2p17s and E3p11s). 'Strength of mind', however, is not necessarily diminished simply by the fact that individuals passively affirm others' ideas of their bodies and thus imitate others' affects, but that one is exposed to the possibility of affirming ideas of oneself that may be inadequate and painful, and thus to imitating the affects of others – the very cause of *animi impotentia*.[35]

In E4p39s, in the business of extrapolating from the well-known Spanish poet example to make the point that one can 'die without becoming a corpse', Spinoza remarks that older people believe babies' natures to be so different from their own that they would never believe that they had been a baby unless they 'drew a parallel from other cases'. In the passage in question, Spinoza is trying to persuade his reader that the case of the Spanish poet is not so exceptional as to be uninformative. In other words, all of us are, at one level, like the Spanish poet. We have a more adequate, 'unified' idea of ourselves as having been the infants we once were, not because we can remember having been an infant, but because we affirm others' ideas of ourselves having been an infant. We do this by seeing other infants grow and mature to adolescence and adulthood all around us. We then reason that our own bodies and minds come of age in the same way. One's reasoning, then, motivates one to affirm others' images' or ideas of oneself as having been an infant one cannot remember being. By this means, the Spanish poet's 'idea of himself' as the 'same' individual and body that authored the works he can no longer remember authoring nonetheless perseveres. It follows that others' images and ideas of one will be, however, more or less painful or pleasurable to the degree that those ideas are more or less adequate. If one passively affirms these ideas, one's agency-constitutive reflexive ideas will involve imitating others' affects. It looks, nonetheless, as though in order to form an adequate enough idea of one's body (or one's 'self') as one individual that exists over a time extending beyond one's memory, one must actively affirm some images and ideas representing one's body that can only form from the perspective of another body, and so, within another mind.

It is clear that Spinoza does not regard affirming others' ideas of oneself, or imitating others' love for oneself, as weakening *as such*. He claims that joy taken from the esteem of others can 'arise from reason' (E4p58). And Spinoza contrasts this reflexive joy to the 'empty self-esteem', which is 'encouraged only by the multitude'. He also claims that the 'powerfully animated', by contrast (in E4app25), will aim to 'arouse others' love without arousing their admiration or envy'. If love is joy together with an idea of its cause (as Spinoza defines it in E3p13s and in E3def.em.6), then others' genuine love, as opposed to their mere admiration, consists in their having a joyful or pleasurable idea of oneself, with an idea of oneself as its cause. If one returns others' hatred with love, and aims to 'upbuild' them, as Spinoza claims a 'powerful spirit' will aim to do, then the joy one causes for another registers in their consciousness the empowering effects of one's love upon them, countervailing their hatred.

When, or under what conditions, does joy taken in another's esteem 'arise from reason'? The answer must be that another's esteem arises from reason when it arises in conjunction with an adequate idea of one's strength of mind or 'virtue'. And genuine self-love (*acquiescentia in se ipso*), as opposed to mere pride or 'empty self-esteem', registers, in one's own consciousness, the empowering effects of one's own activity of mind. Even passively affirming others' warranted esteem, however (esteem accompanying an adequate idea of one's strength of mind), strengthens one's own mind, because one passively affirms a more adequate idea of oneself that becomes (quite literally) a part of the complex idea of oneself that constitutes one's mind. So it follows that recognition on the part of others, and the communication of their recognition, that is, their love or joy that they take in one's own individual strength of mind expressed in effective action, is not only a source of warranted self-esteem, but constitutes genuine self-knowledge.[36] And it follows that recognition engenders autonomy.

Spinoza's discussion of the perseverance of the Spanish poet's idea of himself as the individual who wrote works he cannot remember having written, implies that recognition is a necessary condition for perseverance as the same 'nature' over time. One comes by reflexive ideas and affects that are necessary constituents of one's mind by affirming, either passively or actively, ideas that can only arise in the experience and minds of others, from the perspective of a *different* body. To the degree that friendship and others' esteem and love respond to one's real strength, one's strength of mind, or capacity for self-recognition, is engendered, whether it is (say) a parent's love for their child, a teacher's love of her student or the mutual love of genuine friends.

We have already seen that the contrast to a 'powerful spirit' is one prone to blame, one who seeks to 'criticize mankind and censure vice', whom Spinoza characterises as suffering from *animi impotentia*. Spinoza claims that such individuals are 'stumbling blocks' both to themselves and to others.[37] And he most frequently cites as an example the injurious effects of parents, who are loved deeply by their sons, subjecting their sons to blame, and comparing them unfavourably with others (see E3p55s, E3def.em.27 and E4app13). The result is that their sons find the viciously cruel discipline of, say, the military less painful than the disapproval of their parents (whom they love). The implication is clearly that the 'strong minded' are more likely to form more adequate ideas of others, whoever they are, so responding with joy to whatever genuine strength (i.e. strength of mind, above all) they possess. And even if their idea of another is passively affirmed, and their affect of love imitated, they 'animate' or empower another to have more adequate ideas of their own body and power, and so make their own 'real advantage' the end of their activity. Spinoza describes the aim of the liberated, or strong-minded, individual as the aim that human beings 'moved not by fear or Aversion, but only by an affect of joy, may strive to live as far as they can according to the rule of reason' where they are able to self-consciously further their own 'good' through their own activity or virtue.

Considered together with the image of the social constitution of mind – one's complex idea of one's body – that is reflected in texts such as Spinoza's remarks about the Spanish poet, the implication is that recognition not only engenders strength of mind (and thus autonomy), but is a necessary condition for possessing strength of mind. It not only engenders liberation from the motivational power of painful affects that would move one to act in ways that colluded, under conditions of domination, with the subordination of one's 'good' to that of others. And it is not only that one enjoys friendship and many of the forms of human association that make possible cooperative human activity that optimises the satisfaction of preferences that one happens to have. The image of the constitution of the mind that emerges is one where one, quite literally, and necessarily, comes to recognise or 'know' (form a more adequate and 'unified' idea of) oneself through others' recognition of oneself. Spinoza's deployment of the Spanish poet example also suggests that one never ceases to depend upon the recognition of others, whether through memory or the ongoing engagement with others through friendship.[38]

The critical implication for any attribution of a notion of autonomy to Spinoza is that recognition is a necessary condition for possessing the power of mind to 'regulate one's own will' – for genuine autonomy to direct one's activity toward one's 'real advantage', and not merely the phenomenal autonomy of 'shattered spirits'. And one's regulation of one's own will constitutes autonomy – being *sui iuris* – only to the degree that one can make one's perseverance and flourishing the self-conscious end of one's activity.

For these reasons, Spinoza clearly anticipates critics of (1) proceduralist conceptions of autonomy, in whose view the necessary conditions for autonomy are specified by a description of conditions under which an agent is able to optimise the desires, 'preferences' or values that one happens to have. 'Proceduralist' views also assume that 'agents' morally self-regulate or constrain their own actions if they have in view the conditions or means by which their own preferences will be optimally satisfied. And Spinoza clearly embraces the notion that autonomy is a condition under which individuals who are *sui iuris* realise their own 'ends' without harm to others.

We must see, however, that Spinoza also anticipates critics of 'neutralist' conceptions of autonomy – conceptions according to which the conditions of autonomy can be specified without taking a position about, or implicitly embracing, any 'substantive' conception of human 'good' or flourishing. According to Spinoza, one may well engender one's 'servitude' by acting upon desires and affects formed under the condition of *animi impotentia*. And this risk is greatest when 'agents' act upon the affects and desires they happen to have under the phenomenal illusion of 'free will', unselfconscious of the causes of their affects. Individuals must have a substantive knowledge of one's 'real advantages', which involves having adequate ideas of the natures that yield one's affects and desires, and whether the actions they motivate would actually secure and advance one's power to persevere and extend one's power of mind. Autonomy, then, presupposes a substantive and objective conception of 'the good' as a necessary condition.

Other contemporary theorists of autonomy, such as John Christman, infer that 'autonomy concerns the independence and authenticity of the desires (values, emotions, etc.) that move one to act in the first place'.[39] We have seen, however, that 'independence' of will or the 'authenticity' of an individual's 'desires, values and emotions' cannot, for Spinoza, imply 'will's' 'freedom from' any form of causal dependence. So perhaps it is misleading to attribute to Spinoza the idea that 'authenticity' of 'will' is a necessary condition for being *sui iuris*, or autonomous. Above all, the 'authenticity' of an individual's 'will' cannot, on Spinoza's view, be conceived to consist in overcoming dependence on causes. 'Animating' sources of causal dependence are a necessary condition for autonomy, or a capacity to be *sui iuris*. But we have seen that on Spinoza's view, having (1) adequate ideas of one's own nature or power, (2) adequate ideas of the natures that cause one's motivationally salient affects, and (3) a knowledge of the conditions that optimise one's power to persevere and extend one's 'power of mind' are also required in order to 'own' the affects and desires that will move one to act to the end of one's own 'good' as well as that of other natures that agree with one's own. Spinoza anticipates not only a relational conception of autonomy, and not only for those whose 'autonomy' is merely phenomenal, but a conception of autonomy that presupposes a substantive conception of human 'good'.[40]

Notes

1. This is likely a reflection of Kant's well-known association of autonomy and free will, conceived as 'will' not causally moved by efficient causes, but whose function unfolds according to purely logical 'laws'. See, for example, *Groundwork for the Metaphysics of Morals* (G), iv: 447 (Kant 2002).
2. MacKenzie and Stoljar (2000: 4): 'The term "relational autonomy', as we understand it, does not refer to a single unified conception of autonomy, but is rather an umbrella term, designating a range of related perspectives. These perspectives are premised on a shared conviction, the conviction that persons are socially embedded and that agents' identities are formed within the context of social relationships and are shaped

by a complex of intersecting social determinants, such as race, class, gender, and ethnicity. Thus the focus of relational approaches is to analyze the implications of the intersubjective and social dimensions of self-hood and identity for individual autonomy and moral and political agency.'
3. To see the anticipation of Kant's 'formula' of autonomy most clearly, compare the quoted text from E4p37s2 to G iv: 440, where Kant claims that autonomy is a property of the will to the degree that the will is the source, in itself, of the laws to which it is subject.
4. Lee Rice (1999) argues that we must not just assume that no affect 'that is passively produced could not result in activity' or that 'human behavior either originates within us (in which case it is activity and we are its cause) or it originates outside us (in which case it is a passivity and we are not its cause). Indeed, this is the case with all action of all or any individual modes.' Importing this assumption on the sly merely begs the question against Spinoza. Eugene Marshall has also framed a defence of the notion that some human actions are 'free' in virtue of what he calls explanatory adequacy. See also Marshall (2014: 171).
5. Ursula Renz (2009: 84) has pointed out that talk of 'disposition' or 'dispositional' attributes such as *aptum* (in E2p13s, E4p38s, E2p39 and E5p39s) may seem to fly in the face of Spinoza's claim that everything that occurs cannot have failed to occur, and that every event or occurrence has a sufficient explanation in terms of efficient causes, extending indefinitely backward in time. She argues, however, that without knowledge of efficient causes that we cannot practically have (extending indefinitely 'backward' in time), we can only talk in terms of 'dispositions', or of how individuals are 'disposed' to be effected in specific determinate ways by specific determinate causes acting upon, and through, them – just as Spinoza argues in E4p38, for example. 'Dispositions can in principle be explained in terms of the actual properties of its bearer, or in terms of things affecting its bearer. That someone is inclined to do x rather than y has thus nothing to do with an original power, but with her being the focal point of several (internal and external, direct and indirect) causal relations, which together amount to a certain disposition to do x.'
6. Armstrong (2009: 47).
7. Descartes (1986: 40–1), *Fourth Meditation* §58.
8. Steinberg (2011, 2016).
9. See Lenz's discussion of the sun analogy in his chapter in this volume. Lenz argues that unless there are already ideas in one's mind (an individual's idea of herself and, thus, of the effects of other natures upon her body) that are 'contrary' to the images and ideas that are caused by 'external' bodies acting upon an individual's own body, an individual will be caused 'passively' to form inadequate beliefs.
10. It is critical to remember that pride is placed among the affects that mark or constitute *impotentia animi* because one is vulnerable to affirming ideas of oneself as a source of others' joy or pleasure to the degree that one is already vulnerable to passively affirming ideas of oneself as a source of pain to others.
11. Green (2016: 77–80).
12. Steinberg (2016).
13. Steinberg (2011).
14. Steinberg (2013: 394–7).
15. Implicitly, Spinoza accounts for moral 'normativity' in this way. See Green (2013: 208–16).
16. Paul Benson (1994: 651–2). What 'matters most', in Spinoza's view, is not what

subjects happen to prefer or desire (or, as Benson has it, what they happen to 'care about and value'), but basic conditions of perseverance and power of mind that are necessary conditions for seeking or enjoying any other goods.

17. See Kisner (2008).
18. The definition of oppression which informs this discussion is that of Sally Haslanger (2012: 332). It will become clear, in what follows, that domination and oppression must be distinguished because the former describes the condition under which one's own power, including the power to 'act internally' (to use the language of TTP17) is directed away from one's own persevering and flourishing. Haslanger helpfully defines *agent oppression* in the following way (where O=oppressor, V=victim, and F=any identity which V might bear in O's eyes): 'O oppresses V *as* F by act A in context C iff [*by definition*] in C (V is an F (or O believes V is an F) and, being an F (or believed to be so) nonaccidentally correlates with being morally wronged by O), and A creates, perpetuates, or reinforces the moral wrong' (Haslanger 2012: 334). This definition could not apply clearly to Spinoza as it stands, since moral wrong can only be defined in terms of failing to obey a law enjoined by a sovereign power. But it can be modified to capture a notion of oppression implicit in Spinoza's notion of servility, if being an F non-accidentally correlates with F's persevering being subordinated to the end of O's persevering.
19. On Spinoza's contrast between citizens, subjects and slaves, see Steinberg (2009: 51–2).
20. Pettit (1997: 23–4, 52–8, 110). Domination (as described by Pettit) implies that A has the power (or means), as a matter of fact, to subordinate B's persevering to A's ends, whatever they happen to be, by way of enjoining law and compelling obedience, by whatever means. One can, in principle, be vulnerable to oppression (as defined by Haslanger), though being subject to domination (as defined by Pettit), but without actually being subjected to agent oppression by that 'agent' who has the power to enjoin obedience.
21. See Garrett (2002), on 'contrary to'. See also Lenz in this volume.
22. See Steinberg's discussion of Spinoza's 'compliance' doctrine in his chapter in this volume.
23. Spinoza's account of 'servitude' can, in principle, encompass suffering the effects of institutional oppression. Haslanger's distinction between agent and group (or institutional) oppression helps to see why. Her definition of institutional oppression is paraphrased here: 'For members of some group, F: Fs are oppressed (as Fs) by an institution I in a context C, if and only if: in C, there is a relation R that can be described as follows: being an F nonaccidentally correlates with being unjustly disadvantaged either primarily, because *being F* is unjustly disadvantaging in C, or secondarily, because, for any member of group F, *being F* nonaccidentally correlates with *being G* due to prior injustice and *being G* is unjustly disadvantaging in C, and institution I creates, perpetuates, or reinforces R.' The example Haslanger used to illustrate such a relation is that 'Blacks are oppressed *as Blacks* by child welfare policies in the 1990s in Chicago because in that context, being poor results in having one's family being unjustly disrupted, and being poor nonaccidentally correlates with *being Black* due to a prior injustice. And the child welfare policies cause or perpetuate unjust disruption of families' (Haslanger 2012: 332). Being 'disadvantaged' implies that one's ends are subordinated to ends other than their own perseverance and flourishing, and subordination need not be specifically intended by those whose ends are empowered by the institutions. It is a question of whose perseverance is secured, and whose power to persevere and satisfy desires is extended, in fact, by social arrangements.

24. We should note that Spinoza's arguments, especially for the superiority of democracy in TTP16.29–35 (C2: 288–9; G iii: 195), and in his characterisation of the 'best' or most stable state in TP1.6 and TP5.5–6, is that, whatever form of polity, the most stable state is one in which individuals can self-consciously seek the end of their own persevering and flourishing through participation in the exercise of sovereign power. And we should note that, *ipso facto*, a 'citizen' of a democracy is, by implication, also empowered, from the guidance of reason to seek relief and remediation from historic forms of oppression that are engendered by historic domination.
25. Christman (2011).
26. Steinberg's chapter in this volume.
27. See Don Garrett (1990).
28. See LeBuffe (2004) and Sharp (2015). Not all cases of 'taking pleasure in oneself', or unselfconsciously finding an idea of oneself joyful or pleasurable, are genuinely 'self-love' – that is, it is not a pleasure or joy that tracks the animating of one's own nature, as such, or a part of one. E4p18 and E4p19 should not, however, be read 'egoistically' as the claim that all human beings are always acting out of 'self-love'.
29. See Lenz (2017) for an interpretation of active affirmation as a form of appropriation.
30. Steinberg (2014) on *recta ratio vivendi*.
31. In E4p19, Spinoza claims that 'from the laws of his own nature, every one necessarily wants or is repelled by what he judges to be good and evil'. The reference to 'from the laws of his nature' imply that an individual is only motivated to seek his own 'good' to the degree that his actions are moved by his own nature alone – that is, *in se ipso*. But individuals are never *in se*; their motivationally salient affects are yielded through the effects of stronger natures which may either 'agree with' or 'be contrary to' his own. So this claim authorises no attribution of psychological egoism in the conventional sense, or that might more plausibly be attributed to Hobbes. See Youpa (2009, 2010) for a criticism of specifically 'egoist' readings of E4p18 and E4p19.
32. For a fuller discussion of the senses of 'agreement', specifically '*convenientia*' and '*pactum*', in Spinoza's *Ethics* and in the political treatises, see Steinberg's chapter in this volume. See also Balibar (1997).
33. See Carriero (2014: 37–8), especially the claim that the fact that when people live by the guidance of reason, it is a reflection of the basic 'rationality of the universe' that they 'do not get in each other's way'.
34. See Aquinas, *Summa Theologiae, Prima Secundae Partis (I–II)*, Question 29, Articles 3 and 4. See Green (2007) for a discussion of the phenomenological and motivational priority of love over hatred in Aquinas, and O'Donovan (1980) for a discussion of real versus apparent self-love and self-contempt in Augustine. For Spinoza, see E3p43 and E3p44, by comparison.
35. Spinoza makes this claim explicitly in E4p58s. See also E3p58 and E3p59, and his account of the fall in E4p68 – Adam 'falls' by imitating the affects of animals whose natures do not 'agree' with his own.
36. I use 'recognition' here in the spirit of Honneth and Anderson (2005).
37. E4app13. Note also Spinoza's claim in E4app25 that one who seeks another's good will also seek to avoid giving others cause to envy him.
38. See Oshana (2010, 2015) for a fuller contemporary account of the necessity of memory and self-identity (the importance of how we see ourselves) for agency, at least in the spirit of Spinoza's account.
39. Citing Gerald Dworkin (1988: 13–15, 19–20). Here, one's actions fail to meet what

Paul Benson, Diana Meyers, Christman and other critics of purely procedural conceptions of autonomy call the 'authenticity requirement'.

40. Karel D'huyvetters, Andrea Sangiacomo, Aurelia Armstrong, Heidi Raven and Francesco Toto have patiently read and commented on this paper, saving me from many errors, and generously sharing many insights. Karel, in particular, saves me from critical misquotations in Latin, for which I am especially grateful.

Works Cited

Armstrong, Aurelia (2009), 'Autonomy and the Relational Individual', in Moira Gatens (ed.), *Feminist Interpretations of Benedict Spinoza*, University Park: Pennsylvania State University Press, pp. 43–64.

Balibar, Etienne (1997), 'Spinoza: From Individuality to Transindividuality', Mededelingen vanwege het Spinozahuis, Delft: Eburon.

Benson, Paul (1994), 'Free Agency and Self-Worth', *The Journal of Philosophy*, 91(12), 650–8.

Carriero, John (2014), 'The Ethics in Spinoza's *Ethics*', in Matthew Kisner and Andrew Youpa (eds), *Essays on Spinoza's Ethical Theory*, Oxford and New York: Oxford University Press, pp. 20–40.

Christman, John (2011), 'Autonomy in Moral and Political Philosophy', in Edward N. Zalta (ed.), *The Stanford Encyclopedia of Philosophy*, <http://plato.stanford.edu/archives/spr2011/entries/autonomy-moral/> (last accessed 16 November 2018).

Descartes, René (1986), *Meditations on First Philosophy*, trans. John Cottingham, Cambridge: Cambridge University Press.

Dworkin, Gerald (1988), *The Theory and Practice of Autonomy*, Cambridge: Cambridge University Press.

Garrett, Don (1990), '"A Free Man Always Acts Honestly, not Deceptively": Freedom and the Good in Spinoza's Ethics', in Edwin Curley and Pierre-Francois Moreau (eds), *Spinoza: Issues and Directions*, Leiden: Brill, pp. 221–38.

Garrett, Don (2002), 'Spinoza's Conatus Argument', in Olli Koistinen and J. I. Biro (eds), *Spinoza: Metaphysical Themes*, Oxford and New York: Oxford University Press, pp. 127–54.

Green, Keith (2007), 'Aquinas on Attachment, Envy, and Hatred in the *Summa Theologica*', *Journal of Religious Ethics*, 35(3): 403–28.

Green, Keith (2013), 'Spinoza on Blame and Hatred', *Iyyun: The Jerusalem Philosophical Quarterly*, 62: 195–233.

Green, Keith (2016), 'Spinoza on Self-Hatred', *Iyyun: The Jerusalem Philosophical Quarterly*, 65: 73–95.

Haslanger, Sally (2012), *Resisting Reality*, Oxford and New York: Oxford University Press.

Honneth, Axel and Anderson, Joel (2005), 'Autonomy, Vulnerability, Recognition, and Justice', in John Christman and Joel Anderson (eds), *Autonomy and the Challenges to Liberalism: New Essays*, New York: Cambridge University Press, pp. 127–49.

Kant, Immanuel (2002), *Groundwork for the Metaphysics of Morals*, Allen W. Wood (ed. and trans.), New Haven: Yale University Press.

Kisner, Matthew (2008), 'Spinoza's Virtuous Passions', *Review of Metaphysics*, 61(4): 759–83.

Kisner, Matthew (2011), *Spinoza on Human Freedom: Reason, Autonomy, and the Good Life*, Cambridge: Cambridge University Press.

LeBuffe, Michael (2004), 'Why Spinoza tells People to Try to Preserve Their Being', *Archiv für Geschichte der Philosophie*, 86: 119–45.
Lenz, Martin (2017), 'Whose Freedom? The Idea of Appropriation in Spinoza's Compatibilism', *Zeitschrift für philosophische Forschung*, 71(3): 343–57.
Mackenzie, Catriona and Natalie Stoljar (eds) (2000), *Relational Autonomy: Feminist Perspectives on Autonomy, Agency, and the Social Self*, Oxford and New York: Oxford University Press.
Marshall, Eugene (2014), 'Man as a God to Man: How Human Beings can be Adequate Causes', in Matthew Kisner and Andrew Youpa (eds), *Essays on Spinoza's Ethical Theory*, Oxford and New York: Oxford University Press, pp. 160–77.
O'Donovan, Oliver (1980), *The Problem of Self-Love in St. Augustine*, New Haven: Yale University Press.
Oshana, M. A. L. (2010), *The Importance of How We See Ourselves: Self-Identity and Responsible Agency*, Lanham: Lexington Books.
Oshana, M. A. L. (2015), 'Memory, Self-Understanding, and Agency', in Christopher Cowley (ed.), *The Philosophy of Autobiography*, Chicago: The University of Chicago Press, pp. 96–121.
Pettit, Philip (1997), *Republicanism: A Theory of Freedom and Government*, Oxford: Clarendon Press.
Renz, Ursula (2009), 'Explicable Explainers: The Problem of Mental Dispositions in Spinoza's Ethics', in G. Damschen, R. Schnepf and K. R. Stuber (eds), *Debating Dispositions. Issues in Metaphysics, Epistemology and Philosophy of Mind*, Berlin and New York: De Gruyter, pp. 79–98.
Rice, Lee (1999), 'Action in Spinoza's Account of Affectivity', in Y. Yovel (ed.), *Desire and Affect: Spinoza as Psychologist*, New York: Little Room Press, pp. 155–68.
Sharp, Hasana (2015), 'The Whole Law Consists Only in Loving One's Neighbor: Spinoza on What the Bible Commands of All Mortals,' *Journal of Scriptural Reasoning*, 14(1), <https://jsr.shanti.virginia.edu/back-issues/vol-14-number-1-june-2015-politics-scripture-and-war/the-whole-law-consists-only-in-loving-ones-neighbor-spinoza-on-what-the-bible-commands-of-all-mortals/> (last accessed 16 November 2018).
Steinberg, Justin (2009), 'Spinoza on Civil Liberation', *Journal of the History of Philosophy*, 47(1): 35–58.
Steinberg, Justin (2011), 'Spinoza on Human Purposiveness and Mental Causation", *Logical Analysis and the History of Philosophy*, Special Volume on Teleology, 14: 51–70.
Steinberg, Justin (2013), 'Imitation, Representation, and Humanity in Spinoza's Ethics', *Journal of the History of Philosophy*, 51(3): 383–407.
Steinberg, Justin (2014), 'Following a *Recta Ratio Vivendi*: The Practical Utility of Spinoza's Dictates of Reason', in Matthew Kisner and Andrew Youpa (eds), *Essays on Spinoza's Ethical Theory*, Oxford and New York: Oxford University Press, pp. 178–96.
Steinberg, Justin (2016), 'Affect, Desire, and Judgement in Spinoza's Account of Motivation', *British Journal for the History of Philosophy*, 24(1): 67–87.
Youpa, Andrew (2009), 'Spinoza's Theory of the Good', in Olli Koistinen (ed.), *The Cambridge Companion to Spinoza's Ethics*, Cambridge: Cambridge University Press, pp. 242–57.
Youpa, Andrew (2010), 'Spinoza's Theories of Value', *British Journal for the History of Philosophy*, 18(2): 209–29.

10
A Spinozistic Approach to Relational Autonomy: The Case of Prostitution

Andrea Sangiacomo

> And since you know you cannot see yourself,
> so well as by reflection, I, your glass,
> will modestly discover to yourself,
> that of yourself which you yet know not of.
> (W. Shakespeare, *Julius Caesar*, Act I, scene ii, lines 69–72)

1. Autonomy Qualified

How do the relationships I entertain with others determine my autonomy? According to the traditional account of autonomy that can be traced back to Kant (Schneewind 1998), such a question would not be well formulated. In that view, autonomy should be conceived as a freedom of self-rule. The extent to which an agent cultivates and improves her autonomy determines the kind of relationships she will be able to entertain with others – and not vice versa. However, in the last decades, feminist philosophers (e.g. Friedman 2003; Oshana 2006) have charged the traditional account of autonomy as being too individualistic. They contend that autonomy cannot be understood without taking into serious consideration how social relationships and social bonds affect an agent's autonomy. The notion of 'relational autonomy' has been used as an 'umbrella term' to investigate the social nature of autonomy (Mackenzie and Stoljar 2000: 3–33). From this relational point of view, our relationships with others are necessary conditions for our autonomy.

In today's debate, autonomy can be understood as relational in two senses. On the one hand, 'causal' approaches maintain that the agent's autonomy is causally affected by her relationships and by the socio-cultural environment in which she operates. On the other hand, constitutive approaches hold that social relationships and social embeddedness are necessary conditions of what autonomy is and of how it should be understood.[1]

In this chapter, I contend that Spinoza's moral philosophy not only develops an account of (constitutive) relational autonomy,[2] but it also introduces a further distinction between a *quantitative* dimension of autonomy (i.e. the capacity of an agent to be more or less autonomous) and a *qualitative* dimension of autonomy (i.e. the capacity of an agent to develop better or worse forms of autonomy). I argue that this distinction is important to deal with particularly hard cases that are addressed in the contemporary debate. Before returning to Spinoza, I shall put forward general reasons for taking into serious consideration the distinction between quantitative and qualitative dimensions of autonomy.

On the one hand, it seems important to acknowledge that agents who make self-harming choices may nevertheless have a certain degree of autonomy, despite the fact that they might entertain relationships based on oppression or exploitation.[3] Even if an external observer disagrees with the values and behaviours of agents operating under exploitation or oppression, it is important to implement an account of autonomy able to recognise in which sense the choices of those agents express a degree of autonomy. This approach is particularly important in cases in which an agent herself claims to be autonomous in making her (self-harming) choice.[4] On the other hand, it seems important to maintain that by entertaining different kinds of relationships with other individuals, the same agent could develop (in a better and hopefully less harmful way) the same positive aspects that she autonomously considers to be important in her current behaviours or choices. Self-harm is one of the main reasons to adopt and justify paternalistic interventions. An account of relational autonomy able to take into consideration both the quantitative and qualitative dimensions of the agent's autonomy can lead to rethinking these paternalistic interventions and reconceptualising the idea of self-harm.

In this chapter, I consider so-called 'voluntary' prostitution as a challenging case study to articulate such a view. Because the cause is controversial, I devote section 2 to unpacking the issues it raises. In section 3, I reconstruct the guidelines of Spinoza's approach to relational autonomy. In section 4, I implement Spinoza's account in order to solve the case at hand.

2. Angie's Case

> Angie is a very pretty girl, with blue eyes and hair dyed strawberry blond. A nineteen-year-old, from Moldova, Angie has had 10 years of formal education plus an 8-mont[h] sewing course; however, she has never worked in that field. Her parents remain in Moldova; her mother is a cook and father drives a tractor. Angie sends them money, around $1200 every month, but says they do not know what she is doing in Israel. When Angie was 16, she had sex for the first time, with a boyfriend she loved. A year later, at 17, she began to work in the sex trade. . . . She sees between 5 to 17 clients daily, averaging 11. . . . Her overall self-image is positive, and, except for occasional trouble sleeping, her mental health seems satisfactory. . . . Angie reports that she has not experienced rape or abuse, either as child or in Israel. If clients curse or insult her, she curses them back. She is working of her free will and wants to continue in the trade. She says she likes what she does and feels that she is satisfied with, and had some control over her life. (Chudakov et al. 2002: 308)

Although Angie's case is not unusual,[5] interpreting such cases is controversial. Advocates of the legalisation of prostitution claim that Angie's choice of being a 'sex worker' is fully compatible with her autonomy. Moreover, Angie seems able to use her activity as a sex worker to achieve positive goals. For instance, she economically supports her family. Prostitution seems to her a way to raise her status or at least does not provide her with a negative overall view about her life and work. According to this view, instead of condemning or blaming prostitution, we should

> (1) pay more attention to the socioeconomic conditions that promote sex work, (2) focus on unfree labour rather than prostitution per se, (3) faithfully represent workers' varied experiences in prostitution, and (4) identify concrete ways of enhancing workers' health, safety, and control over working conditions. (Weitzer 2007: 467–8)

Abolitionists (e.g. Miriam 2005), on the contrary, would claim that Angie is not a 'sex worker' but that she is a victim of 'sex trafficking'.[6] Although she appears to be fully aware of the dangers and implications of her choice, and her decision is fully voluntary, her decision is nothing but the result of relationships of oppression and domination (eventually joined with economic difficulties) diminishing her autonomy. Accordingly, abolitionists invoke paternalistic interventions to limit the number of young women who follow Angie's example. One of the main arguments to legitimate paternalistic prostitution laws in liberal democracies is that

> prostitution is psychologically destructive and results in the loss of important opportunities, and that prostitution laws reduce this harm, by reducing the number of people who do this work and by reducing the amount of prostitution that is done by those who do it. (De Marneffe 2010: 4)

Specifically, emotions such as worthlessness, shame and self-hatred are considered a specific form of (self-)harm that prostitutes commonly suffer. Although abolitionists do not deny that Angie is conscious and voluntarily accepts being a prostitute, they object, for instance, that mere consent is not enough in granting the autonomy of Angie's decision (e.g. Widdows 2013). Moreover, abolitionists contend that Angie is simply not aware (or she tries to hide) the (self-)harm that her activity inflicts on herself. However, the fact that she is not aware of the dangers of her activity does not count as a sufficient reason not to intervene by preventing her from continuing such an activity.

Supporters of relational approaches to autonomy seem to have two major contributions to bring to this debate. On the one hand, a relational approach is likely to be used to show that Angie is not really autonomous even if she might satisfy individualistic criteria to ascribe autonomy to her decision (e.g. she has not been forced against her will, she does not suffer from particular mental diseases, and she seems able to undertake rational reflections and the like).

Actually, the relationships of oppression and domination, in which Angie grew up, undermined her autonomy. In this sense, relational approaches can be used to support abolitionism. On the other hand, John Christman has drawn attention to the fact that relational accounts 'raise new and challenging issues for the application of standard norms of anti-paternalism' (Christman 2013).[7]

Specifically, Christman has focused on the attitude that an 'aid worker' should assume toward a young woman, Irina, in a condition very similar to Angie's. In this case, the aid worker should facilitate Irina in taking an autonomous decision concerning her future (e.g. by returning to her country or entering specific programmes). According to Christman's view, a relational account of autonomy leads to the realisation that:

> [T]he aid worker's actions have a constitutive role to play in the structure of Irina's potential autonomy, not merely as a means for determining whether she is autonomous (in the traditional individualist sense). If the paternalist withholds such recognition or fails to engage with Irina in mutually trusting and respectful ways in order to come to a cooperative decision based on dialogically structured reflection, Irina may fail the test for autonomy if viewed through a relational lens. (Christman 2013)

If we apply this view to Angie's case, the aid worker's intervention becomes a constitutive element of Angie's own autonomy. This claim, however, can be understood in different ways. From a strictly *quantitative* point of view, we might think that the relationships Angie entertained with others before encountering the aid worker were such that she was less autonomous in her decisions. If the aid worker will be able to address Angie's situation appropriately, she will become *more* autonomous in her choices and she will decide to quit prostitution. The 'aid' provided by the aid worker (at least) enables Angie to become more autonomous in her decision. From this point of view, we must assume that Angie's decision to become a prostitute could not have been a *fully* autonomous decision (or at least it was a *less* autonomous choice). Otherwise, if Angie had been perfectly autonomous even from a relational point of view, the aid worker would not provide 'aid' but would simply constrain Angie to do something that she autonomously would not have done. In this sense, a strictly quantitative account of autonomy might support an abolitionist approach by conveying the idea that Angie's decision to become a prostitute was not, after all, an autonomous decision.

However, there is something unsound about such a reading. On the one hand, it seems plausible to grant that the kind of relationship that Angie entertains with the aid worker is different from (and hopefully better than) that entertained with, say, her clients or with a pimp. The aid worker aims at engaging with Angie through a 'dialogically structured reflection' intended to stress this difference, and it is for that reason that the aid worker's behaviours and attitudes towards Angie are so important from a relational point of view. On the other hand, there is phenomenological evidence in Angie's case that she voluntarily chose to be a prostitute. Apparently, Angie was not pushed to this decision by her family or by any previous traumatic experiences. She seems to have autonomously decided to engage in sex work to provide herself and her family with better economic resources.

Angie's case entails that she had a certain degree of autonomy when she decided to become a prostitute but, at the same time, she could also acquire a *better* kind of autonomy through the help of the aid worker. Through her relationship with the aid worker, Angie can better grasp her own goals and reassess whether and to what extent her choice of being a prostitute is really the most conducive means to achieve these goals. The aid worker does not simply allow Angie to make more autonomous choices about her future by providing options that were not previously available to her. Rather, the aid worker's ultimate goal is to strengthen Angie's own ability to assess the extent to which Angie's decision to be a prostitute is the most conducive to the fulfilment of Angie's genuine advantage. The aid worker's intervention might result in a quantitative *increase* of Angie's autonomy, but this quantitative increase as such does not capture the core of the aid worker's intervention. Independent of the options that the aid worker proposes to Angie, the *quality* of the relationship they entertain will affect the quality of Angie's own capacity to reflect on her own choices and decide what to do. In sum, the role of the aid worker is not to help Angie to become *more* autonomous (assuming she was less autonomous before), but rather to achieve a *better* form of autonomy more conducive to her *genuine advantage*[8] (independent of her becoming more autonomous). Quantitative and qualitative aspects may well go hand in hand, but there is still no reason to assume that they are the same. In fact, as I shall argue, Angie's case is better approached if qualitative and quantitative dimensions are not conflated.

Taking into consideration the qualitative dimension of the aid worker's intervention requires a redefinition of the aid worker's own goals. In Christman's portrait, the aid worker is a paternalist who aims to allow Angie to quit prostitution. The paternalist is substantially convinced that this is the best choice that Angie could undertake. The moral judgment at the basis of this assumption is not really under discussion. Rather, what needs to be negotiated is *how* the paternalist can help Angie in making this choice, for instance by returning to her home country or by entering a specific programme. This approach presupposes a fundamental, although implicit, moral disagreement between the aid worker and Angie concerning Angie's values and her motivations for becoming a prostitute.[9] Such a fundamental disagreement is indeed a problem from Christman's point of view:

> It may by unclear what should be done if there is abiding disagreement between the aid giver and subject about the wisdom of her decisions. The standard liberal position on this issue, which is still at work here, is that paternalism is not justified if the only issue is the substantive value judgments of the subject. The carer in such cases must be especially judicious in separating his or her own judgment about the wisdom of those value commitments (for a life of selling one's sexual services for money, say) and the support that must be provided

to the subject to effectuate her autonomy itself in making those judgments. (Christman 2013)

The aid worker's objection to Angie's decision to be a prostitute (and possibly continuing as such) underpins the very idea of undertaking a paternalistic intervention in Angie's case. The reason for the aid worker's intervention is motivated by her conviction that prostitution is a self-harming choice and that a fully autonomous subject should not embrace it. Separating this judgment from the aid worker's intervention seems highly difficult, if not impossible altogether. After all, the aid worker is a paternalist and paternalism is never perfectly value-neutral.[10] Should the aid worker fail to *change* Angie's belief and decisions concerning her choice to be a prostitute, the aid worker would not obtain the paternalistic goal of 'saving' Angie from prostitution. From this point of view, I do not see how a clear solution to the problem of 'abiding disagreement' can be provided by adopting a strictly quantitative relational approach. 'Abiding disagreement' remains an (at least) implicit starting point of the paternalistic intervention and presupposes that the aid worker wants to raise Angie toward higher degrees of autonomy, by so assuming that her self-harming choices result from lower degrees of autonomy.

Considering the qualitative dimension of autonomy can offer a different perspective. From a qualitative point of view, the aid worker should not focus on the fact that Angie is engaging in an activity that can be shown to be (self-)harmful. On the contrary, the aid worker should first help Angie to focus on her own reasons for considering prostitution a somehow convenient choice that expresses her autonomy. Second, the aid worker should help Angie to envisage alternative ways to foster the same goals that motivated Angie to become a prostitute without exposing her to the same dangers. The aid worker's role in fostering Angie's autonomy results not only in allowing her to evaluate new options for her future (by increasing the range of her possible choices), but also in building up a relationship that creates *better* options (i.e. solutions more suitable for her own goals). The aid worker succeeds in her enterprise not principally by convincing or enabling Angie to quit prostitution, but by enabling her to have security and a way to pursue her genuine advantage without having to expose herself to risks to health or diminished social standing. At a basic level, Angie and the aid worker build their relationship on some shared goal or aim, such as living with an income and hopefully without threat to one's life and health. The qualitative strengthening of Angie's autonomy consists in helping her (in any number of possible ways that do not entail constraining her activity or power of choice) to realise goals that they share and to reassess to what extent prostitution is actually conducive to their achievement. This is indeed the approach to Angie's case suggested by Spinoza's account of relational autonomy, to which I shall now turn.

3. Spinoza on Quantitative and Qualitative Dimensions of Autonomy

As the contributions of this volume show, there are several reasons for considering Spinoza a supporter of a relational account of autonomy. In this section, I shall focus mainly on those aspects of Spinoza's thought from which his distinction between quantitative and qualitative dimensions of autonomy emerges more clearly. I first introduce a few basic notions of Spinoza's moral theory, and then I develop in which sense they lead to the distinction at stake.

There is an essentialist assumption in Spinoza's ontology, according to which everything has its own essence that determines the capability of the thing itself. I am not interested here in discussing the metaphysical foundation of such a claim.[11] For present purposes, it suffices to assume that every individual possesses a core set of commitments, beliefs, desires and values that she considers 'essential' to herself. I shall refer to this as the individual's 'essential core'. Insofar as the individual is able to act and produce effects in accordance with her essential core, the individual is active; otherwise, she is passive. When Spinoza refers to the 'nature' of something, we can understand him as referring to this essential core. According to Spinoza each individual always strives, as much as she can, to act in accordance with her essential core. This is the so-called *conatus* principle, according to which 'the striving by which each thing strives to persevere in its being is nothing but the actual essence of the thing' (E3p7). Again, I would like to leave aside the metaphysical foundation of this claim. For present purposes, I would rather like to emphasise that for Spinoza the existence of every individual fundamentally consists in her striving (which the individual may conceive of more or less adequately depending on her cognitive ability and condition) to bring about the effects embedded or dictated by her essential core.

For many philosophers, autonomy has to do with freedom of choice. Freedom seems to be required in order to grant that a certain action is not forced upon the agent by any other external cause, and thus it is actually an 'autonomous' choice. Spinoza strongly rejects freedom of choice or *liberum arbitrium* (E1app, E2p49). Nonetheless, he captures the same intuition at the basis of the notion of autonomy (i.e. the idea that an autonomous act follows somehow from the agent herself and it is not imposed upon her) by relying on the idea that every agent strives to bring about the effects that follow from her essential core. Insofar as these effects follow from the agent's essential core, they are not externally imposed or forced upon her.

I take Spinoza as understanding autonomy as the agent's power of bringing about her own effects. In this sense, I grant that every agent, insofar as she exists, is always autonomous to some extent. One might object that Spinoza's account makes autonomy somehow trivial since every agent would always be autonomous (at least to some minimal degree), whatever she does. However, I do not think that Spinoza's rooting of autonomy in the agent's *conatus* makes the notion of autonomy trivial. What is crucial to Spinoza's account is that autonomy comes in degrees. Spinoza's point is not to demonstrate that we are autonomous. Spinoza would grant that every agent, insofar as she exists, is always somehow autonomous. The crucial point is that we can increase not only our autonomy, but we can also aim at *better* forms of autonomy. Let me explain this point in more detail.

Spinoza maintains that insofar as a thing exists, it is constantly determined by external causes (E1p28). External causes have different natures and, depending on the degree of compatibility or incompatibility that they have with the agent that they determine, they can help or hinder the agent's own power of bringing about her own effects. The agent's power thus depends on the way in which her striving to bring about her own effects is composed (and interacts) with the power of the external causes. Interactions that lead the agent to increase her own power are expressed as affects of 'joy', while interactions that lead the agent to decrease her own power are expressed as affects of 'sadness'. Moreover, the same causes can determine the same agent in different ways, depending on the circumstances. For instance, human beings can interact on the basis of what they share and of common interests, or they can oppose each other on the basis of different passions and external motivations. To capture this point, Spinoza bases his account of causal interactions on the notion of 'agreement in nature' (*convenientia*). Human beings, for instance, agree in nature insofar as they are determined by rational ideas that they share, while they disagree in nature when they are led by passions originated by different external causes.[12]

This picture leads to three different scenarios: (1) interactions with external causes, based on agreement in nature, which lead to an increase of power; (2) interactions with external causes, based on disagreement in nature, which lead to a decrease of power; and (3) interactions with external causes, based on disagreement in nature, which lead to an increase of power.[13] Case 1 corresponds to what Spinoza calls 'active affects of joy', and they represent the highest degree of autonomy and lead to the highest degree of power and to the best way of interacting with external causes (i.e. interaction based on agreement). Case 2 corresponds to what Spinoza calls 'passive affects of sadness', and they represent the lowest degree of autonomy, in which the agent undergoes a decrease of her own power due to a disagreement in nature with the external causes that determine her. Case 3 corresponds to what Spinoza calls 'passive affects of joy' in which the agent undergoes an increase of power which is *not* due to agreement in nature with external causes. Before showing the relevance of this latter case, let me emphasise two main points that emerge from Spinoza's account.

First, in Spinoza's moral theory, autonomy is a notion broader than the notion of 'activity' conceived in a strict sense. According to Spinoza, 'activity' in the strict sense is defined as follows:

> I say that we act when something happens, in us or outside us, of which we are the adequate cause, that is [by def1], when something in us or outside us follows from our nature, which can be clearly and distinctly understood through it alone. On the other hand, I say that we are acted on when something happens in us, or something follows from our nature, of which we are only a partial cause. (E3def2)

The distinction between 'activity' and 'passivity' in this definition is not due to the fact that an agent is merely 'inert' when she is passive and really producing effects when she is active. On the contrary, both when the agent is passive and when she is active, the agent is constantly striving (whether or not she is aware of it) to bring about the effects that follow from her essential core. Moreover, activity cannot entail isolation from external causes, since Spinoza demonstrates that everything, insofar as it exists and operates, is constantly determined by external causes (E1p28). The distinction between activity and passivity is rooted in the different ways in which the same agent can be determined by external causes. Activity results from determinations based on agreement in nature. In this case, the agent is determined by external causes on the basis of properties that are common to both the agent and to the external causes, and thus fully understandable through the nature (or essential core) of the agent alone. On the contrary, passivity results from determinations based on disagreement in nature. In this case, the agent is determined by external causes on the basis of properties that are not shared, and thus the effects that are produced cannot be understood without also referring to the nature of external causes *insofar as* they are different from the nature of the agent herself.

An agent is always autonomous to some extent insofar as she exists and strives to bring about her own effects. However, an agent can be autonomous in different ways (i.e. she can be active or passive to different degrees), depending on how she is determined by external causes. For this reason, 'autonomy' (i.e. striving to bring about one's own effects) is broader that 'activity' (i.e. striving to bring about one's own effect on the basis of agreement in nature with external causes).

Second, Spinoza's distinction between the agent's increase of power of acting and the agent's activity in the strict sense is the ground for distinguishing between the quantitative and qualitative dimensions of autonomy. Spinoza's notion of autonomy captures the intuition that agents, insofar as they exist, strive to bring about effects that follow from their own essential core. Depending on how agents are determined by external causes, agents are more or less successful in this striving. Spinoza's notion of autonomy is *constitutively relational* because whatever an agent does depends on the way in which the agent interacts with external causes. However, according to Spinoza's account, an agent can increase or decrease her power of acting (and thus her autonomy) while remaining purely passive and thus without increasing her overall agreement in nature with external causes. Active passions of joy express a greater degree of power (and thus autonomy) than passive affects of sadness. Nonetheless, Spinoza maintains that both kinds of affects remain passions. Only insofar as interactions are based on agreement in nature do they qualify properly as 'actions' in the strict sense. Since Spinoza understands 'reason' as the mind's capacity to act on the basis of common notions (which maps onto common properties and agreement in nature), activity in a strict sense coincides with 'rational activity', and active affects express and presuppose 'acting under the guidance of reason' (E4p59s). According to Spinoza, rational activity is qualitatively *better* than passive affects of joy, although rational activity is not necessarily stronger in a quantitative sense. To fully appreciate why active rational affects are qualitatively better than a mere passive (quantitative) increase of power, it is useful to compare passive joy with rational activity.

Insofar as passive joy determines the agent to produce effects that increase her power of acting, passive joy determines the agent to do something that she can strive and desire to do for herself. Passive joy entails an 'active' dimension with respect to its content, that is, the specific action that it brings about. Nonetheless, passive joy is a *passion* insofar as the agent would not act in such a way without the determination of those external causes acting on her. In this sense, passive joy is 'passive' with respect to the way in which the agent is led to operate. Specifically, the effect produced by a passive joy is symptomatic of a certain weakness of the agent, who would not be able to produce the same effect without the support of those external causes acting upon her. The effect she produces is actually coherent with her essential core and could become a proper action, but the agent is unable to bring it about without being supported by certain external causes. This can happen because the agent does not know how to bring about such an effect or because she does not know how to bring it about without referring to the specific external causes that determine her.

A passive affect of joy depends on the operation of a particular external cause. When the agent experiences a passive affect of joy, her condition is such that this affect could not be produced by the agent alone or by the agent's interaction with any other cause. This entails that the passive affect of joy cannot be explained or accounted for by the agent's nature alone. Hence, when the agent undergoes a passive affect of joy, the agent *disagrees* in nature (to some extent) with the external cause that causes the affect. More precisely, the agent disagrees with the external cause insofar as the agent's own nature is different from the external cause's nature and without that external cause the agent could not produce the same affect (i.e. the agent is only a *partial* cause of her passive affect of joy).[14]

Joyful passions imply a form of addiction to the particular external causes that produce them. The agent desires and strives to obtain the increase of her power of acting produced by the determination of the external causes, but she is not able, at the same time, to produce the same increase of power without them. Accordingly, joyful passions will create not only a desire to increase the agent's power of acting but also a specific desire towards the specific external causes that appear necessary to the agent to achieve her goal. This leads the agent to a form of fixation and obsession with certain particular external causes that the agent regards as necessary for her own striving. This condition leads to a decrease of the agent's ability to foster her striving in different conditions and makes it rather dependent on the presence and effects of specific external causes. For present purposes, I shall call 'passionate autonomy' the kind of autonomy supported by joyful passions.

Rational autonomy (i.e. autonomy based on rational activity) is always better than passionate autonomy (i.e. autonomy expressed by passions of joy) because it creates better conditions to foster the agent's power of acting without relying on particular external causes or circumstances but rather on common features shared among many things. According to Spinoza, 'no thing can be evil through what it has in common with our nature; but insofar as it is evil for us, it is contrary to us' (E4p30). If something turns out to be evil for us this is because it interacts with us according to some aspect of its nature that differs from our own nature. Insofar as the external cause determines our power of acting on the basis of those aspects of its nature that are different from our own nature, such an external cause will determine our power of acting in a way that cannot be conducive to the improvement of our own power of acting. This implies that sad passions are harmful insofar as external causes exploit our power of acting to bring about effects that benefit the external causes' nature insofar as it is different from our own nature. However, difference in nature comes in degrees. Things are more or less similar and more or less able to share common properties. Causal interactions can foster what things have in common or what instead differentiates them. In the first case, the result will be an increase in the power of acting of both external causes and the agent. In the second case, external causes will decrease the agent's power of acting by exploiting it to bring about effects in contrast with her essential core. Insofar as we act in accordance with reason, we act in accordance with what we have in common with external causes. This is why actions based on reason can never be harmful.

Rational activity is always better than passionate activity because it is based not only on a positive interaction with external causes but also on a community of nature. This community implies that the agent not only interacts with external causes but actively cooperates with them in such a way that the realisation of her essential core is conducive to the strengthening of external causes and, vice versa, the strengthening of external causes is conducive to the agent's own strengthening. In this sense, 'only insofar as men live according to the guidance of reason, must they always agree in nature' (E4p35).

Rational activity has a further benefit as well. Insofar as reason focuses on what is shared, reason is not bound to what is singular and specific. Insofar as an agent is guided by reason, she can cooperate with external causes for what they share with her essential core and irrespective of their differences. This implies that the agent is less dependent on the presence of a specific external cause, and she is more able to interact with several different external causes in various circumstances, provided they can share a common nature. While joyful passions are 'passions' insofar as they make the production of a certain effect dependent on the presence of certain singular external causes, rational activity fosters the agent's independence from the specificity of certain external causes by supporting her adaptability to different circumstances and kinds of interactions (E5p11–12, E5p20s).

Spinoza discusses at length (E4p35–7) the benefits that follow from rational activity. Although rational activity is not necessarily stronger than passionate activity, it leads the agent to become the active and adequate cause of her own increase of power. Passionate activity, insofar as it relies on specific external causes, supports the agent's activity without enabling her to become the adequate cause of her self-improvement. Rational activity does not necessarily support a higher degree of activity because certain external causes might produce stronger passions. However, rational activity always supports the agent's striving to interact in an active way with external causes by countering the kind of addiction implied in passionate autonomy. Instead of hoping for the external causes' support without being able to act without them, rational activity enables the agent to actively cooperate with external causes. In this sense, rational activity must be evaluated as our 'supreme good' (E4p36) because it undermines the basis of every sad passion (that is, of every 'evil') insofar as it grounds our action on what we can share with external causes (and from which no evil can follow).

To summarise, Spinoza's moral philosophy portrays autonomy as the agent's striving to bring about those effects that follow from her essential core. Moreover, Spinoza distinguishes between a qualitative and a quantitative dimension of autonomy. The quantitative dimension corresponds to the degree of power and success with which an agent brings about her own effects in interactions with external causes. The qualitative dimension corresponds to the degree of agreement in nature that supports the agent's interaction. The greater the degree of agreement in nature between the agent and the external causes with which she interacts, the greater her degree of rationality. Since passive affects of joy can produce increases of power that nonetheless entail side effects such as addiction, fixation and other forms of limitations of the agent's power, rational activity is *better* than passionate autonomy, although not necessarily *stronger*.

4. The Spinozistic Approach at Work

In this section, I apply Spinoza's framework to Angie's case discussed in section 2. The preliminary question that the Spinozist approach urges us to address is whether Angie operates on the basis of joyful passions or rational activity. To approach this question, it is necessary to examine whether and to what extent Angie's voluntary engagement in prostitution relies on some form of actual cooperation with others based on some shared or common value or need. The evidence adduced by those who consider prostitution a self-harming choice could demonstrate that prostitution cannot be understood as a 'rational activity' in Spinoza's sense because it entails an asymmetrical relationship of exploitation, or addiction to certain external conditions that hinders the agent's capacity to engage and take part in many other kinds of social interactions. For instance, prostitution makes Angie's activity so dependent on her relationships with certain kinds of external causes (such as her clients or her pimp) that she progressively loses her ability to increase her power of acting without them. Eventually, these external causes do not aim at interacting with Angie on the basis of a shared nature but rather on the basis of a relationship of exploitation resulting from disagreement in nature (i.e. Angie has to 'sell' what others want from her). This question cannot be settled a priori but clearly needs empirical examination. If the result of this examination is that Angie's decision is in fact a form of rational activity, there cannot be any reason (from a Spinozistic point of view) to consider Angie in need of any help.

However, for present purposes, I shall grant to the supporter of paternalistic intervention that prostitution entails some form of addiction or exploitation. In the rest of this section, I shall thus elaborate on the way in which a Spinozistic approach would deal with the case in which Angie is in fact led to prostitution by joyful passions and how the aid worker may provide support to help Angie reconfigure her choices on the basis of a rational form of autonomy.

From a Spinozistic point of view, the aid worker's role should be that of enhancing Angie's rational activity. To do so, the aid worker should start from Angie's passionate autonomy by providing a cooperative way of developing it without exposing Angie to the exploitation of the external causes that abuse her power of acting. The starting point is what Angie herself recognises as good for her, namely what she envisages as conducive to increase her own power of acting. While such good is usually provided by external causes that exploit Angie, the aid worker should provide Angie with an alternative way to achieve the same good. For this purpose, the aid worker should actively cooperate with Angie in such a way that the joyful affects perceived by Angie in that cooperation would be stronger than the joyful affects perceived by Angie in her activity as a prostitute.

A Spinozistic approach to Angie's case entails that the aid worker should start from examining Angie's affective life (i.e. her passive affects of joy, which encompass everything Angie does with the aim of remediating pain or sorrow or securing a better condition). Angie and the aid worker analyse Angie's passive affects of joy and aim to identify those effects that are proper to Angie's essential core. Angie's genuine advantage is to be able to produce these essential effects in the best possible way (i.e. in the most active and rational way). By clarifying what is Angie's genuine advantage, the aid worker can collaborate with her to achieve it. This approach presupposes the need for both Angie and the aid worker to find some *shared* goal that they can both strive to achieve. From this point of view, the aid worker will not play the (more or less explicit) role of someone who is entitled to 'judge' Angie's activity and eventually teach her why it is wrong or dangerous. Rather, the aid worker will appear first of all as a 'peer' of Angie and as someone who shares some basic interest or goal and who is willing to collaborate with Angie to achieve those goals together.[15] In this way, the aid worker will approach Angie from the beginning on the basis of some shared feature, from which only joyful emotions and an increase of activity can follow. This is in fact preferable to an approach in which the aid worker addresses Angie by simply trying to convince her that her activity is wrong. In this latter case, it is likely that the aid worker will not be able to help Angie distinguish between her core commitments and the way in which prostitution supports them. By confusing the aid worker's (more or less explicit) blame of prostitution with a contempt for her own core commitments, Angie will probably not perceive the aid worker as someone who can cooperate with her own goals. In this case, she will not perceive any shared nature among them and thus no basis for true cooperation.

Empathy will surely be an important aspect on which the aid worker can build this cooperation with Angie. Empathy facilitates the sharing of emotions (E3p27) and, as such, it strengthens the perception of a common nature between Angie and the aid worker. Nonetheless, empathy without concrete cooperation cannot be successful in bringing Angie from a passionate to a rational activity. Indeed, Angie's relationship with the aid worker should be *qualitatively* different from her previous relationships with, say, her clients or her pimp, in order to determine her to undertake a different path. This is the reason why empathy should not be limited to a paternalistic effort by the aid worker to be sympathetic with Angie's own emotions. Rather, the aid worker must know how certain forms of cooperation can increase Angie's own power of acting and how this will result in joyful emotions. The aid worker must be able to share these joyful emotions with Angie to stimulate their collaboration and make it stronger than the emotional bonds that other external causes exert on Angie.

By engaging with Angie in this way, the aid worker is no longer determined by an abiding disagreement with Angie because the focus of their relationship no longer depends on whether prostitution is 'wrong' or not. Rather, the focus is now on what Angie defines as her own good and how the aid worker can cooperate with Angie in fostering it. Angie's relationship with the aid worker can be different because the aid worker must be a person trained in playing a 'prosthetic' role (Silver and Francis 2009) to support her rational autonomy. The aid worker must be able to understand the nature of Angie's own good (that is, what Angie herself considers good for her essential core and what is conducive to Angie's genuine advantage) by analysing her joyful feelings and emotions. The aid worker must also be able to assist with the production of such good by sharing its achievement with Angie. In this sense, Angie's good must also become the aid worker's good. This presupposes that the aid worker has a flexible and adaptable nature. By cooperating with Angie to achieve *their* shared good, the aid worker provides Angie with new powers and skills that will enable her to cooperate with others.

This process can be divided into three steps. At first the aid worker is introduced to Angie as an exceptional figure, who compensates the other external causes that act upon Angie. Then, Angie and the aid worker identify what their shared nature is and how they can both actively cooperate to achieve Angie's good, which becomes *their* common good. In this moment, Angie starts to become rationally active in her interaction with the aid worker. The final step consists in Angie's acquired ability to interact with other individuals in the same way she interacted with the aid worker, that is, by seeking rational cooperation intended to achieve a shared good.

This process is surely demanding on both Angie's and the aid worker's side, and the stronger the external causes acting upon Angie, the more demanding this process will be. Moreover, the way in which the process will be articulated in detail and its specific goals cannot be predicted a priori or through armchair speculations. Only a thorough analysis of Angie's emotional life can reveal in which direction her autonomy points and enable the aid worker to cooperate with Angie in order to foster her own power of acting in a *better* way.

Nonetheless, it should be stressed that from a Spinozistic perspective emotions are reliable indicators of the degree of the agent's power of acting. One might object that Angie could simply be a victim of some adaptive preference that deeply affects her way of thinking about her life and her goals, by associating positive feelings with activities that Angie should instead avoid. If passive emotions of joy imply a form of addiction, why should we not consider Angie's positive feelings about her being a prostitute as the result of a form of addiction? Should we not treat Angie in the same way in which one might expect to treat a case of drug addiction, namely by simply helping the subject to quit her use of drugs?

From a Spinozistic point of view, the positive feelings produced by addiction are indeed the expression of passive emotions of joy. This means that the agent actually seeks to improve her power of acting through the addiction, although the *way* in which she strives to achieve this goal turns out to be self-defeating. By distinguishing between *qualitatively* different kinds of autonomy, a Spinozistic approach aims to produce the same improvement of power of acting by adopting a different kind of interaction with external causes and eventually avoiding addiction as such. What produces addiction is not the goal that the agent seeks but the means that the agent uses, in certain situations, to achieve her goal. Drugs are not ends in themselves, but substances used to achieve certain states of mind that the agent feels desirable. In the same way, the objectives and effects sought because of adaptive preferences are not ends in themselves but means that the agent believes to be necessary to live in a certain socio-political context. Accordingly, although passive forms of joy presuppose a form of addiction, they still encapsulate crucial information about the agent's ultimate goals. It is upon the analysis of these ultimate goals (which is the expression of the agent's essential core) that the aid worker should plan her intervention. The very fact of being addicted does not deny that, behind the addiction as such, the agent still acts and strives to improve her power of acting. The aid worker should understand what is the kind of activity that the agent seeks to improve (even through some means that lead to addiction), in order to provide her with an alternative path to achieve the same goal in a better way.

To conclude, a Spinozistic approach to relational autonomy can improve our research agenda by drawing our attention to the way in which we can improve the *qualitative* aspects of autonomy by fostering rational activity. In this attempt, Spinoza's account focuses on the role that emotions play in revealing the degree of the agent's power of acting. Such an approach reinforces the need to rethink the standards used to implement paternalistic interferences. These interferences need to take seriously into account the agent's own goals as they are expressed by the agent's emotional feelings about her own choices. The aid worker can successfully fulfil her task only by actively cooperating with the aided subject. Finally, 'abiding disagreement' between the two will be overcome by the activity in which they should mutually engage. In this way, paternalistic interventions would cease to appear as interferences with the agent's choices by appearing as efforts to improve the *quality* of the agent's own autonomous activities.

Notes

1. For further discussion of this distinction see Christman (2004); Mackenzie (2008); Baumann (2008).
2. Armstrong (2009) and Kisner (2011) have already noted this point.
3. This point is connected with the 'agency dilemma' discussed by Mackenzie in the first chapter of this volume.
4. One may distinguish an agent's autonomy from the voluntariness of the agent's choices. The voluntary nature of a choice may reflect the way in which the agent herself perceives her not being forced by others towards a certain decision. One may claim that voluntariness does not entail that the agent is not somehow coerced or constrained by some oppressive system or external factor(s). However, the point I would like to advance in this chapter is that whenever an agent (phenomenologically) claims to make a voluntary choice, this fact should be taken into serious account in assessing the agent's autonomy. Even in conditions of oppression, the agent's voluntary choice should not be dismissed on the basis that the agent does not really know what she is doing and why she is doing it. For this reason, I maintain that voluntariness is directly connected to autonomy. I aim to underscore a different *qualitative* dimension of autonomy in order to assess to what extent voluntary choices may reflect a degree of autonomy, even if this is not the *best* kind of autonomy that an agent may develop. For a further discussion of the distinction between 'phenomenal' autonomy (i.e. how the agent herself or other agents perceive her autonomy) and 'metaphysical' autonomy (i.e. the degree and kind of autonomy that an agent actually has in a given condition), see Green's chapter in this volume.
5. The survey presented by Chudakov et al. (2002) among fifty-five prostitutes reveals that Angie's case represent 36 per cent of them, and 41 per cent of the participants think they have at least partial control over their lives. Moreover, 'almost all women reported engaging in sex work of their own volition and reported that they knew before leaving their country of origin that this was to be their occupation upon destination' (p. 307). Furthermore, 27 per cent of the group is described as 'uncomplicated', that is 'education level was medium to low, psychosocial problems were not prominent, and motivation appeared economic and ego-syntonic. Despite the present satisfaction with their works, most of these respondents wanted to leave prostitution after acquiring a specific amount of money' (pp. 308–9). Similar results are suggested by the case study conducted in India by Sinha (2015), which also shows that 'quite a few women reported that, in comparison to other jobs, sex work provides them with more control and autonomy over their lives' (p. 226).
6. Sex trafficking entails exploitation and coercion of the victims (see Crawford 2017; Cox 2017). There is evidence that sex trafficking causes a wide range of mental health issues in survivors (Levine 2017). In this chapter, I do not deal with uncontroversial cases of sex trafficking, but rather with agents who seem to enter sex work without being apparently coerced or acting against their own will.
7. For a similar relational approach see also Meyers (2014), which advocates for 'a weak paternalist, feminist approach designed to enhance the autonomy of trafficked sex workers'.
8. I use the expression 'genuine advantage' to indicate that the goal of the ethical progress should be that of identifying what is actually conducive to the full development and achievement of the agent's essential core and commitments. This 'genuine

advantage' may be different from what a certain agent wishes to achieve at a particular point of time and in a particular circumstance.
9. The aid worker's intervention cannot be motivated by her simple concern about the 'dangers' or 'risks' of prostitution because the fact that something is dangerous or risky does not entail that it cannot be the object of an autonomous choice. Smoking is dangerous, but we would not claim that he or she who smokes is not autonomous in taking this decision.
10. De Marneffe (2010: 133–53), while supporting paternalistic intervention against prostitution, is rather dismissive concerning the importance of neutrality for a liberal policy.
11. See, on this topic, Viljanen (2011); Sangiacomo (2013).
12. Concerning Spinoza's notion of 'agreement' see Sévérac (2005) and Sangiacomo (2015).
13. On Spinoza's view, it is impossible that interaction with external causes based on agreement in nature can lead to a decrease of power since similar things, insofar as they interact on the basis of what they share, cannot destroy each other (E3p4–5).
14. The essential feature of Spinoza's account is that, in every causal interaction, agreement and disagreement are co-present to different degrees. This is the reason why the same interaction can cause an increase of power (which depends on agreement) while at the same time remaining a passion (which expresses some disagreement in nature). Moreover, an interaction may increase the power of some part or feature of an individual, without necessarily increasing the power of the whole individual. Insofar as the excessive increase of power of a single part disrupts the overall balance in the individual's power, this increase of power may be dangerous. Spinoza calls this phenomenon *titillatio* (translated by Curley as 'pleasure') (see E3p11s, E4p43).
15. For further discussion, on this point, see Meyers (2014).

Works Cited

Armstrong, Aurelia (2009), 'Autonomy and the Relational Individual: Spinoza and Feminism', in M. Gatens (ed.), *Feminist Interpretations of Benedict de Spinoza*, University Park: Pennsylvania State University Press, pp. 43–64.

Baumann, Holger (2008), 'Reconsidering Relational Autonomy. Personal Autonomy for Socially Embedded and Temporally Extended Selves', *Analyse & Kritik*, 30: 445–68.

Christman, John (2004), 'Relational Autonomy, Liberal Individualism, and the Social Constitution of Selves', *Philosophical Studies*, 117: 143–64.

Christman, John (2013), 'Relational Autonomy and the Social Dynamics of Paternalism', *Ethical Theory and Moral Practice*, 17(3): 369–82.

Chudakov, Bella, Keren Ilan, R. H. Belmaker and Julie Cwikel (2002), 'The Motivation and Mental Health of Sex Workers', *Journal of Sex and Marital Therapy*, 38: 305–15.

Cox, Carole Beth (2017), 'Sex Trafficking in Cyprus: An In-Depth Study of Policy, Services, and Social Work Involvement', *International Social Work*, 61(6): 867–83.

Crawford, Mary (2017), 'International Sex Trafficking', *Women & Therapy*, 40(1–2): 101–22.

Friedman, Marilyn (2003), *Autonomy, Gender, Politics*, New York: Oxford University Press.

Kathy, Miriam (2005), 'Stopping the Traffic in Women: Power, Agency, and Abolition in Feminist Debates over Sex Trafficking', *Journal of Social Philosophy*, 36: 1–17.

Kisner, Matthew (2011), *Spinoza on Human Freedom. Reason, Autonomy and the Good Life*, Cambridge: Cambridge University Press.
Levine, James A. (2017), 'Mental Health Issues in Survivors of Sex Trafficking', *Cogent Medicine*, 4(1).
Mackenzie, Catriona (2008), 'Relational Autonomy, Normative Authority and Perfectionism', *Journal of Social Philosophy*, 39(4): 512–33.
Mackenzie, Catriona and Natalie Stoljar (eds) (2000), *Relational Autonomy. Feminist Perspectives on Autonomy, Agency and the Social Self*, Oxford: Oxford University Press.
Marneffe, Peter de (2010), *Liberalism and Prostitution*, Oxford: Oxford University Press.
Meyers, Diana Tietjens (2014), 'Feminism and Sex Trafficking: Rethinking Some Aspects of Autonomy and Paternalism', *Ethical Theory and Moral Practice*, 17: 427–41.
Oshana, Marina (2006), *Personal Autonomy in Society*, Cambridge: Cambridge University Press.
Sangiacomo, Andrea (2013), *L'essenza del Corpo. Spinoza e la scienza delle composizioni*, Hildesheim, Zürich and New York: G. Olms.
Sangiacomo, Andrea (2015), 'The Ontology of Determination: From Descartes to Spinoza', *Science in Context*, 28(4): 515–43.
Schneewind, Jerome (1998), *The Invention of Autonomy. A History of Modern Moral Philosophy*, Cambridge: Cambridge University Press.
Sévérac, Pascal (2005), *Le devenir actif chez Spinoza*, Paris: Honoré Champion.
Silvers, Anita and Leslie P. Francis (2009), 'Thinking about the Good: Reconfiguring Liberal Metaphysics (or Not) for People with Cognitive Disabilities', *Metaphilosophy*, 40(3–4): 475–98.
Sinha, Sunny (2015), 'Reasons for Women's Entry into Sex Work: A Case Study of Kolkata, India', *Sexuality & Culture*, 19: 216–35.
Viljanen, Valtteri (2011), *Spinoza's Geometry of Power*, Cambridge: Cambridge University Press.
Weitzer, Ronald (2007), 'The Social Construction of Sex Trafficking: Ideology and Institutionalization of a Moral Crusade', *Politics & Society*, 35(3): 447–75.
Widdows, Heather (2013), 'Rejecting the Choice Paradigm: Rethinking the Ethical Framework in Prostitution and Egg Sale Debates', in S. Madhock, A. Phillips, K. Wilson and C. Hemmings (eds), *Gender, Agency and Coercion*, London: Palgrave, pp. 157–80.

Notes on Contributors

Aurelia Armstrong, Lecturer, School of Philosophical and Historical Inquiry, University of Queensland

Keith Green, Professor, Department of Philosophy and Humanities, East Tennessee State University

Matthew Kisner, Professor, Department of Philosophy, University of South Carolina

Martin Lenz, Professor and Department Chair, History of Philosophy, Faculty of Philosophy, University of Groningen

Catriona Mackenzie, Professor of Philosophy; Director, Research Center for Agency, Values, and Ethics, Macquarie University

Heidi M. Ravven, Bates and Benjamin Professor of Classics and Religious Studies, Hamilton College

Ursula Renz, University Professor, Institute for Philosophy, Alpen-Adria-University-Klagenfurt

Andrea Sangiacomo, Assistant Professor, History of Philosophy, Faculty of Philosophy, University of Groningen

Justin Steinberg, Associate Professor, Department of Philosophy, Brooklyn College, City University of New York (CUNY)

Ericka Tucker, Assistant Professor, Department of Philosophy, Marquette University

Caroline Williams, Visiting Senior Research Fellow, Political Theory Team, School of Politics and International Relations, Queen Mary University of London

Index

Note: 'n' indicates chapter notes.

abjection, 8, 172, 179
accidental properties, 76–7, 87–8, 91n10, 94n41
activity, 2, 3, 75–6, 79–80, 90n8, 201–3
   passive, 76, 77, 79, 83, 87
   rational, 202–8
Adams, Suzy, 128n12
adaptive preferences, 2, 19, 25, 207–8
addiction, 203, 205–6, 208
affects, 118, 124, 127, 154, 155–8, 160n2
affirmation, 164, 169–73
agency, 6, 10–12, 15, 16, 20, 21, 24, 26–7, 76, 77, 116, 118, 200–2
agency dilemma, 3–4, 12–14, 19, 21, 25
agents, 4, 8, 165, 168–9, 172–6, 179, 187–8, 195, 202
agreement in nature, 7–8, 60, 133, 140–4, 143, 147n34, 147n38, 182–8, 191n32, 201–5, 210nn13–14
alienation/non-alienation, 16–17
altruism, 7, 138–40, 142
anima see impotentia animi; 'strength of mind'
Aquinas, Saint Thomas, 60, 76–7, 90n4, 90n9, 91n10
Arendt, Hannah, 115–16, 119, 127n3
Aristotle, 6, 34, 45n5, 52, 59, 60, 74, 75–7, 81, 83, 88–9, 90n3, 90nn6–8, 92n23
Armstrong, Aurelia, 87, 94n46, 94n48, 95n55, 117, 149, 156, 169
attributes, 78, 81

authenticity, 15–17
autonomy, 1–3, 10–13, 27n1, 27n2, 28n12
   concept of, 6, 115–19, 126–7
   constitutive, 149–50, 194
   degrees of, 118
   myth, 12, 28n5
   passionate, 203, 206
   phenomenal, 164–5
   politics of, 118–20, 125–6
   project of, 119–21
   qualitative, 194–5, 198, 199, 200–5, 207, 208
   quantitative, 194–5, 197–9, 200–5
   rational, 203–4, 207
autopoiesis, 120–1

Bacon, Francis, 60
Balibar, Etienne, 3, 37, 46n9, 94n47, 98–9, 111, 112n13, 113n32, 118, 120, 122, 147n43, 158
Balling, Pieter, 40
Barbone, Steven, 133–4, 145n12, 145n16
beliefs, 2, 50, 52, 57–8, 66–9, 107
   confirmation bias, 50, 51, 54, 65, 67–9
   'necessary beliefs', 106
   priority of belief principle and exclusion principle, 50, 51–4
   see also ideas
belonging uncertainty, 27, 28n20
Bennett, Jonathan, 142–3
Benson, Paul, 20, 27, 176, 189n16, 191n39

bias, confirmation, 50, 51, 54, 65, 67–9
bioethics, 17
blame, 8, 166, 175–6, 183, 186–7
blessedness, 152–5
body, the/bodies, 6, 35, 36–8, 55, 57–8, 60–3, 100–4, 109–10, 113n17, 119–25
   and mechanism, 5, 74, 75, 78, 81, 82, 88–9, 91n21, 93n32, 94n49
   social and political, 105, 107
bondage, 6, 150, 183
Brandom, Robert, 66
Butler, Judith, 3

capabilities theory, 24, 28n17
Castoriadis, Cornelius, 121, 128n12
causal dependence, 165, 168–9, 182, 184, 188
causal networks, 99, 111, 112n13
causation, 75–6
causes, external, 2, 59–60, 81, 92n22, 123, 146n23, 154, 166, 171–4, 179–80, 182, 200–8, 210n13
change, 75–6, 78, 79–80, 92n28
Christman, John, 14–15, 16–17, 181, 188, 191n39, 197
civility, 132–3, 144
Coady, Anthony, 33
cognitive dissonance, 107
cognitive psychology, 40–1, 44, 46n23, 68, 71n39
communitarian epistemology *see* social epistemology
competence, 15, 17–18
competitive interaction, 61, 64
compliance, 137–40, 146n26
conatus principle, 4, 5, 6, 74, 80–5, 87, 88, 92n30, 92n32, 93n34, 93n39, 93n42, 95n54, 102–5, 108–10, 112, 115–27, 128nn15–16, 134, 135, 138, 145n12, 151–2, 154, 155, 200–2, 206
   of ideas, 50–67, 70n21
   see also essences; nature
confirmation bias, 50, 51, 54, 65, 67–9
contrariety of ideas, 51, 59–65, 70n21, 70n28
convergence, 138–40, 144
cooperation, 8, 133, 141–4, 206–8

critical race theory, 16, 25
Curley, E., 91n12, 147n36

death, 121, 128n13
Deleuze, Gilles, 3, 118, 123, 127n9
Della Rocca, Michael, 7, 53, 56, 61, 138–9, 143
democracy, 158–60, 191n24
Den Uyl, Douglas, 133, 135, 146n20, 156
Denkungsarten (manners of thinking), 44
dependence, causal, 165, 168–9, 182, 184, 188
dependency, 4, 6, 11, 86–7, 116, 120
Descartes, René, 4, 5, 34–6, 38–9, 41, 42, 44, 45n2, 52–4, 60, 74, 75, 77–81, 87–8, 90n3, 91n12, 91n15, 91n17, 91n18, 91n19, 91n21, 92n23, 92n24, 92n28, 94n50, 122
desires, 123, 154, 155–7, 160; *see also* passions
determinism, 117, 127
disadvantage, 190n23
dispositions, 184, 189n5
domination, 165, 176–8, 180, 182, 187, 190n20, 196, 197

effects, 5, 74, 84, 89, 93n42
egoism, 4, 56, 69n9
emotions, 26, 28n18, 40, 41, 60, 66, 86, 100, 102, 107, 108, 110, 111, 154–7, 160, 207–8; *see also* affects
empathy, 206–7
endorsement, 16–17
enlightenment, 41–5
Enlightenment, 6, 11, 33, 36, 119
environment, 98, 102, 108–9, 110
   social, 12, 13, 18, 19, 24, 25
epistemology, 4, 33–45
essences, 77, 78, 80, 82, 88, 90n6, 91n18, 91n21, 92n29, 92n30, 151–3; *see also conatus* principle; nature
exclusion principle, 50, 51–4, 65, 67, 68, 70n18
exploitation, 195, 205–6
extension, 77–81, 88
externalism, 13–14, 18, 20–2, 23, 24, 28n9

fanaticism, 98, 105, 107–9
fear, 106–7

INDEX

feminist philosophy, 1, 3, 11, 12, 16, 25, 28n17, 116, 158, 194
Fineman, Martha, 11, 12, 28n5
Frankfurt, Harry, 15
free will, 6, 115, 119, 151, 153, 164, 165–9, 171, 188n1
freedom, 2, 3, 6, 8, 10, 11, 23–5, 85, 86, 89, 94n43, 99, 108, 115–19, 126, 127n3, 149–60, 164, 167, 169–70, 172–4, 177, 178, 184, 188, 200
Fricker, Miranda, 26–7
Friedman, Marilyn, 15, 16, 17, 19, 94n45

Gabbey, Alan, 59–60
Garber, Daniel, 92n25
Gatens, Moira, 3
Gelfert, Axel, 42
Giglioni, Guido, 60
Gilbert, Daniel, 68
Goclenius, Rodolphus, *Lexicon philosophicum*, 34–5, 36
God, 5, 55, 77, 78, 81–2, 92n25, 100–1, 112, 145n19, 151, 153
good, 7, 8, 188, 191n31, 205, 206, 207
Grey, John, 147n39
group mind, 37, 98, 99, 104–8, 110

habitus, 34–6, 42, 44, 45n4
happiness, 42
Haslanger, Sally, 190n18, 190n23
hierarchisation, 15–16
Hobbes, Thomas, 81, 88, 90n3, 92n25, 93n34, 159, 166, 169, 180
holism, 5, 39, 41, 53, 61, 65, 66
homology, 143
hope, 106–7
humility, 8, 172–3, 175, 179, 183
hylomorphism, 77–8, 91n15

ideas, 2, 4–5, 50–69, 82–3, 100, 154, 155–7, 160
  competitive interaction of, 61, 64
  conatus of, 50–67, 70n21
  contrariety of, 51, 59–65, 70n21, 70n28
  dual content of, 63
  interaction of, 51, 59–65, 67
  normativity of, 66–7

and philosophies of mind, 65–9
priority of belief principle and exclusion principle, 50, 51–4, 65, 67, 68, 70n28
see also imagination; thought
identity, 2, 3, 12, 13, 15, 16, 17
ideology, 67–9
imagination, 6, 98–112, 118, 123–4, 127, 129n19, 129n20, 170, 179–80, 183
imitation of the affects, 154, 155–8
implicit bias, 25–6, 68
impotentia animi ('weakness of spirit'), 164, 165, 169–77, 178–9, 185, 188, 189n10
individual natures, 5, 74–5, 85, 87, 89, 94n49, 95n54, 95n55, 95n56
individualism, 2, 4, 10, 11, 33–45, 45n2, 45n3, 45n4, 55–8, 65, 67, 99, 115, 118–20, 126–7, 194
  Restrictive Individualism, 7, 133–6, 139, 144, 146n23
  state, 132–44, 146n23, 146n25, 153–5, 158–9
  see also transindividuality
individuum, 37, 119, 122
injustice, social, 11, 12, 20, 21, 25–7
integration, 28n11
interactions of ideas, 51, 59–65, 67
internalism, 13–14, 18, 22
intersubjectivity, 4–5, 26, 40
intuitive knowledge, 39, 99, 111

joyful passions, 203–7

Kant, Immanuel, 27n2, 33, 41–5, 115, 166, 167, 169, 188n1, 189n3
King, Martin Luther, Jr., 22
Kisner, Matthew, 86, 117, 167–8

laws, 132–4, 137–40, 144n2, 145n17
learning, 35–6, 41, 42
LeBuffe, Michael, 55, 69n9
Lenz, Martin, 41, 46n10, 70n12, 189n9
Lewis, Charlton T., 141
liberalism, 2, 10, 11, 126, 149, 156–7
libertarianism, 23–4
local motion, 78, 91n20, 92n22
Luker, Kristin, 19

Macherey, Pierre, 118
Mackenzie, Catriona, 28n16, 28n17, 116, 118, 164, 188n2
Maimonides, Moses, 6, 105–6, 113n17
Mandelbaum, Eric, 68
Manning, Richard, 70n21
Marion, Jean-Luc, 45n5
Marshall, Eugene, 189n4
Marxism, 118, 127n2, 127n8
Massumi, Brian, 129n21
Matheron, Alexandre, 3, 36–7, 41, 135
mechanism, 5, 74, 75, 78, 81, 82, 88–9, 90n2, 91n19, 92n23, 92n27, 93n32, 95n52
Meier, Georg Friedrich, 42
Melamed, Yitzhak, 59, 70n18, 103, 113n17, 145n19
Mercier, Hugo, 68, 69
merger, unreflective, 107–8
Meyers, Diana, 16, 17–18, 28n11, 191n39
Mill, John Stuart, 27n2
mind, the, 2, 4–5, 37–9, 46n12, 51, 83, 123
    group mind, 37, 98, 99, 104–8, 110
    philosophies of, 65–9
    transindividuality of, 6, 98, 100–2, 109–11
    will/striving of, 55–8, 64, 67, 69n9, 70n11
    see also ideas; imagination; thought
modes, 4, 86, 87–8, 94n51
Moore, Jason, 126
Morfino, Vittorio, 118
motions, 78–9, 81, 92n25, 94n49
multidimensional theory, 4, 10–14, 23–7, 28n17
Myth of the Given, 66, 70n34

Nadler, Steven, 117
Nancy, Jean-Luc, 121, 125, 127n3, 128n14
nature, 6–8, 10, 57, 59–61, 64–5, 70n28, 99, 100, 102–5, 107–11, 117–19, 122–6, 127nn7–8, 133–6, 138–43, 145n17, 145n19, 147n34, 147n38, 147n40, 151–4, 156, 159, 164–72, 174, 176, 178–88, 191n28, 191nn31–2, 194, 200–7, 210nn13–14
    of mind, 3, 4, 5, 33, 79, 100–2
    of things, 51, 70n18, 75–9, 80, 82–5, 87, 89, 90n4, 93n42, 111, 138–41
    see also conatus principle; essences
natures, 5–6, 61, 74–89, 92n30, 92n32, 93n39, 93n42, 95n54, 120, 138–9, 164–6, 168–71, 174–6, 178–82, 184, 185, 188, 191n31, 191n35, 201; see also essences
Negri, Antonio, 3, 118
normative individualism, 11–12
normative priority, 7, 133, 134, 136
normativity of ideas, 66–7
norms, false, 19–20

occasionalism, 92n25
O'Neill, Onora, 43
opportunity, 23–4, 28n17
oppression, 3–4, 12–16, 17, 19–22, 25–7, 164, 177–81, 184, 190n18, 195, 196, 197
Oshana, Marina, 18, 21, 24, 149

parallelism, 63, 83
Pasnau, Robert, 90n6, 92n27
passions see desires
passivity, 3, 74, 86–7, 93n40, 99, 107, 108–10, 154, 202–3
paternalism, 4, 13, 14, 195, 196, 198–9, 205–8
penitence, 8, 172, 173, 175, 176
perception, 52, 81–2, 100
perfectionism, 36–42, 152–5, 160
Pettit, Philip, 24, 178, 190n20
phenomenal autonomy, 164–5
politics, 98, 99, 104–8, 115–16, 119, 123–4, 127
    'politics of autonomy', 118–20, 125–6
    tyranny, 105, 107
potentia, 83, 84, 88, 89, 93n36, 93n37, 93n39, 95n54, 120, 122; see also power
power, 2, 3, 6, 118, 121, 122–6, 153–5, 200–8, 210n14
    and freedom, 8, 149–60, 161n4
    of mind, 165, 167, 171–2, 178, 180, 188
    relational, 8, 153–5
    social, 155–8

state, 7, 134–5, 138–40, 143, 146n22, 158–9
see also potentia
pride, 172, 173, 175, 179, 186, 189n10
prime matter, 91n10
priority of belief principle, 50, 51–4, 66, 68
proceduralism, 8, 13–15, 19–20, 181, 187
prostitution, 195–208
    quantitative/qualitative autonomy framework, 200–5
psychology
    cognitive, 40–1, 44, 46n23, 68, 71n39, 134
    social, 25, 26, 27

rationalism, 2, 11, 12, 38–9, 68
Raz, Joseph, 24
reason, 43–5, 86, 99, 125, 152–3
Reid, Thomas, 33
relation, 115, 128n11
relational autonomy, 1–4, 10–27
    causes, 194
    debate on, 13–22
    multidimensional theory of, 4, 23–7, 28n17
    overview, 10–13
    sources of, 85–9, 94n45
    term, 85, 188n2
relational power, 8, 153–5
religion, 98, 99, 104, 106–7
    fanaticism, 98, 105, 107–9
Renz, Ursula, 70n11, 71n36, 180, 189n5
republicanism, 23–4
Restrictive Individualism, 7, 133–6, 139, 144, 146n23
Rice, Lee, 133, 145n4, 145n8, 168, 189n4
Roessler, Beate, 26–7

Sangiacomo, Andrea, 60, 69n9, 147n40
scholasticism, 90n3, 90n4, 90n9, 91n12, 91n17
scientia, 34–6, 39, 45n3, 45n4, 45n5
Scotism, 90n9
self-authorisation, 4, 13, 20, 22, 26–7
self-definition, 17–18, 28n11
self-determination, 4, 10–13, 22, 23–5, 27
self-direction, 17–18
self-discovery, 17–18
self-esteem, 20, 26

self-governance, 4, 10–14, 17, 22, 25–6, 27
self-harm, 195, 196, 199, 205
self-love, 8, 182–4, 186, 191n28
self-respect, 20, 26
self-trust, 20, 26
self-worth, 20, 27
Sellars, Wilfrid, 66, 70n34
senses, 45n2
servitude, 165, 177–8, 181, 182, 188, 190n23
shame, 8, 172, 173, 175, 176, 183
Sharp, Hasana, 57, 65
'shattered spirits', 164, 172–81
Short, Charles, 141
similarity, 125, 140, 143–4
Simondon, Gilbert, 120
slavery, 107–8
Smiglecius, Martinus, 52
Smith, Steven, 156
social interaction, 150, 151, 154, 157–8
social power, 155–8
social psychology, 25, 26, 27
social recognition, 20, 26
social relationships, 12, 13, 17, 22, 85–7, 89, 132, 194, 195
social/communitarian epistemology, 33, 37–43, 47n24
society, 104–8, 110
soul, the, 76–7, 91n15
Spanish poet example, 185–7
Spinoza, Baruch de
    Epistolae, 40
    Ethica more geometrico demonstata, 4, 37, 39, 51–2, 53, 54, 55, 57, 60–1, 69, 98, 99, 104, 106–9, 119, 122, 124, 132, 141, 151, 152, 153, 155, 156, 165, 168, 179–80
    Principia Philosophiae Cartesianae, 122
    Tractatus Politicus, 7–8, 104, 106, 132, 133, 137, 141, 160, 167
    Tractatus Theologico-Politicus, 98, 99, 104, 106, 107, 108, 124, 132, 137, 166
Springborg, Patricia, 93n34
state, the, 7, 132–44, 158–9, 191n24
Steinberg, Diane, 54, 57, 59, 70n18, 142, 143
stereotype threat, 25–7, 28n20
Stoljar, Natalie, 19, 188n2

'strength of mind', 8, 173–5, 179, 181–8
striving, 2, 6, 7, 51, 83, 89, 117, 122–3, 125, 136, 139–40, 145n12, 145n16, 168, 174, 177, 180–1, 200–3, 205
   of the mind, 55–8, 64, 67, 69n9, 70n11
structuralism, 126–7
Suárez, Francisco, 52, 76–7, 79, 87, 91n12, 91n18
subjectivity, 116, 118–21, 124, 126, 127
subjects *see* agents
subordination, 26, 136
subservience, 99, 107, 108–9
substantial forms, 76–7, 78, 79, 81, 87, 88, 90n4, 90n9, 91n10, 91n13, 92n27, 93n31, 94n50
substantivism, 12–14, 18–20, 160n1
   strong/weak, 19–22
sui iuris (a law unto oneself), 164, 165–7, 169, 172, 175, 178, 181, 182, 187, 188
suicide, 179, 180
sun analogy, 183
superstition, 105, 107

testimony, 33, 34, 39, 42–3, 46n17
things, 3, 5, 6, 34–5, 37, 42–3, 50–5, 57, 59–61, 63, 65, 74–84, 86–9, 93n40, 93n42, 94n49, 117, 129n22, 132, 135, 138–44, 145n16, 146n23, 147nn39–40
thought, 6, 77–80, 81–2, 100–1
   solitary, 43–4
transindividuality, 2, 3, 4, 6, 37, 46n9, 98, 100–4, 108–12, 120
triangulations on the body, 62–3
tyranny, 105, 107

'unfreedom' *see* freedom
unreflective merger, 107–8

Varela, Francisco, 120–1
Velleman, J. David, 16
virtue, 152–5
Vlastos, Gregory, 90n7
Voetius, Gisbertus, 92n23

Walther, Manfred, 37
Warriner, Jennifer, 20–1
Waterlow, Sarah, 92n23
weak substantivism, 19–20, 22
Westlund, Andrea, 28n12
Wolff, Christian, 42
Wollstonecraft, Mary, 28n16

EU representative:
Easy Access System Europe
Mustamäe tee 50, 10621 Tallinn, Estonia
Gpsr.requests@easproject.com

www.ingramcontent.com/pod-product-compliance
Lightning Source LLC
Chambersburg PA
CBHW070352240426

43671CB00013BA/2471